1,000,000 Books
are available to read at

Forgotten Books

www.ForgottenBooks.com

Read online
Download PDF
Purchase in print

ISBN 978-1-333-56674-6
PIBN 10520575

This book is a reproduction of an important historical work. Forgotten Books uses state-of-the-art technology to digitally reconstruct the work, preserving the original format whilst repairing imperfections present in the aged copy. In rare cases, an imperfection in the original, such as a blemish or missing page, may be replicated in our edition. We do, however, repair the vast majority of imperfections successfully; any imperfections that remain are intentionally left to preserve the state of such historical works.

Forgotten Books is a registered trademark of FB &c Ltd.
Copyright © 2018 FB &c Ltd.
FB &c Ltd, Dalton House, 60 Windsor Avenue, London, SW19 2RR.
Company number 08720141. Registered in England and Wales.

For support please visit www.forgottenbooks.com

1 MONTH OF FREE READING

at

www.ForgottenBooks.com

By purchasing this book you are eligible for one month membership to ForgottenBooks.com, giving you unlimited access to our entire collection of over 1,000,000 titles via our web site and mobile apps.

To claim your free month visit:
www.forgottenbooks.com/free520575

* Offer is valid for 45 days from date of purchase. Terms and conditions apply.

English
Français
Deutsche
Italiano
Español
Português

www.forgottenbooks.com

Mythology Photography **Fiction**
Fishing Christianity **Art** Cooking
Essays Buddhism Freemasonry
Medicine **Biology** Music **Ancient Egypt** Evolution Carpentry Physics
Dance Geology **Mathematics** Fitness
Shakespeare **Folklore** Yoga Marketing
Confidence Immortality Biographies
Poetry **Psychology** Witchcraft
Electronics Chemistry History **Law**
Accounting **Philosophy** Anthropology
Alchemy Drama Quantum Mechanics
Atheism Sexual Health **Ancient History**
Entrepreneurship Languages Sport
Paleontology Needlework Islam
Metaphysics Investment Archaeology
Parenting Statistics Criminology
Motivational

THROUGH UNKNOWN
NIGERIA

BOOKS OF TRAVEL

Demy 8vo. Cloth Bindings. All fully Illustrated

LIFE IN AN INDIAN OUTPOST.
By Major Casserly. Fully Illustrated. Demy 8vo. 12s. 6d. net

ALONE IN WEST AFRICA
By Mary Gaunt. 15s. net

CHINA REVOLUTIONISED
By J. S. Thompson. 12s. 6d. net

NEW ZEALAND
By Dr Max Herz. 12s. 6d. net

THE DIARY OF A SOLDIER OF FORTUNE
By Stanley Portal Hyatt. 12s. 6d. net

OFF THE MAIN TRACK
By Stanley Portal Hyatt. 12s. 6d. net

WITH THE LOST LEGION IN NEW ZEALAND
By Colonel G. Hamilton-Browne ("Maori Browne"). 12s. 6d. net

A LOST LEGIONARY IN SOUTH AFRICA
By Colonel G. Hamilton-Browne ("Maori Browne"). 12s. 6d.

MY BOHEMIAN DAYS IN PARIS
By Julius M. Price. 10s. 6d. net

WITH GUN AND GUIDE IN N.B. COLUMBIA
By T. Martindale. 10s. 6d. net

SIAM
By Pierre Loti. 7s. 6d. net

A GATEWAY IN THE WALL OF KANO.

The wall, which is made of mud, is 40 feet in thickness, 50 feet high, and 7 miles in circumference.

Photo by the Author.

THROUGH UNKNOWN NIGERIA

BY

JOHN R. RAPHAEL
LATE TRAVEL EDITOR OF "THE AFRICAN WORLD"

ILLUSTRATED FROM PHOTOGRAPHS BY THE AUTHOR

LONDON
T. WERNER LAURIE LTD.
8 ESSEX STREET, STRAND

DT 515
R2

PREFACE

NIGERIA is in process of change, in some places rapid change. Since this book has been written Southern and Northern Nigeria have been amalgamated administratively. The two colonies, or protectorates, whichever title be preferred, are being unified. The public service have been fused. What were the Lagos Government Railway, the Baro-Kano Railway and the Bauchi Light Railway recently received the comprehensive designation of Nigerian Railways. The volume was in too advanced a condition for the alterations to be made; and perhaps use of the old names will give a better idea of the efforts to open up the youngest dependency brought under the Crown.

Linking rich Southern Nigeria with her Northern sister provides money for railway and other development, which is to be pushed on vigorously. Many of the conditions of the country must necessarily alter. The locomotive is to whistle through regions where few white men have trod. Wild areas are to be penetrated by trains. Naturally the character of the inhabitants will be affected: no doubt many superstitious rites and, incidentally, cruelty and inhumanity in social customs be dispelled. Pagans will catch the passing fashions, or an imitation, and clothe, or at least cover, themselves.

These and other material benedictions are sure to radiate from the emblems of civilisation. Let us hope we shall not also be the means of dispensing many of the blessings taken by Europeans to the Coast towns of West Africa in former centuries and in evidence to-day by the moral and physical degeneration of adult natives, as well as by children saturated with hereditary disease.

Contact with aborigines may be a very fine thing for them. Let care be taken that their second state is not worse than the first. That is likely to be avoided if the policy followed by Sir George Taubman Goldie and Sir Frederick Lugard with the Fulani and the Hausa population of Northern Nigeria be scrupulously continued: that of encouraging and fostering all which is good in tribal life, repressing only those features which violate the principles of human existence.

No attempt has been made in the following pages at an historical survey or at a deep examination of the difficult problems that confront the administration. There are a number of books in which both subjects are treated excellently. Recent ones occurring to mind are Lady Lugard's, " A Tropical Dependency"; Colonel Mockler-Ferryman's, " British Nigeria "; Captain Orr's, " The Making of Northern Nigeria "; Mr E. D. Morel's, " Nigeria: Its People and Problems "; and the several publications of Major Tremearne.

PREFACE

This volume is no more than impressions taken from a quiver of them gained in the course of a rather long visit, part of it through country not well known. Most chapters were written during the journey, either at the close of a day's trek or whilst detained at various spots.

My obligations are manifold for the courtesy, kindness and assistance shown in various quarters. If all to whom I feel indebted were stated several pages would be required.

I cannot, however, allow the volume to go to Press without again tendering thanks to my former Editor and present friend, Mr Leo. Weinthal, of *The African World*, for the opportunity given to carry out the expedition and for allowing me to incorporate in these pages matter printed in his paper; Sir Walter Egerton and Sir Hesketh Bell, ex-Governors respectively of Southern and Northern Nigeria, for the letters of introduction which proved an open sesame to the good-will of the high officials administrating each colony; Mr F. Seton James, C.M.G., and Mr A. G. Boyle, C.M.G., both of whom in the course of my stay were in turn Acting Governors of Southern Nigeria; Mr F. W. Waller, Acting General Manager, Lagos Government Railway; Mr Charles L. Temple, C.M.G., Acting Governor of Northern Nigeria; Captain G. C. Kelly, temporarily in command of the 1st Battalion Northern Nigeria Regiment; Captain C. F. S. Maclaverty, in charge of the Battery; Mr C. Maclean, Agent of the Niger Company at Zungeru; Mr E. M. Bland,

PREFACE

Deputy Director of Railways, Northern Nigeria; Mr Joseph E. Trigge, Managing Director of the Niger Company; the late Mr Walter Watts, its Agent General; Mr Robert Lenthall, also Agent General of same Company; Mr W. P. Byrd, and Captain J. J. Brocklebank, D.S.O., of Kano, and also my native friends of that city, Adamu Ch'Kardi and Suly; Mr F. Beckles Gall, Resident at Naragutu; Mr F. D. Bourke, Manager of Naragutu Tin Mine; Mr S. E. M. Stobart, Resident at Bukuru; Mr T. H. Driver, Manager of the Anglo-Continental Mines; Mr A. C. Francis, Acting Resident at Zaria; Major E. M. Baker, temporarily in command of the 2nd Battalion Northern Nigeria Regiment; Mr W. H. Hibbert, of Lokoja; Mr Bertram D. Byfield, Cantonment Magistrate there; and Mr A. E. Price, of Burutu. Although not strictly within the scope of this book, I add Mr J. B. McDowell, Managing Director of the British and Colonial Kinematograph Company, who gave special care and attention to the apparatus and material which enabled me to bring back unique moving pictures of people in whose country no instrument of the kind had ever been taken.

J. R. R.

CONTENTS

CHAPTER I

OUTWARD BOUND

Call of the Coast—Mal-de-mer—Coasters afloat—From 78°
to 90°—The Kru sailor—His civilised degeneration—
Laundryman's discipline—A dangerous stretch—The
skipper—From ship to train 1

CHAPTER II

FROM THE COAST BY TRAIN—THE WEST AFRICAN PULLMAN

Iddo Wharf—Strange sights and thoughts—Umbrellas—
"Niggers"—Train luxuries—Liquor permits—The
iron-horse at the Niger—Ferry and bridge—Budget
details 12

CHAPTER III

ZUNGERU—THE CAPITAL OF THE PROTECTORATE

A garden-city Capital—"Ikey" square—Autocracy thorough
—Circumscribed accommodation and doubled-up quarters
—Young administrators—Strict, stern, severe economy
—The Governor's "Palace"—Job-lot furniture—His
Excellency's 1s.-an-hour, Bank-Holiday motor-car—
Pooh-Bah Cantonment Magistrate 19

CHAPTER IV

ZUNGERU—THE CAPITAL OF THE PROTECTORATE—(continued)

Native settlement—Rents and Treasury—A model prison—
Northern Nigeria Constabulary—Mails paid time-work—
Sport at the door—Up-country and Coast natives—
Selection of Zungeru—The future Capital . . . 33

CONTENTS

CHAPTER V
ZUNGERU TO KANO

Everybody his own porter—Religion and missions—Divining water—Carriages patchy in parts—Native passengers—In the track of the slave-raider—Engine sustenance—Kaduna Bridge—A tight-rope performance—Close cultivation—" The lazy negro "—Two civilisations—At Kano 43

CHAPTER VI
ARRIVAL AT KANO

Plans and expectations—Small water-famine—The handy man—Change of quarters—Ants as sauce—Niger Company 57

CHAPTER VII
FASHIONS, GOVERNMENT, ADMINISTRATION

An Empire builder—The country and population—Hausa tribes—Moslem and Pagan—Sartorial distinctions—Ruling through natives—Election of their own rulers—Lugard's peaceful persuasion—A modern Earl of Warwick—The genius of Taubman Goldie and Lugard—Native administration — Residents — Taxation — Law Courts 63

CHAPTER VIII
KANO PROVINCE AND CITY—BRITISH TRADE PROSPECTS

Town and country—Officials and traders—Belgravia and Bermondsey—A housekeeping budget—European stores—Buying and selling—A Syrian in the fold . . . 72

CHAPTER IX
A GENTLEMAN ADVENTURER

The London and Kano Trading Company—The Captain intervenes—Army, Civil Service, Commerce—Discarding appearances—Contrast of mansions—The pleasure of business—" Traders " and others 80

CONTENTS

CHAPTER X
KANO CITY

The founder—Hunter and prophet, too—The city wall—Warfare and slave hunts—Provocation and defiance to the British—The Emir's challenge—March on the city—First check—Renewed attempt—Entry—A new ruler ... 86

CHAPTER XI
KANO CITY—(continued)

Houses and rents—From 1s. 6d. to £5 a year—Mud mansions—No. 1 Kano—When to build and repair—Advice on building—A contract and a surprise ... 93

CHAPTER XII
KANO MARKET

A cosmopolitan rendezvous—Arab merchants—The desert route and the iron-horse—War and commerce—Local industries—Arts and crafts—Skilled workers—Camels, cattle, sheep, horses—Pitiful brute suffering—An appeal ... 100

CHAPTER XIII
KANO MARKET AND CITY—(continued).

Deference to the Englishman—A sagacious policy—Administration of justice—An Alkali's judgment—The native Treasury—Kano municipality—Money matters ... 112

CHAPTER XIV
SOME ASPECTS OF SOCIAL LIFE

Wives of the upper-class—Women and the mosques—Polygamy—Its difficulties in the home-circle—How to maintain peace—Hints on management of the feminine character—A domestic diplomat—Slavery—The former and the present position—Status of a slave ... 119

CHAPTER XV
THE MISSIONARY QUESTION

Missions and Moslems—Strong comments—Bearings of the situation—Present practice—The British solemn promise—The alternative ... 125

CONTENTS

CHAPTER XVI
THE BAUCHI LIGHT RAILWAY

Zaria and other stations—The two gauges—Through new country—Second-hand rails—A new post for Sir Frederick Lugard—A relic of tribal warfare—Sport for the gun—A derailment—Blend of tongues—Smart re-railing work 130

CHAPTER XVII
AT RAHAMA RAILHEAD

Engaging carriers—How to facilitate getting away—Hausa horse coupers and political economy—Bullock transport—Donkey carriage—The man who belies a fable . . 139

CHAPTER XVIII
ON TREK—RAHAMA TO JUGA

Heavyweight and overweight—The white barred—Collective displeasure—Getting off—A doki boy—Tin-mine pilgrims—A scion of royalty—The rest-house—Village elders—Acrobatic horsemanship—The carriers—Headman Hanza—Over the edge of the Pagan belt 146

CHAPTER XIX
RAHAMA TO JUGA—(continued)

Stopped by a stream—A volunteer—Amadu the carrier—Sun heat—Across the river—" Kow abinshi "—The doki boy's experiment—The climate and granite—Domestic details on trek—A chilling downpour—Mark Tapleys—Sun and warmth—Hanza's command—A dignified procession 156

CHAPTER XX
JUGA TO NARAGUTA

Native feminality and the cavalry spirit—Scarcity and economy—A house of straw—Carriers, professional and other—Diversified panorama—Parting with the first carriers 169

CONTENTS

CHAPTER XXI
TWO SHORT JOURNEYS

Man proposes—A narrow river barrier—Travellers this side of the stream; beds, the other side—Pagan cultivation—A postal description—Headmen and Headmen—Gotum Karo 175

CHAPTER XXII
THE NIGER COMPANY'S JOS CENTRE

Jos and St Peter's—A wet and dry object—Fashion in stationery—Smoking and writing materials—The cost of money—Coin in transit—Tin-mine labourers and food—Inception of European transport—Linguistic stimulus and aptitude—Donkey caravans—The animals' acumen—Double-distilled philosophy 181

CHAPTER XXIII
MINES—MEDICAL

Tin-mining—First Exclusive Prospecting Licence—Early tin-winning—Mr Law's work—Health and economics—Feminine nursing—The medical service . . . 194

CHAPTER XXIV
A MURDER TRIAL

Mining licences and leases—The Government Inspector of Mines—Nine years without doors—Two Residents—Poisoned arrow welcome—A murder trial . . . 202

CHAPTER XXV
TROUBLES OF THE TREK

Philosophers' test—At the back of white men's minds—Human calculations—Blows to plans—Oje leaves—The servant problem—Short, severe rations—Doki boy Kolo—A Pagan pony—Its performances—Injury to insult—Human and equine elements 209

CONTENTS

CHAPTER XXVI
INCIDENTS ON TREK

The changed seasons—End of the rainy season—Bush fires—Rolling downs and kopjes—A 25-miles march without food or drink—Return journey commenced—Ascent of the escarpment, 2,200 feet—A Hausa and Pagan affray—An ugly situation 221

CHAPTER XXVII
INCIDENTS ON TREK—(*continued*)

Information and advice in West Africa—Different men, different manners—Ritz by comparison—A Samaritan by the way—Dried streams—Primitive transport—A visitor from Rhodesia—Omitting anti-fever precautions . . 230

CHAPTER XXVIII
CLOSE OF THE TREK

Character of carriers—The only blow given—Native grooms' monetary transactions—Material for a *cause célèbre*—Dispensing justice on the road—Headman Dan Sokoto—Dan's sharp practices—A long march 237

CHAPTER XXIX
TOWARDS THE PAGAN COUNTRY

Hausa and Pagan—Distinction of dress—Deeper divisions—The price of peace in former days—Public highway—Revenge and brotherhood—Scope of an Assistant Resident 243

CHAPTER XXX
IN A PAGAN TOWN

Bukuru Residency—Bukuru town—Its ingenious defences—Traps for an attacking force—The blacksmith—Musical instruments—Pagan orchestras—A royal male Pavlova—The Court band—A King's reward—Pagan homesteads—The sleeping apartment—Farming—Incentives

CONTENTS

to obtain money—Enhancing nature's charms—Male and female decorations—Bareback and bitless horsemanship—Races—Care of horses—The hunt—Sign language 247

CHAPTER XXXI
ADMINISTERING JUSTICE AND TAXATION

Direct rule—Cases in a Resident's Court—Wife and " another man "—Trial by ordeal—Modification of that method—Kidnapping for slaves—" The liberty of the subject "—Extenuating circumstances and even-handed justice—Benefits that are not welcomed—The joy of fighting—Graduated taxation—How to express numerals to people who have no such terms—Two tax collectors—First lessons in administration . . . 260

CHAPTER XXXII
MARRIAGE AND DEATH CUSTOMS

Fashions—A wedding-ring warning—The former way with undesirables—Succession to a Chiefship—Marriage—Dowries — A perpetual leap-year — Widows — Burial usages—Cannibalism—Eating those who die from natural causes—Etiquette of the practice—A credit and debit account 269

CHAPTER XXXIII
SOLDIERS AND THEIR SPORTS

British-trained troops—Little-known Mr Atkins—Swearing-in recruits—Hausa and Pagan oaths—Native priests on active service—Number of wives allowed—Artillery on men's heads—Gun drill—Dipping for toroes—Mounted infantry—Signalling tuition—Teaching the band—Inculcating self-reliance—The military classification of white civilians 278

CHAPTER XXXIV
ZARIA CITY AND PROVINCE

Prominence of Zaria—As a produce and trading centre—The gold discoveries—Opposite deductions—Model, native town-planning—Various taxes . . . 291

CONTENTS

CHAPTER XXXV

THE BARO-KANO RAILWAY

Emir's assent—Compensation for palm trees—A locomotive's food—Engine whistling preferred to Caruso—Official opening—Natives' curiosity—A Mallam's impressions—Horse *v.* train 299

CHAPTER XXXVI

BARO ON THE NIGER

Baro port—A Selfridge-Whiteley 400 miles up the Niger—London frock-coats in West Central Africa—Fretwork and ladies' garments—An untutored eye and its guide—The rat a table delicacy—Oje's local patriotism—Baro and Jebba; hygienic problems—A superfluous hospital 306

CHAPTER XXXVII

LOKOJA

First stage down the Niger—Lokoja's past—The discovery of the brothers Lander—Previous theories—McGregor Laird's enterprise—Eighty per cent. mortality—The 1841 expedition—Richardson, Barth and Overweg—Laird's second endeavour—The House of Commons scuttle policy—Its reversal—First Fulani battle—Imperial control—Commerce of Lokoja—Vessels at the beach—Loading boats—Freedom of contract 312

CHAPTER XXXVIII

LOKOJA—(*continued*)

A cosmopolitan town—A Baron Haussman—The Cantonment Magistrate—Some of his duties—Expenditure and economy—King Abigah—A plea for generosity—The hospitals—A black Bishop's legacy—The missionary question—Critics and the converse 324

CHAPTER XXXIX

NAVIGATING THE NIGER

Rise and fall—A tideless stream—Comfort afloat—The uncertain river—Nasaru the Pilot—Altered channels—When aground—Breakdown of machinery and smart repair—Tropical scenery—The crocodiles' rest—Riverside villages—Where money is ignored—Estimation for old bottles and tins—Harmattan fog—An island trading station—Hazard and skill to maintain a time-table . 334

CHAPTER XL

BURUTU

A port in a swamp—Training native engineers—A composite village—Social grades—Medical provision—Mr John Burns on a Nigerian river—Back to the sea . 348

LIST OF ILLUSTRATIONS

A Gateway in the Wall of Kano . .	*Frontispiece*	
The Rt. Hon. Sir George Taubman Goldie, Founder of Nigeria	*Facing page*	64
One of the Emir's Trumpeters	,,	78
Native Skin-merchants with Transport, Kano	,,	78
Captain J. J. Brocklebank, D.S.O. . .	,,	82
The Premises of the London and Kano Trading Company at Kano . . .	,,	82
Sir Frederick Lugard, D.S.O., First Governor of Northern Nigeria	,,	92
Houses in Kano City. The cheapest type, rent 1s. 6d. a year	,,	94
Houses in Kano City. A detached dwelling, rent 1s. 9d. a year	,,	94
House in Kano City, rent 2s. 6d. a year . .	,,	96
No. 1 Kano. The houses in the city are numbered to facilitate taxation . .	,,	96
An Arab Merchant who trades from the Shores of the Mediterranean to Kano .	,,	102
Ex Sergt.-Major Dowdu, a Beri-Beri from Barum	,,	102
The Magistrate's Court in the Market. His worship is on the steps . . .	,,	108
A Detachment of the Emir's Police . .	,,	108
A Corner of Kano Market. Note the stocks	,,	112
A Section of the Market with Open-air Stalls	,,	112
The Principal Mosque	,,	114
An Entrance to the Courtyard of the Emir's Palace	,,	114
The Royal Courts of Justice	,,	116
The Native Treasury, known as the Beit-el-Mal	,,	116
A Street in Kano	,,	118

LIST OF ILLUSTRATIONS

Doctor's Shop in the Market . . . . *Facing page*	118
Hausa Woman-trader. Her clothes are silk and her rings silver . . . . ,,	120
A Hausa Belle . . . . . . ,,	120
Tureg Traders from Lake Chad. They are reformed robbers . . . . . ,,	122
Abigah (seated) and his Two Wives . . ,,	122
"Zaki!"—Natives giving the usual salute to a white man . . . . . . ,,	128
Respect to the Aged is shown by removing the Shoes and Curtsying . . . . ,,	128
The Religion of the Mohamedan forbids the use of soap, as it contains fat. Shaving therefore is done with the aid of water only ,,	138
Specimen of the Barber's Art . . . ,,	138
Carriers ready to start . . . . . ,,	168
A Bridge which is swept away by the stream each year during the wet season . . ,,	168
A Government Rest-house . . . . ,,	174
The Headman's House at Toro, where the Author slept . . . . . . ,,	174
Approach to a Pagan Town. A maze of impenetrable cactus . . . . ,,	248
A Pagan Homestead, built against a rock to prevent rear attacks . . . . ,,	248
Pagan Farmer using his only implement, a spade-hoe . . . . . . ,,	250
The King of the Jarawa Pagans dancing in Honour of the Author's Visit. The accompaniment is by his Court band in State uniform . . . . . . ,,	250
A Naked Pagan riding his pony barebacked ,,	256
Pagan Horsemen . . . . . . ,,	256
Bukuru Sign Language . . . . . ,,	258
Mr S. E. M. Stobart, the Resident at Bukuru, and His Staff . . . . . ,,	268
Bukuru Residency . . . . . ,,	268
Pagan Feminine Fashions . . . . ,,	270
A Pagan Beauty of the Dass Tribe . . ,,	272
A Girl of the Jarawa Tribe. The cuts in the face are made when she reaches the age of puberty . . . . . . ,,	272

LIST OF ILLUSTRATIONS xxiii

Jarawa Pagans. The marks are produced by the flesh being cut and charcoal placed in the incision	*Facing page* 276
Signalled message	*Page* 290
A Beri-Beri Woman with an elaborate head-dress	*Facing page* 290
Swearing in a Pagan and a Mohamedan for the Northern Nigeria Regiment . .	,, 290
Hausa Boy playing the molah, a kind of banjo	,, 298
Fiddle with Strings and Bow of Horsehair rubbed with Gum	,, 298
Hausa House-Building with Grass. The foundation	,, 310
The Finished Mansion. It is put up, including cutting the grass, in a couple of hours	,, 310
Manicure. The fee is twenty cowries, i.e., about one-fourteenth of a penny . .	,, 338
A Nupé Pilot on the Niger	,, 338
A European Trading Station on the Niger .	,, 342
On a Creek of the Niger	,, 342
The Niger Company's Wharf at Burutu .	,, 348
Shipping Palm-oil for Direct Transit to Liverpool	,, 348

THROUGH UNKNOWN NIGERIA

CHAPTER I

OUTWARD BOUND

Call of the Coast—Mal-de-mer—Coasters afloat—From 78° to 90°—The Kru sailor—His civilised degeneration—Laundryman's discipline—A dangerous stretch—The skipper—From ship to train.

WHAT induces that mysterious, elusive "call to the Coast" to which few who have been to West Africa remain unresponsive? None deny its existence, even those who remain unaffected. Yet no conclusive answer has been given for a strange, fascinating attraction to revisit a part of the world which is regarded as uninviting. The "call" cannot be one of mere novelty, for it is only men and women who have lived in West Africa—perhaps suffered there—who are impelled to return, in spite of its drawbacks and talked-of risks, some real, some unduly and unnecessarily magnified.

Whether I felt the "call" strongly, overpoweringly, or merely preferred the country as a change to England has been tested. Not long ago my Editor enquired was I willing for a journey to

Egypt, with its splendid climate and the charm of looking on the land of Bible stories; he asked whether I cared for a trip through East Africa, with the delightful flora and fauna of a new colony. Neither attracted me. The mention of each created no eagerness. But when, one Wednesday afternoon, he called me into his room and spoke of West Africa I was all agog.

"You will be there in the rainy season," he warned.

"I know, though I should prefer another period of the year; but do not ask anybody else if you wish me to go."

"All right. When would you be ready to start?"

"From London next Tuesday if you urgently desire, but I should like a little longer, to fulfil a special engagement."

The conversation took place at 2.30 p.m. By 5.30 the following afternoon everything had been settled.

Another prospective journey in West Africa filled me with delight, and no more blithesome soul stepped on the Elder Dempster liner *Akabo* the morning she left the Princes' Quay at Liverpool.

A smooth course through the Irish Sea takes us next morning round Land's End and across the mouth of the English Channel, which is in anything but a friendly mood; and, as usual on the second day out, the chronicler promptly goes into involuntary retirement. In previous similar experiences he had not troubled the ship's doctor, but on the present occasion a slight trouble not yielding to the applications from his own medicine-case, he thinks it well to utilise skilled, professional treatment.

As promptly as if he were carrying out a three-guinea visit, Dr Hanington appears. A British Columbian with an exceedingly rapid delivery of words, before you have finished your explanation, not a look at tongue nor a touch at the pulse, he has darted out of the cabin and almost instantaneously returns, holding a tube of gelatine in the left hand and a tumbler of water in the other. You cannot gulp down drug and liquid and splutter or stammer your thanks in time for them to catch the swiftly disappearing doctor, who whilst you have been employed in the operation of swallowing has ejaculated, with a delightful Irish brogue, "That will put you right. You will be skipping about the deck to-morrow."

Three times that day Dr Hanington came unsolicited to see the patient, the two later visits extending to interviews with conversations. They were of the bright, cheery kind, such as, "The Channel is always beastly. I am usually sick there myself. We shall be through the Bay to-morrow noon. It will be smoother than this choppy water" —a glance through the glass of the porthole—"and then you will be running along the promenade deck." That seems a far-distant vision to the helpless victim of grievous mal-de-mer, though its manifestation is limited to intense headache.

Meanwhile prompt attention is forthcoming from the berth steward, W. Harrison. The measure of your suffering is indexed by your feed. The first morning of being down Harrison enters the cabin and asks tenderly, "What can I get you for breakfast, sir?" holding out a menu-card. "Don't show me that" is the shuddering reply. The sight certainly the thought, of it provokes an internal protest against food. "My stomach no fit for chop," as the natives down the Coast would say. Anglise: "I cannot possibly eat."

Midday Harrison appears in an enquiring attitude, "No, thank you; not now."

The evening brings him again. The situation is slightly on the mend, for a few grapes are requested and a large bunch is sent in by the chief steward, Mr James Toner. Next morning there is a brighter outlook. Life appears worth living. Dry biscuits and grapes are readily asked for. The doctor makes a call, which is repeated a few hours later, and each time he insists, in his quick manner of expression, that the still-stricken patient is appreciably nearing the stage of tearing about the deck.

Lunch-time the menu-card, which Harrison on his calls has evidently been holding behind him, out of sight, no longer creates the former revulsion, and a little cold meat, mashed potatoes and biscuits are selected. The fulfilment of the doctor's prophecy still, however, feels a long way off, but he urges the powers of the sea, the fresh air and the breeze, adding that "the close breathing in a cabin gives as much trouble as the rolling waves."

Two efforts were made to dress. They had to be abandoned. The prone position was the only one endurable. An hour or two and a third endeavour. Very laboured was each stage of the toilet. There were strong indications that internal influences would prevail. Fortunately the perpendicular balance was maintained until the last touch had been given, and then a washed-out looking object crawled upstairs and huddled itself in a deck chair. Dr Hanington's declaration was not as far removed from justification, after all, for the fresh air proved wonderfully recuperative, and by the following morning the patient was, like Richard, himself again. It was the shortest of his many terms of mal-de-mer, the limited span entirely due to the excellent doctor of the *Akabo*.

Now there is opportunity to look at one's surroundings. We have not many trippers aboard. Half-a-dozen for the Canary Islands. The rest are Coasters, the term given to men employed in West Africa, either in the Government service or in commercial concerns. Some are going out for the first time; others have served many years and are returning after the home leave which is given at the close of every twelve months, eighteen months, or two years, according to the agreement. Government men are allowed four months in England, on full pay, for every twelve spent in West Africa. It sounds pleasant and easy, but, although marvels have been wrought in the health statistics by the discoveries of Manson, Ross and Boyce on the transmission of malarial fever; and the splendid medical staff in the colonies, with the hospital Sisters, have multiplied many times the chances of life, still, under the best conditions the climate must remain a trying one, and an unduly long sojourn in it is likely to undermine the constitution of the strongest.

Contact with another civilisation, or years passed in places where there is none, has not made coarse the tender chord of sentiment in these outward-bound Coasters. Look in at their cabins and you will frequently discover the framed photograph of a female figure and perhaps the voyager in front of it, bent, writing. Possibly the original in some English home is similarly occupied towards this direction.

It must not be assumed, however, that people whose days are spent in West Africa have a more serious view of life than the rest of mankind. As a body, they are a happy, light-hearted community, with the colonial spirit of good-fellowship. No fears of the unhealthiness of the climate affect them. If fever or worse is to come, time enough when it puts in an appearance. They are not men to meet trouble half-way. Part of the battle in warding off climatic disease is not to think of it. They act on that principle. Whether as Government officials or those associated with mining or commerce, nearly all are physically above the corresponding class in Europe.

One quickly realises why the men are the few chosen from the many called. They have been selected with care. There is no place for wasters in West Africa, either from the health or the business aspect. A few may get there. They are soon found out. In recruiting their staffs the trading firms select those likely to justify the expense of being sent. The salary to be earned as an "agent" —manager of a store—attracts persons who have not the opportunities in England which present themselves in West Africa. There are drawbacks, but the recompense is not small for a man who can make his way. Everybody must weigh the pros and cons for himself.

A sharp change of temperature occurs as we pass Cape Verde, nine days out. A little beyond this point is the great Gambia River, which comes out heated by the scorching winds of the Sahara Desert, and at the mouth of the river there are also flowing up towards us warm currents from the south. It is not uncommon for hardy voyagers to be weakened and temporarily knocked over by the sudden rise of temperature. These are the figures we experience:

Thursday 10 a.m. 72° off Cape Blanco.
Friday 10 a.m. 78° approaching Cape Verde.
Saturday 10 a.m. 82°.
Saturday 4.40 p.m. 86° in a well-ventilated cabin with an electrical fan running.
Saturday 4.40 p.m. 90° on deck of the ship at full speed, under a stout awning.

At Sierra Leone—eleven days from Liverpool—the ship's company is augmented by a number of Kru sailors, who proceed to a spring-cleaning with a zest and enjoyment unmistakable.

The Kruman is the seaman of West Africa. His villages are on the seashore. He is put in the water and made to swim from babyhood. He can be seen coming to a ship, on rough, rolling waves, in a frail canoe crudely cut or burnt out from the trunk of a soft-wood tree. A couple of small boys will paddle such a canoe two or three miles out to sea. At certain parts of the Coast the lads dive for coppers thrown from an anchored vessel, and do it as unconcernedly as though they were in a calm river instead of a place frequented by sharks. Yet no fatalities are known, which is probably due to the noise the youngsters make. Should a shark be espied hovering near, several of the boys will even swim towards it, shouting, yelling, and splashing, and the brute, who is a coward, slips away.

At Axim, Gold Coast, three days beyond Sierra Leone, a further complement of Krumen are shipped. Each batch is of a different tribe. That from Sierra Leone consists of Nana Krus; at Axim they have come from the Beri-Beri country, on the French Grain Coast. Some years ago they clandestinely left French territory, where they were compelled to labour on public works, and founded a small settlement near Axim, for the purpose of serving on British ships. At one time the French prevented shipment from their own shore unless at a tax per man, but now there is no objection to enlistment at recognised ports of entry. Krus who have made homes in the British sphere prefer to remain there.

Considerable difference is noticeable between the two tribes mentioned. The Nanas are greatly inferior in physique and stamina. The degeneration is due to evils resulting from the "civilisation" to be found in certain districts of Sierra Leone. The Beri-Beris, who have been freer from these influences, are a much better type. In a set period, fifteen of the latter will do more work, with less effort, than can be carried out by twenty-five of the former in the same time.

Each body of Krus is under its own Headman, who will be either a village Chief or appointed by the Captain of the ship. The Headman can usually be relied upon to keep his folks up to the mark. He receives instructions from the officers as to what is required. They leave him to have it done, and, as a rule, it is sure to be done well. The Headman is given tea and other small luxuries, in addition to the usual rations of rice and fish, and he is allowed to bring a small boy, usually his son, to assist him in cooking.

At Sierra Leone there has also come on board the black laundryman and his " boys," who deal with passengers' linen. It is not turned out in the finished style of a first-class establishment in England, but what is lacking in other respects is made up by very liberal starching. A couple of collars feel they could support an anchor.

The laundryman frequently walks round with a broom. The article is not for professional use in connection with the tub; the handle is utilised for gentle persuasion and is applied to the cranium of the delinquent who needs stimulus or correction. When applied, the thwack can be heard many yards distant and is only rivalled in sound by the ship's siren. A thin skull would be crushed by such a blow. The "boy" who receives one shakes it off as nothing, and sometimes gets a succession of them for laughing at the first. There is "Home Rule all round" for the various black departments of the vessel, and he is a wise man who does not attempt to interfere with local customs and usage.

The night after leaving Sierra Leone we are passing the Kru Coast, Liberia, probably the most uncertain and dangerous four hundred miles stretch along West Africa, because of the outlying rocks and reefs and the irregular insetting currents. Except at Monrovia, Grand Bassa and Cape Palmas, and even there the lights are of minor power, no illuminations or beacons mark the dangers. Often without warning the currents set towards the land. No precautions on the ship are considered superfluous. The deep-sea lead is cast at not longer intervals than every four hours, and anybody who owing to the heat has made his bed on deck and is awake may see the figure of the Captain frequently flit from his cabin during the night to join the officer on watch on the bridge.

When we are in calmer waters and the dark night has shut out surroundings and made us feel we are a little world to ourselves, we are now and again reminded of the vigilance maintained for our safety, as the look-out sings to the officer of the watch, "Light on the starboard bow, sir," and you see, miles away on your right front, a small gleaming lamp which tells of another ship on these trackless areas. And if the officer of the watch is in light mood you may hear him humming the doggerel of the "rule of the road" at sea:

"If all three lights I see ahead, I port my helm and show my red,
For green to green and red to red are perfect safety, 'Go ahead.'
But if to starboard red appear, it is my duty to keep clear.
To act as judgment says is proper, port or starboard, back or stop her.
But when in danger or in doubt I always keep a good look-out.
In danger with no room to turn, I ease her, stop her, or go astern."

Skippers of these West African liners become well known to the voyagers who pass backwards and forwards at regular intervals, and it is my good fortune to sail with one of the most popular of them. The manner Captain Pooley is regarded by travellers may be gauged from the fact that three on this journey are making the third voyage designedly on his ship and another had altered the date of starting by a fortnight to again be with him.

Twenty years along the West Coast of Africa and among its native population has not dulled the sympathy of Captain Pooley towards that race. All that can possibly be done for the deck passengers, taken on at the various ports, is effected. Canvas awnings are put up to protect the men " and especially the women and babies," as he explains, from the downpours of the wet season.

The skipper is a storehouse of stories about the Krumen. He tells a tale related by a fellow Captain against himself. He was carrying two white, Rotterdam hogs to the Oil Rivers and noticed one of his Kru sailors seated on the ground, gazing into the pen where the animals were kept. Placing his hand on the Kruman's woolly pate, he said, " Hullo, my frien', you look your brudder, eh ? "

Turning his face upwards the Kruman answered, " Massa Capin, he no be my brudder," adding, with a twinkle, " he be white."

Secondee, Cape Coast and Accra are the further ports at which stops are made, and at 7 a.m. on the sixteenth day from leaving Liverpool we are at anchor about four miles off Lagos, the capital of Southern Nigeria. Passengers going up-country tranship to a branch steamer of about eight hundred tons which takes them over the sand-bar, which the liner cannot pass, and across the large lagoon, depositing them at Iddo Wharf, the railway terminus.

CHAPTER II

FROM THE COAST BY TRAIN—THE WEST AFRICAN PULLMAN

Iddo Wharf—Strange sights and thoughts—Umbrellas—"Niggers"—Train luxuries—Liquor permits—The iron-horse at the Niger—Ferry and bridge—Budget details.

PASSING the length of the lagoon—a mile wide at its broadest point—leaving the town of Lagos, with its busy wharves and crowded streets, on his right, less than an hour's steaming from the Roads and the traveller is at Iddo Wharf. The train is drawn up near the water, and passengers walk a few steps from marine to land locomotion.

Strange sights appear to the traveller as he stands at Iddo Wharf. The strangest—or the strangest thought—of all is that there should be a train running in West Africa on which there is every reasonable comfort and luxury, and that this train should be in existence—the first of its kind in this part of the world—a few months after the extension of the line had been opened. First, however, a word or two on the surroundings at the terminus.

The train leaves at 9 p.m. on whatever day the ocean ship arrives. The vessel is due in the morning, but people have not the inconvenience of loafing about a strange town for hours. The boat train is an ark, available all day as a resting-place

FROM THE COAST BY TRAIN

for the sole of the foot. All its resources for meals can at once be utilised.

By nightfall most of the luggage will have been stowed in the vans. A few late arrivals, perhaps persons who have not come by the ship, will be having their belongings attended to. Black wharf labourers, who have been working late and are going home, put their umbrellas on the ground in order to give a hand in packing the vans. These labourers, whose attire is usually like that of the Wandering Minstrel in "The Mikado," "a thing of shreds and patches," almost to a man carry an umbrella as they go home o' nights—bless you! not for protection against rain, but as an article of adornment. It is as much a matter of course with them as the clay pipe and the cloth cap are with their counterpart in Great Britain. Different countries, different customs.

Nearly all the other officials at Iddo Wharf are also indigenous West Africans—clerks, inspectors, foremen, porters. There are as many grades and degrees of education among any one Coast people as there are with our folks in Europe. Were this fact always recognised and remembered, perhaps a little more tact might be exercised by individuals who regard all black men as "niggers" and suit their actions to the word. I stand as no apologist for the smatteringly-educated native, who dressed in uniform takes up an attitude truculent and offensive towards white men. It is British policy and systems of education which are responsible.

There is also at Iddo Wharf at least one first-class, white railway official on duty to attend to any matter requiring his attention.

The train usually consists of eight coaches, some of them fifty feet long, and therefore easy running at the fairly high speed over certain portions of the line. Meals are served en route, and every attention is received from the inspector of restaurant cars, who was formerly a chief steward in the Elder Dempster fleet. In the course of the journey I witnessed his solicitude, and that of the European head guard, Cyril Richards, for passengers who were not well and unable to take the table meals. The inspector, whose name I regret to have mislaid, had light food brought instead, the charge for which was, in instances, less than a quarter that of the regular menu. Perhaps the action does not appear surprising, but it means a deal in a country where a man feels weak and knows he has little margin of strength to withstand the effect of the climate.*

The term sleeping saloon means provision of bed, blankets, and linen. Couches are fitted for rest during the day. Electric light is in all compartments, which are provided with electrically-driven fans and have mosquito-proof windows. Shower baths are another luxury for which there is no extra payment. No doubt it all sounds prosaic enough to the trotter across the European continent. Let him " pad the hoof " in the tropics, or so much as be in an ordinary West African train for several days where he is entirely " on his own," with a temperature ranging from 90 degrees to 112 degrees in the shade, or with the Harmattan winds bringing

---

* I have since learned that what was done was quite in accordance with the spirit of the instructions that are laid down from the boat train. They are, in effect:—" We do not seek to make a profit, but we do wish to have no complaints."

FROM THE COAST BY TRAIN

scorching dust into his ears, nostrils and the pores of his skin, covering every mouthful before it can enter that avenue. Should he have experienced these things, have a memory, and is inclined to gratitude, then he will take off his hat to the Administration of the Lagos Government Railway, if he does not go so far as to be Biblically impelled and rise up and call the work of their hands blessed.

The traveller wakes for early morning tea to find himself traversing the palm belt. There is a continuous line of the tall, thin, bare trunks, surmounted by the graceful, drooping palms beneath which cluster the kernels which are the main wealth of Southern Nigeria. Palm kernels and palm oil are to Southern Nigeria what coal is to England. There are rumours that that mineral has been located on the lower Niger. Possibly I may be able to say something on the subject as I come down the river on the return journey.

Running through at night, several features of interest are unseen, prominent among them the exceptionally pretty view towards the Sacred Hill at Olokemeji and Ibadan, the largest town in West Africa, though not nearly so frequently spoken of as the much smaller ones of Zaria, Bida, Sokoto and Kano. Each has had the advertisement of war.

A short stop for water—not the first—is made at 6.45 a.m. at Oshogbo, 187 miles from Lagos, and still one of the hopes of the British Cotton Growing Association. Little more than an hour later the line enters Northern Nigeria. At Offa, the station over the frontier, permits have to be shown to take wines or spirits into the Mohamedan land, even for personal consumption. We are now 1,500 feet above sea level.

Jebba, 306 miles, is reached at noon, and here one of the stiff difficulties of railway construction which faced the engineers can be seen. The Niger must be crossed. The easiest way of doing so is from the south mainland to a large island, thence to the north mainland. The south channel is 1,100 feet broad, the north one rather less. The latter has been bridged; the former is still under that operation, which will not be finished for two years, making three in all.

The length across the river is the least of the obstacles to be solved. Heavy rises and falls of the water—in a month it may alter from 15 feet to 50 feet—made the work not only hard and hazardous, but impossible at certain periods of the year. But with hundreds of miles of rail completed south and north last November, it would have been an exasperating position to have to wait a further two and a half years for through connection. A civil engineer will tell you that nothing on earth is impossible. It is only a matter of money and time.

Well, the same train which carries you from Lagos to its destination at Minna, 161 miles beyond Jebba, covers its course without the traveller having to leave his carriage. The train goes over the Niger by means of a ferry. That, however, is itself a difficult subject by reason of the varying height of the river. The question at issue was how to transport weights, too heavy to be safely lifted, from a fixed level to an alternating one.

FROM THE COAST BY TRAIN

The carriages are run to the head of an inclined plane and a wire rope fastened to each coach, the other end encircling a winding drum. Another rope bound to the further end of the carriage draws it on the slope of the plane, and the winding machine lets it down. The plane carries the carriages to a trolly bridge resting on the river, and rising and falling with it. The trolly bridge fits to a steam ferry which bears four carriages, so that the entire train is taken over in two journeys. At Jebba Island the reverse process is followed, and a freight engine being coupled up the train proceeds over the north channel bridge and thus onwards.

Kooty-Wenji should be made by daylight, and there a halt is made till next morning, as the line has not yet been ballasted, and is therefore not safe to be used at night.

At 6 a.m. the train is again on the move, and in less than an hour-and-a-half we draw up at Zungeru, 430 miles from Lagos. The course has been covered in thirty-six hours. A week later the boat twenty-four hours.
train attained a record by doing the journey in

I am making a short stay at Zungeru; but perhaps it will make a better connected narrative if a few additional railway particulars are given now. Midday the train leaves for Minna, which is its destination. A journey straight ahead can be made by ordinary train to Kano, 282 miles from Zungeru. The traveller for the tin fields in the Bauchi and the Nassarawa Provinces will alight at Zaria, 90 miles south of Kano. From Zaria, the Bauchi Light Railway will in seven hours take him the $88\frac{1}{2}$ miles to Rahama railhead.

B

Appended are the through fares by the boat train, including sleeping accommodation and attendance:

	£	s.	d.
Lagos to Ibadan	3	0	6
,, ,, Zungeru	6	7	3
,, ,, Zaria	8	12	4
,, ,, Rahama	9	14	7
,, ,, Kano	9	14	10

First-class passengers by the boat train are allowed the following weight of luggage, excess of which is placed at heavier rates:

```
              2 cwts. free.
              20  ,,  at 7s. 2d. per cwt. to Zungeru.
              20  ,,  at 9s. 3d.   ,,   ,,  to Zaria.
              20  ,,  at 9s. 11d.  ,,   ,,  to Kano.
Additional    20  ,,  at 10s. 6d.  ,,   ,,  to Zungeru.
     ,,       20  ,,  at 13s. 6d.  ,,   ,,  to Zaria.
     ,,       20  ,,  at 14s. 6d.  ,,   ,,  to Kano.
```

Meals are charged: early morning tea, 6d.; breakfast, 2s.; lunch, 3s.; afternoon tea, 1s.; dinner, 4s. 6d.

Doubtless very mundane details, but useful to the man who desires to know before setting forth from Europe how he is to fare financially in small matters.

CHAPTER III

ZUNGERU—THE CAPITAL OF THE PROTECTORATE

A garden-city Capital—" Ikey " square—Autocracy thorough—Circumscribed accommodation and doubled-up quarters—Young administrators—Strict, stern, severe economy—The Governor's " Palace "—Job-lot furniture—His Excellency's 1s.-an-hour, Bank-Holiday motor-car—Pooh-Bah Cantonment magistrate.

I EXPECTED to find Zungeru a town more or less roughly divided into official, business and residential quarters, with clearly-defined and named roads and thoroughfares. The Capital of Northern Nigeria—the administrative headquarters—is, however, a city in a garden; and a very small city at that, probably the smallest in existence, much smaller than Monrovia, the Capital of the Republic of Liberia.

Still, power is seated at Zungeru—power strong, clear, absolute. The Governor of Northern Nigeria is given fuller authority over the people and the country than is in the hands of the Kaiser of Germany or the Czar of Russia. Without giving a reason he can decide questions of life and death; cancel a lease held by European or native; deny entry of or expel white or black; make law by simply issuing a Proclamation. He has not even a nominated Legislative Council, as in Crown Colonies. The form of government for natives in Northern Nigeria will be dealt with in a separate chapter.

Zungeru consists of a few bungalows dotted irregularly amidst trees in open grass and bush country. The roads, made by the Public Works Department, are very good: gravel, 10 to 30 feet wide and excellent for cyclists. The thoroughfares are all unnamed. You do not say that you live at such-and-such a house in such-and-such a road, or avenue, or street, but that your address is number one, two, or three, or any other number, as the case may be, Zungeru.

One point must not be included in this generalisation. Leaving out the Secretariat, five of the principal Government buildings face the same centre, and are designated by the natives Aiki—pronounced Ikey—Square. Aiki is the Hausa word for work, and the name therefore means " the place where the work is done." Gratifying to the persons whose hours are spent there.

Certainly there is an official quarter, but it comprises the whole of the town, with the exception of the Niger Company's store, and the native village, which is a recent creation. Midway between the two points are the native clerks' houses. Distinct from all the places stated are the military lines and the police barracks. That, in outline, is the story of Zungeru to-day.

It is ten years old, and previous to the advent of the British, in 1901, was scarcely a " geographical expression," for few maps gave the place. The population is made up of seventy officials, two hundred native officials, and four white members of the staff of the Niger Company and the Bank of Nigeria.

The extension of the Lagos Railway from Jebba

to Kano via Zungeru last January has brought the last-named within two days of the sea, instead of between three and four weeks, according to the state of the rivers. But the character of Zungeru is unchanged, and is likely to remain so. There is no prospect within sight of its becoming a city or even a town, as understood in Europe. More passengers may pass up and down the line, for commercial or other reasons, than formally travelled through, and a number of individuals may consider it necessary to come to Zungeru to see Government officials about mining matters—though the total of these is not likely to be large, as the Government Inspector of Mines, who advises the Governor, is located at Naraguta—but there is nothing at present to indicate an appreciable influx of population to Zungeru.

Let there be no mistake about the accommodation in Zungeru. It is extremely limited. If anybody thinks to arrive by train and " roll off " to an hotel he will be grievously disappointed. Only in one town of Southern and Northern Nigeria—territory 333,300 square miles in extent—is there an hotel. That is at Lagos. Men come without previous notice or inquiry to Zungeru and expect provision to be made in the way of board and lodging. It simply cannot be done. Bungalows are few and nearly all are overcrowded, from Government House down. The Chief Secretary to the Government, the Chief Justice, the Attorney-General, the Commandant, the Treasurer, the Director of Public Works, the Principal Medical Officer, the Chief Transport Officer, the Inspector-General of Police, and the Commissioner of Police alone have separate housing, very circumscribed. The rest of the Government staff are "doubled-up," i.e., two men to every three-roomed bungalow. As matters stand, there are not sufficient bungalows to go round even on this plan. It is not uncommon for an official to be moved from one to another as a man returns to duty, just finding room where somebody is going on vacation.

Four rest-houses are provided for visitors staying temporarily. The structures are rather primitive, of dried mud walls and thatched roofs. The stranger within the gates must bring all his daily requirements with him: bed, table, chair, cooking utensils, groceries, etc. Fresh meat can be bought in the native market at certain hours of the day.

Happy in the enjoyment of hospitality at a large private house, I felt quite a twinge of unworthiness at going to interview at one of these rest-houses a President of Chamber of Mines, Colonel Judd, who in England probably dines at the Carlton, the Ritz, or the Midland Grand, and who, even in Northern Nigeria, wearing a bush shirt, was still spruce, with a gold-rimmed monocle. A dozen people would have been glad to pay him the compliment of an invitation as guest, but there was simply no room in Zungeru where he could be placed. Colonel Judd was the least concerned of anybody. He expressed himself as quite content, and told me, as we both sat on the arm-rests of the single deck-chair available, that he had had to put up with much worse places in the course of his journey and that I would be fortunate to get as good in the areas I shall shortly cross.

These four rest-houses are frequently all occupied

to the fullest extent. The advent of a stranger, perhaps bent on business with a Government department, creates a painful situation.

Everything in Zungeru has been done on the lowest price scale, which is perhaps not the cheapest. From the first, Northern Nigeria has been short of funds. The Imperial grant-in-aid was kept down to a minimum, and that minimum much less than it should be in justice to the men who serve here at great risk to life and health. Not a penny has been spent that could be avoided. With the exception of the railway bungalows, which are of brick, but for which rich Southern Nigeria paid, all the others are of wood which has been exposed to a wasting climate for ten years. Several are in a dilapidated condition. They are occupied by men holding high posts whose work is essential to the administration, the finances, and the peace of the country; yet we make them live in dwellings—there are none other—which are a daily challenge to health and provocation to disease. This is not economy; it is gambling with men's lives for the sake of a miserable few shillings capital outlay. Sanitary housing—houses of the proper material and with ample air and protection against the insect and accompanying pests of the land—is second only to good food in keeping "fit." It is high time the necessary measures were carried out.

Excuses have been made for the situation. The future of Zungeru is uncertain as the Capital of the Protectorate. I will deal with that as a separate question. On the ground that the Capital may eventually be located elsewhere, the word went forth five years ago that no further building was to take place beyond what was absolutely necessary. It is only what is absolutely necessary that I advocate.

The high invaliding and death-rate which formerly obtained amongst officials in Northern Nigeria is to be attributed to the bad housing to which they have been subjected. The rate has lowered greatly. But too strong a deduction should not be drawn from the latest figures. An unhealthy station may enjoy long immunity. Tropical illnesses will not always arrange their appearance in the arbitrary terms of twelve months. To facilitate statistical argument, they more frequently rise and fall in a cycle of years. Let the proper steps be taken in Zungeru before the old high percentage of mortality reasserts itself.

Northern Nigeria is a country of and for young men.

The Postmaster-General strikes you as a fair-haired boy of twenty-two. He tells you, with pride, he is "much older than that." He is thirty-two. The Acting Chief Justice is no "potent, grave, and reverend seigneur," but is of an age when in England he would probably be fulfiling the rôle of "devil" to a leader in the High Court. The cool, clear-headed, and obviously capable officer temporairily in command of the 1st Battalion (1,314 men) Northern Nigeria Regiment, Captain G. C. Kelly, would, elsewhere, in these days of slow promotion, be lucky to have got his company. His colleague in charge of the battery of four light guns, Captain C. F. S. Maclaverty, could not hope to discharge anything like that responsibility at home. The Deputy Director of Railways, under the famous

ZUNGERU

John Eaglesome, might pass as a youth who had not long finished his articles.

Those at the head of affairs are not much older in years. I do not venture to ask the Acting Governor his age, and there is no "Who's Who" within reach, but I should judge Mr C. L. Temple, C.M.G., to be on this side of forty; and the next in rank, the Acting Chief Secretary, Mr H. S. Goldsmith, who recently temporarily carried out the duties of the highest position—with absolute rule over a territory containing 10,000,000 inhabitants—is, I learn from a friend, thirty-eight.

He started thirteen years ago, when Northern Nigeria was taken over by the Crown from the Niger Company. He began, as there was urgent demand for getting the administrative machinery into working order, in a very junior post in the Protectorate. In the course of his first year he had to give help wherever it was most pressing, going from one office to another: Stores, Transport, Treasury, and the Marine Department. All his willingness and eagerness were not wasted. Although seemingly unnoticed at the time, it marked out the kind of officer Sir Frederick Lugard wanted. In the last birthday honours list Herbert Symond Goldsmith, Acting Chief Secretary to the Government of Northern Nigeria, received a C.M.G.

Yes, the country has still opportunities for the man who is ready and keen. But it is not the place where "the lotus life" can be lived. The tradition of plenty of work and responsibility which Lugard established still obtains. Government office hours end at 2 p.m., with an hour's interval from nine to ten for breakfast. But they start early, and you may be startled at first at finding that an appointment for which you asked has been fixed for 7 a.m.

The time for official hours does not mean that it is a case of "down tools" as the clock points. I have found the Chief Secretary still hard at his duties at 5.30 in the afternoon, and one Sunday morning, when I went to see Captain Kelly at his bungalow, I learnt that he was closely engaged at the Brigade Office on a defence scheme.

The Secretariat has only a few constituting the personnel, nothing like the number one might look for at the Capital of such a large and well-populated territory. In Northern Nigeria the Government is greatly decentralised. Wide discretion is left to the Residents, who in some distant and not easily accessible places, such as Bornu and Sokoto, occupy the position of well-nigh sovereign kinglets. Further, actual and daily rule is left to the hereditary Emirs of the Provinces, subject to the advice and guidance, when necessary, of the Residents.

Another cause of the limited staff at the Secretariat is that in Northern Nigeria strict, stern, severe economy remains the order of the hour. There is evidence of it all round. The Secretariat is a poor building indeed. Bare brick whitewashed walls and cement floor crumbling in places, and in others worn into holes. Not a roll-top desk or anything approaching it in the place. Old, plain wooden tables, and, at the farther edge of each, roughly-made pigeon-holes. By way of contrast, the tables are of a light colour and the pigeon-holes have at some time or other been given a single daub of green paint, now faded. The Chief Secretary's room is just like the others. His table is covered by a bit of threadbare green baize which a messenger at Whitehall would not think fit to wipe his boots upon and for which no Hausa trader would give a handful of cowries.

At present occupied by the Acting Governor, Mr Temple—whose wife shares his " plain living "—the Governor's " Palace " is a mean shanty. A sevenroomed, wooden bungalow, it has stood " the battle and the breeze " for nine years and shows signs of the ordeal in all directions. It looks as though it could be easily shaken to bits. The dining-room is walled with boards which once received a single dash of brown staining. This apartment, however, is luxurious compared with the Governor's office adjoining, the plank partition of which has not its ugliness improved by a sparse covering of green paint, of the quality used in England on the garden fences of thirty-pounds-a-year houses. Nor does His Excellency recline on soft velvets or plush cushions, as might be expected of the ruler of Emirs and Kings who turn out in splendour. As I talked with him he sat in a plain chair, the hardness of the seat of which was somewhat relieved by an old horse-blanket folded.

The furniture at Government House is of the same nondescript character. It might have been picked up in job lots at public auction rooms. In order that I might take a group photograph six chairs were brought into the grounds from the drawing-room and I noticed that the six were made up of three different styles. Before the picture could be composed I had to do a temporary repair to one of the chairs.

The motor-car in which he gets about Zungeru,

and which is used for traversing distant roads the railway does not cover, is an old shambling machine making as much noise as a traction engine. The motor-cabs of Europe, and even the vehicles of the London General Omnibus Company are smart and ultra-fashionable by comparison. I should say that a suburban shopkeeper would scorn to hire it at a shilling per hour on a Bank Holiday to take his family round Battersea Park or Hampstead Heath. Well-to-do natives in Lagos use better.

These latter things are not written in any mere fault-finding, jeering spirit. They are set out in heartfelt admiration of the manner in which unnecessary hardships are cheerfully accepted by the members of the Government of the Northern Nigeria Protectorate, from the highest to the humblest. Millions have been spent on the country, but the money has gone in building railways, facilitating commerce, bettering the material opportunities of the native population and assuring them protection that they may pursue their ways in peace. The question may fairly be asked whether the time has not come when something should be done for the men who have put this policy into actual operation. John Bull stands to gain a great deal by the acquisition of Northern Nigeria. I am sure he would willingly acquiesce in more liberality on the part of those who act for him.

A figure which pervades Zungeru at every turn is the Cantonment Magistrate. The Governor is a commanding person, of whom everyone, from the visiting Sultans and Emirs to resident and travelling Europeans, stand much in awe. But the Governor is on a pedestal away from the general, daily run of affairs. Excepting on special occasions, when Government House is opened to hospitality, or an audience is sought, the ordinary individual does not come in contact with the Governor.

The Chief Secretary, as the leading member of the administrative staff, is pretty prominent, yet unless a matter is of importance he will not personally appear on the scene, though his name or signature will be used.

But the Cantonment Magistrate! You cannot get away from his authority. His functions seem interminable. He is a dozen individuals rolled into one. He is a veritable " Pooh-Bah " without, as it was darkly hinted to me, the emoluments of that Gilbertian creation.

Here are some of the parts carried out by the Cantonment Magistrate of Zungeru, formerly Captain, now Mr, J. Radcliff:

> He is President of the Cantonment Court, and tries small cases at law.
> He is Coroner within the area of the Cantonment.
> He is an ex-officio Commissioner of the Supreme Court.
> He is the Public Trustee, being charged with administration of the estates of all deceased Europeans.
> He is the Borough, or Town Council, for to him falls the levying of rates on all houses in the Cantonment, excepting those occupied by Government officials.
> He is Public Treasurer, as keeper of the Cantonment Fund.

He is Registrar General, for he must keep a register of all residents.

He is the local London County Council, as he regulates all streets and buildings. You may not cut down a tree without the permission of the Cantonment Magistrate.

He is the Highways Committee of the local London County Council; he constructs the roads.

He is the Local Government Board, for the work of the public department in England in the matter of sanitation is at Zungeru discharged by the Cantonment Magistrate.

He bears another duty of the L.C.C., in issuing licences to domestic servants, who are all males.

He does what is performed over post-office counters in England at certain times, for he gives a licence to keep a dog.

He supervises the native quarter of Zungeru.

He is the outside Master of Ceremonies of Government House, as he arranges communications and interviews between the local native notables and the Governor.

See the Cantonment Magistrate in his own court. Note the side glance of scepticism, scorn, and unbelief as a voluble female pours out her tale of woe. It is just the glance of the stipendiary on the bench at home. Looking at the lady, one would be driven to the conclusion that, after all, human nature is pretty much the same the world over, and that there is no great difference between Bridget or Mary Ann in England and Amina, Fatima, or Rekia in Zungeru.

Every Wednesday morning the local native Council consult with the Cantonment Magistrate. I chanced to be at his office as the four of them and the Chief came up. They salaamed by kneeling and bending their heads to the ground, and then arose and followed the Englishman into the building. Conversation ranged over several subjects. The C.M. lightly reminded the Chief that rents of market pitches were not being collected with that regularity, thoroughness, and completeness which the Governor liked. The Chief responded that people complained of little business, but that he would see to the arrears forthwith, and he improved the occasion by pointing out to the C.M. that certain parts of the market needed repair and money spent on improvements. The C.M. answered that it would be the first thing to be put in hand as soon as the arrears were received.

The talk branched into another channel. The Chief proceeded to say that he had been somewhat troubled in mind of late. The slightest trace of a questioning smile came on the visage of the Cantonment Magistrate. The Chief continued that it was so long since he had paid his respects to the Acting Governor that he was commencing to feel quite uneasy. His Excellency might consider him indifferent to politeness and his obligations.

The Cantonment Magistrate gravely told him to sleep well at nights on that score, as the Acting Governor was thoroughly aware of the Chief's loyalty. All the same, the C.M. would ascertain His Excellency's convenience for the audience and would promptly inform the Chief.

Then the visitor asked about the health of the

Acting Governor. The C.M. gave satisfactory assurances on that point. The next enquiry was as to the well-being of Mrs Temple. The C.M. rendered an equally gratifying report, and diplomatically remarked that she was looking forward to the pleasure of meeting the Chief, at which his face showed that he rejoiced exceedingly.

With similar ceremony to that at the commencement of the visit it ended.

CHAPTER IV

ZUNGERU—THE CAPITAL OF THE PROTECTORATE—
  (*continued*)

Native settlement—Rents and Treasury—A model prison—Northern Nigeria Constabulary—Mails paid time-work—Sport at the door—Up-country and Coast natives—Selection of Zungeru—The future Capital.

THE only European trading establishment in Zungeru is the store of the Niger Company. It adjoins the Cantonment. With a white population composed entirely of Government officials, all of whom bring their main requirements for a twelvemonth's term, it cannot be said there is room for another firm. The store is a great convenience, as men frequently miscalculate what they will need, or occasionally run out of some article of diet or clothing. The store is comprehensive, and stock is kept of provisions, hardware, men's wardrobes, and wines.

During one of my purchases over the counter a man who had been up-country for a considerable period, and whose attire was much the worse for what it had undergone, came in to be equipped for a visit to comparatively fashionable Lagos. He was fitted literally from head to foot, if not in Bond Street style, at least in striking contrast to what would pass muster in the bush districts.

The store stands in a compound wherein grow trees bearing paw-paws, limes, oranges, mangoes, cactus and rubber shrubs.

A mile or so from the Cantonment is the native town, which shows in miniature the principle on which the government of the country is carried on, that of ruling the natives through and by natives. At Zungeru a native settlement came as a sequence to the selection of the place as the administrative headquarters. The people were given plots 100 feet by 50 feet. The town has been designed on thoroughly sanitary lines and wells were sunk. A market, with iron roof and concrete floor, is in the centre of the town. For a pitch in it two shillings and sixpence per month is paid. Another market has been put up with thatch-covered stalls, and here ninepence per month is the due.

These market dues go entirely to the native Treasury, which has to render a strict account to the Cantonment Magistrate, and are used for the upkeep and improvement of the native town and for payment of native officials who are appointed by the Chief, including the market and the Alkali's court officials and the town police.

First-class plots for houses are rented at sixteen shillings a quarter, second-class plots eight shillings a quarter. Half the rent goes to the Government and half to the native Treasury.

Reverting to the direct British administration, Zungeru possesses a model prison, where the inmates have humane treatment without being made so comfortable that they welcome a sojourn within its walls as a place where the tasks are light and regular food is in larger quantities than they would get "on their own." The prison, which is used for convicts sent from various parts of the country to serve long sentences, is controlled by Captain A. E. Johnson, D.S.O., who is also Inspector-General of the Northern Nigeria Police. He is making good use of his hobby as a skilled amateur gardener. Prison labour has been used to lay out a rubber plantation of 100 acres, started $3\frac{1}{2}$ years ago and added to annually. It promises to yield good results.

He has also had fruit trees set along the left bank of the Dago: orange, lime, mango, guava, banana, covering 30 acres, all of which are doing well; and these at the proper stage will give Zungeru and surrounding districts the luxury of fresh fruit supplies. It may be asked why the step has been left to the Director of Prisons to utilise suitable soil. The answer is that with an 8 months' severe drought in 12, the necessary watering could never be done by private and paid labour at a remunerative sum.

The interior organisation of the gaol is equally estimable. Whilst a number of prisoners are put to road-making, railway construction—they made the first five miles from Zungeru to Minna—the best behaved are taught trades. There are five workshops—detached structures of brick, put up by delinquents—where carpentry, blacksmithing, tailoring, boot and slipper making, and grass mats (coloured and used as window and door screens) are turned out.

In the blacksmith's section curios are made. I saw a pair of native stirrups produced from old aluminium water bottles. Used cartridge cases are converted into various articles; they are hammered into one piece and a fancy plate shaped from it. The plan in all these trades is for a long-term man of commendable conduct to be taught a trade, and he teaches others. The system makes honest labour of more monetary value than malpractices to the discharged convict.

The Emirs and Chiefs throughout the Protectorate raise and maintain their own native police, but there is also a force under the central Government, termed the Northern Nigeria Police. It was started in 1900 by Sir Frederick Lugard, with 50 men selected from the Royal Niger Company Constabulary. It now consists of an Inspector-General, the aforesaid Captain A. E. Johnson, a Deputy Inspector-General, 4 Commissioners, 14 Assistant Commissioners, and 838 non-commissioned officers and men, the training being on modified military lines. The Sergeant-Major of the Zungeru detachment is the best-looking negro I had met to the time of visiting the town, and his intelligence is equal to his position. Several times I asked the Commissioner, Captain F. A. E. Godwin, to alter the position of the body paraded to be photographed. In every instance the request was transmitted to the Sergeant-Major, who promptly gave the proper order in military terms, never once failing to bring the 40 men into the required situation.

The force is recruited chiefly from ex-soldiers of the West African Frontier Force. Among the representative races the proportions are: Hausas, 60 per cent.; Yorubas, 30 per cent.; the remainder is comprised principally of Daka-Keri, Kukuruku, and Bauchi Pagans. For night duty the constables

ZUNGERU—continued

carry tell-tale clocks with dials for pricking at certain hours, and there are similar clocks in fixed spots where they must also register. The rank and file live together in lines, each man having his separate house. There are no bachelors in the Zungeru detachment.

The 1st battalion of the Northern Nigeria Regiment and 4 guns of the artillery are quartered at Zungeru. The training and efficiency of the troops are dealt with separately in Chapter XXXIII.

The Postmaster-General of Northern Nigeria, Mr H. M. Woolloy, is located at Zungeru. Mail services are by rail or river, where practicable. In many instances, however, runners have to be employed. Where possible, they are mounted on Bornu ponies. The runners are specially selected and work by contract; the faster they travel the more their pay. This is found more expeditious than providing relays. Thus the road from Zungeru to Sokoto is really a 17 days' journey. It is covered by the mail runners, afoot, each carrying a 40 lb. to 50 lb. bag, in 11 days. The postal and telegraph services were originally designed solely for administrative and strategical purposes and were not calculated to prove revenue-producing until a remote period. In spite of this, whilst the income in 1901 was £842, last year the value of the work performed amounted to over £20,000, obtained with an expenditure of £16,000. Apart from the Naraguta and the Kano telegraphs, none north of Zungeru can be regarded as of any commercial value.

The little white community of Zungeru try to make life pass pleasantly. The Games Club provides for tennis and golf, and there are similar associations for angling, polo, and races. A horse costs about £8. Sport with the gun abounds, though it must not be indulged within 3 miles of the Cantonment, or, figuratively, the hand of the C.M. would be on your shoulder.

Anybody may walk beyond the limit and easily find plenty of warthog, hartebeest and winged game, and sometimes bigger prizes. These occasionally visit the Cantonment. The other evening a large leopard stood looking contemptuously at the bungalow in which I am staying but elected not to jump the low palings. Had he, no doubt the C.M. would have taken a merciful view of the use of a couple of rifles which were cocked and ready. Nearly every evening at the same distance there is a vocal performance by a company of hyænas.

There is an extremely pleasant aspect in Zungeru, typical of Northern Nigeria, of the respect and good feeling shown by the coloured population to the white, and reciprocated. I say "coloured" instead of "native," for there are a fair number of "foreigners" from the Gold Coast and from Sierra Leone, imported for routine clerical work. The native Moslems invariably salute a European. The form of salute is generally that of removing sandals, followed by a low bow. The Gold Coast and Sierra Leone clerks are affected by the environment and custom. They scarcely ever fail to raise their hats and utter a "Good morning" or "Good afternoon, sir." In the Coast towns the prototypes of these young men are too frequently gratuitously arrogant and needlessly insolent towards an Englishman. Problem: Why is the up-country native in all British West African colonies, be he Moslem or Pagan, in nearly every case a gentleman by nature, whilst the output of the Government and missionary schools, with the possible exception of Catholics, too often a creature who makes himself hateful to white men?

The theme could be enlarged by analysis of the proportion contributed by the clerk class in Europeanised towns to the criminal calendar. Elementary education on English lines in West Africa is certainly not a success, decidedly not in the aspect of honesty and morals.

Does the respectful salutation of the Moslem to the English mark the subserviency of one to the other? Emphatically, no. It is a token of respect towards a race standing in the position of a Protectorate Power, exercising its position in the interest of the inhabitants and safeguarding their traditions, their customs, their religion.

Now, a few words on a question which has been discussed in West Africa and, to a certain extent, in England, namely, the selection of Zungeru as the administrative headquarters and its future. Sir Frederick Lugard has been criticised for the choice, though, considering what he did in and for the country with the means at his disposal, I marvel at any nature hardy enough to comment in an adverse sense. Still, I suppose the former High Commissioner would be one of the last to complain of his actions being scrutinised. I can write without subjecting myself to the suggestion of personal influence, for I have never met Sir Frederick Lugard. I merely speak as one who for several years has been a close student of West African affairs, who has had the advantage of looking at matters on the spot, and who for a long period wrote publicly on military operations. I make bold to assert that all the complaints on the selection of Zungeru are made by persons who do not study what the conditions were in 1902 when Jebba was discarded.

Let any reader take a map of Northern Nigeria and argue out the question for himself. Zungeru was decided upon, not, I should say, solely because it was in a central position, but on the strategic ground that it occupied a point extreme north of the territory then actually controlled, with an excellent administrative base from which movements of troops and political officers could be directed. It was also comparatively easy of access from the south.

No man was less ready than Sir Frederick Lugard to fussily interfere with the petty acts of subordinates. One of his primary principles was that of delegation and personal responsibility. But in the critical years between 1900 and 1907 the presence of the High Commissioner was continually essential in the Provinces northwards of Zungeru, and in those days of bush trekking, when covering 100 miles would be calculated at little less than a week, being as much "on the spot" as possible was a weighty consideration. The Sultans and Emirs to be visited or to be installed would regard nobody in the same light as they would the High Commissioner, whose name and fame had spread through the land. What Kitchener was and Wingate is in the Sudan, Lugard has been to Northern Nigeria.

Take a map and consider the situation in 1902. The Provinces of Sokoto, Kano, Bauchi, Nassarawa, Kantagora (although the town of that name had been taken), and the walled city of Zaria, and the large town of Bida, were all either actually or passively hostile. One of 3 courses: They would have to be brought into line with the rest of Northern Nigeria or there was the alternative of maintaining a large standing army or of retiring south. Zungeru was the best pivot on which to turn wherever attention might be required. Why, it has been asked, select a place which was not easily accessible in the dry season and a low river? No other spot presented even the qualities of Zungeru. It was within 10 miles of the navigable part of the Kaduna River—with which it was connected by a steam tramway—and through the town itself there ran a stream of pure water all months of the year. The climate has proved to be as healthy as at any other station.

Sooner or later, however, a decision must be taken whether Zungeru is to be retained as Capital. On it being now the most suitable spot I do not feel qualified to give an opinion. But Lokoja and Jebba, which have each been spoken of as the "natural Capital" may be dismissed. Both have been tried. Kano has also been referred to in the same connection, so put forward for the glamour of its name and the prominent place it has become in recent history, as well as for its commercial importance.

The very qualities cited operate against the central authority being established in or near Kano. A largely populated centre is not the best situation for a government. The local powers-that-be are unfairly dwarfed and the neighbouring population likely to exercise an undue influence on the executive. Possibly, London is an example of these drawbacks. On the one hand, the L.C.C., bearing in mind the interests and area it represents, is overshadowed by its towering legislative big brother at Westminster. On the other hand, an outdoor demonstration of large dimensions in the metropolis has more influence on the Cabinet than a similar gathering five times the size in Lancashire, Dublin, or Glasgow. South Africa has shown wisdom by not locating the Parliament at Johannesburg.

The Bauchi Highlands have been brought forward as the coolest, best temperature for a new Capital. Much water will flow down the Niger before any such scheme is practicable. At present the main obstacle to Bauchi is lack of transport. When a railway makes it like Zungeru, within a few days of Lagos, instead of two or three weeks, then Bauchi will come within the sphere of practical politics. Lastly, the administrative headquarters of Northern Nigeria may, in the near future, be of less importance than it has been, for by the union with Southern Nigeria, the seat of the Lieutenant-Governor of each—assuming that be the form adopted—will obviously fulfil quite a secondary rôle. And to me it seems inevitable that Lagos will become the capital of United Nigeria.

CHAPTER V

ZUNGERU TO KANO

Everybody his own porter—Religion and missions—Divining water—Carriages patchy in parts—Native passengers—In the track of the slave-raider—Engine sustenance—Kaduna Bridge—A tight-rope performance—Close cultivation—" The lazy negro "—Two civilisations—At Kano.

"THE line is the thing," to modify Hamlet's phrase. To get the track into working order at the earliest possible day, that is the object of all concerned in the construction of a railway, once it has been started. You must have rails laid, locomotives, carriages. All subsidiary matters can be improvised provisionally. It is not necessary to wait until "the last button on the soldiers' leggings" has been fixed. Thus, on the section from Zungeru to Kano a number of things remain to be done before there is the completeness which is seen south of the Niger.

To anybody with whom time is a consideration, a railway, instead of the old method along the cart-road of 282 miles to Kano, is an unspeakable boon.

Some novel travelling features appear on Zungeru Station. There has not been sufficient time to enrol a full staff and therefore one must make one's own arrangements for getting heavy packages into or from the train. First-class passengers can enjoy the unusual experience of obtaining from the Stationmaster partly printed labels, writing on them the destination, then hunting for a glue-pot and themselves affixing the labels. It is a case of every man his own porter. We are not at a fashionable resort, and all who have to do the job undertake it in a laughing spirit.

Directly the train moves off you realise you are on your own resources. Private, or even official, hospitality cannot extend to a train where everybody is expected to look after himself in all things for nearly half a week. A 50-foot coach is partitioned into four divisions, all quite bare. In a division—you may be fortunate in having two—you must rig up your little home: a sitting and dining-room by day; a sleeping apartment at night. Each end of the coach has a stove, where the cooks can prepare meals.

Minna—38 miles—is reached in two hours, and here the night is spent. In the hot weather passengers put their camp-beds on the open platform, arranging them under the projecting roof if rain threatens.

Arrival of the train at Minna marks a busy time, for the line upwards from Baro joining, passengers who have come by the river route are waiting to continue the journey northwards, or others may have come down from that direction.

Amidst all the bustle of people coming and going, of the excitement of sorting baggage for carriers, of piles of bales and boxes being moved, of loud whistling of locomotives and of shunting engines, I saw a white-robed figure go on his knees, turn his face to the east and bend his head in devotion. It was a Mohamedan silently offering up evening prayer. Religious duty was louder to him than the babel resounding around. He was not ashamed to speak with his Maker in sight of the multitude.

Yet there are worthy folks at home who seek to send missionaries to these people to teach them to worship the same God but in a different way. Why is the money and the energy expended on such missions—which are practically hopeless in Mohamedan countries like this—not deflected to the better purpose of mitigating the vice, the crime and the preventible poverty in the great cities of the United Kingdom, where the triple evils stalk abroad in the daylight, unabashed, unashamed.

At Minna Station one must see Mr A. Newport, the stalwart traffic inspector. I say one " must," because the first time travelling over the line there are enquiries which have to be satisfied. For instance, change of train is made for the journey continued early next morning. Further, it may not have occurred to a traveller, even thinking out all requirements to the most minute detail, that wood for a fire on the train to cook food would be necessary. Finally, one's filter may not be within easy access and condensed water be needed for preparing the evening meal.

In all these, and perhaps other instances, Mr Newport is of incalculable aid and value. Whatever the multitude of matters pressing upon him for immediate attention, he always seems willing to accept one more without impatience or irritation. But if everybody going through Minna leaves all these things to be supplied by Mr Newport, it is likely that he will not have a sufficiency of them to satisfy everybody's expectations. Maxim and moral: When travelling in Nigeria never depend on supplying from another's provisions that which you have wilfully neglected to provide for yourself.

At Minna Station one may also meet Mr E. H. Biffen, Traffic Superintendent of the Baro-Kano Railway, uniformly genial and courteous, and ever ready to do all in his power to help a traveller; and on the platform there will probably be Mr J. Oldfield, Traffic Assistant, who seconds the manner of his chief.

On waking up at Minna Station one realises more fully than on the previous afternoon what it is to be on one's own resources for bodily needs. Sufficient condensed water had been economised for breakfast, but, in a tropical country above all, some kind of wash, at least once a day is almost as necessary for comfort as food, and for preference the operation is performed on getting out of bed.

Just at 6 o'clock, as I was wondering, after an hour's cogitation, what was to be done in a distinctly uncomfortable predicament, mental relief came. Looking out of the window I saw my native servant —for the time being maid-of-all work, cook, steward, and general factotum—Oje, trudging along towards the stationary train with a pail on his head, and by the manner of balancing the utensil it was clear that it contained water. Without being told, Oje had set out and discovered water.

How did he come to divine its presence in a place where he had not previously been and of which he had never heard? I asked him. He said he saw a footpath from the railway and sagely concluded it must lead somewhere. That somewhere, he deduced, was likely to be a native village. A village was sure to be near a stream or other water. He would go and investigate.

I do not mean that Oje argued all these points in their logical sequence, after the manner of a Sherlock Holmes; instinct told him at once.

The water had come from a shallow, stagnant, well-nigh dried-up water course. It looked yellow, and on being shaken took the consistency of thick soup. Still, it was water, and for that relief much thanks.

Oje—poor, friendless Oje, hundreds of miles from home and parents—had more prescience than his master—employer is a word I would sooner use—more prescience than any white man on the train. A chapter could easily be written of Oje. He deserves it, is worthy of it. He is always helpful, frequently a pleasant companion to speak with, and occasionally a comfort to talk to in the silent evenings when flying insects make writing impossible, in spite of his limited vocabulary of even pidgeon English. His devotion is staunch and unmistakable. I shall remember Oje with many kindly sentiments when thousands of miles of sea and land separate us, and when, perhaps, I am tramping through the lands of another continent.

The prospect of an unwashed state happily past, as the train spins along one can heartily enjoy the free-and-easy existence, as one sits on a camp chair and, facing the open door of the " saloon," tries to catch the breeze stimulated by the running train. It seems more enjoyable than the luxury of the boat express. Your pail containing water may leak; no matter, you *must* effect a repair on the spot, and that is done by drawing a rag into the hole. You discover that you have no bread for breakfast and that none was to be bought at Minna Station; no matter, a tin of biscuits from your food boxes will serve instead. You find out that the firm who made up the food boxes have omitted the sugar; no matter, some other passenger will help you out. Whatever your petty troubles, they are lost sight of in the feeling that you are in your own little compartment, within its walls living in your own way, distant from the stilted and artificial manners which clog life at home.

The celerity with which the Baro-Kano Railway was constructed—its junction with the Lagos Railway is at Minna—and the instant and remarkable success it has proved have caused an "overrunning of the constable" in the provision of rolling stock. You may notice that the first-class coaches are patched up in parts. As a matter of fact, I believe that a number were to have been broken up, having been discarded by home lines, but the call for accommodation was so pressing that as many as could be made serviceable were again put on the rails. So you see the result of two or three worn-out carriages being made into a single sound one; sides and floor, with some doors from other carriages screwed on to form a complete article.

The demand on the part of third-class passengers —of course, all natives—was much greater. It was not merely a case of the construction of the finished track outstripping the supply of carriages; the number of passengers carried had exceeded the utmost expectations. It was estimated that the total receipts for the last financial year, 1911-12, April to March, would amount to £10,000, but they totalled

ZUNGERU TO KANO

£46,000. It is clear that on this line, as in the case of most in the United Kingdom, the third-class passenger is to be the stand-by of income for human freight. Apart from the fact that there are few Europeans in the country—I should say less than 700 to a native population of 10,000,000—averaging the 255 miles between Minna and Kano, the respective proportions are: first-class, seven Europeans; second-class, two or three Europeans; third class, 150 natives.

The supply of ordinary third-class coaches was utterly insufficient. Every type of truck has had to be used in addition, or the passengers left. All canvas sheetings obtainable for roof coverings did not suffice, and as native travellers clamoured to be carried in any way so long as only they were carried, low side trucks were put on, and then high ones, containing coalite and other goods in transit on which the passengers wished to sit.

It should be borne in mind that these people have always been in the habit of moving from one place to another—these Hausa traders—and they quickly grasped the advantage and the comfort of riding in trains at a low charge instead of tramping along bush paths or caravan roads. By means of using the railway they could do as much business in one day, with less marching, as they formerly did in a month.

And how these people enjoy the train ride! No party of school-children on their one-day-a-year excursion more so. See them crowded as the proverbial sardines, laughing, joking, happy, with legs dangling over the sides of the goods trucks. When Lugard projected, Girouard put in hand, and Eaglesome carried out the railway from Baro to Kano they builded better than they knew.

The track between Zungeru to Minna takes a gentle rise; the latter is 500 feet higher than the former. The country traversed is wooded and fertile, but depopulated, the effect of the cruel slave-raiding descents from the north, which devastated districts, leaving, as evidence of the visitation, burnt-down villages, the inhabitants all either dragged off to slavery or put to the sword on the spot. The land sunk into disuse and desolation.

British power has stopped it for ever, at least, as long as British power is supreme. But decades must pass before tillers are again on the soil. When they are the wide acres of Northern Nigeria will give agricultural produce on a scale that will bring great prosperity to the Protectorate and render it of value to territories beyond its borders, exporting perhaps foodstuffs, and certainly those essential oils for which manufacturers in Europe are searching the tropics.

Immediately after leaving Minna, in the first six miles the rise is 300 feet. The track then becomes fairly level, frequently crossing tributaries of the Kaduna River, the largest of which is the Kogin Serekin Pawa. From this the line follows the valley of the Kugo River, climbing 30 miles to the Zaria Plateau, which is touched at Bakin Kasua, 70 miles south of Zaria City and 19 before reaching the Kaduna. Then a drop of approximately 400 feet to Kaduna Station.

Over certain parts of the track, where temporary work has quite recently been superseded by that of a lasting character which has not yet hardened and

ZUNGERU TO KANO

settled, the train proceeds very gingerly, for it is heavily laden and must needs be hauled with caution and knowledge.

Most of the stations consist of a bank of gravel, levelled as a platform would be, with a 10 feet by 12 feet corrugated iron box, which holds telegraph instruments—the eyes and ears for safe conduct of the line—and is also the Stationmaster's office. Two or three huts near by are the domiciles of the staff, comprising a telegraphist, a pointsman, and a labourer, all natives. A pointsman is necessary, as, although the line is a single track, every station has a loop for trains passing each other. At stations of a very minor type the Stationmaster is also telegraphist.

At intervals the engine halts for sustenance. A tank is set up, sometimes quite in bush country but always near streams which are never completely dried up, and water forced into the tank by a handpump worked by "boys," who live in huts near by. The railway engineers have made small dams across the streams as safeguards for supply.

Every three or four miles are gangs of eight to ten "boys," who live in a small settlement of their own, and, under a headman, pay attention to the track, supervised by a European platelayer, who has charge of 25 to 30 miles of line.

There is unmistakable evidence of approaching Kaduna. The line broadens out to four tracks and there are other adjuncts of a locomotive depôt. Kaduna has also the importance of being the headquarters of the Director of Railways. In the absence on vacation of Mr Eaglesome, I spent the evening—the train stays overnight—with the

Deputy Director, youthful Mr E. M. Bland, referred to in the Zungeru chapter.

Among the entertainments in the way of sight-seeing and instruction which he gave me was a walk across the adjacent Kaduna River railway bridge. I was lured on unsuspectingly and, I am sure, innocently on the part of Mr Bland. He never guessed—nor will he know until he sees these lines in print—of the ordeal it was to the visitor. The Kaduna Bridge is 660 feet long. The rails are fixed to sleepers the spaces between which are open to the river below.

In the middle of the track is a narrow sheeting of iron and along this Blondin-like tight-rope strode the Deputy Director, I tremulously following. Had I half an idea that he intended going beyond the first few inches I would either have invented some excuse for turning back or have boldly asked to be excused on the score of a sudden headache or something of the kind. I certainly expected every minute that this exasperatingly cruel guide would stop. When we reached midway across I wondered why on earth he was continuing the walk. Only that I did not trust myself to turn round on the narrow pathway I would have returned forthwith.

Mr Bland never ceased to speak of points of interest left and right, throwing a directing finger first in one direction and then in another, I more or less mechanically answering in monosyllables, the slippery, heavy nails in my boots striking the narrow metal pathway ominously, and, scarcely lifting my eyes from it all the time, I thought of people I knew in England, conjuring up what they would say to my having come to my end by falling through into

ZUNGERU TO KANO

the waters beneath Kaduna Bridge, instead of going under by the more heroic malarial fever.

Once Mr Bland, indicating a notable landmark, turned round to make the matter clearer, and on my quickly replying with a "Yes," as though I saw and understood everything—earnestly praying he would get over the bridge at the earliest possible moment —he remarked that I was looking the wrong way and that the object to which he referred was half-a-mile off the opposite side of the bridge.

At last we were across, and I glanced around to discover a boat by which we could row or paddle back. Before I could gain breath to utter a word out spake Mr Bland. He said how sorry he was that he could not indulge in canoeing, as he did at home—he is a Canadian—as there was no craft of any kind for miles.

Then we must go back over that few-inches-wide iron path! Why were engineers so madly stupid as to place such an ordeal under the uncertain feet of an enquiring journalist? However, there was no alternative. A repeated 660 feet of mental tribulation and we were safe on the other bank.

Immediately I developed a wonderful power of conversation and comment on all the Deputy Director had told me during those horrible perambulations from bank to bank. In my exuberance of spirits I felt I wanted to slap him on the back. Oh, yes, I now saw quite distinctly and with eagerness the concrete piers on which the temporary bridge was laid for construction purposes, and a little higher up the river I recognised, visually, the ford used in the old days of the caravan road from the north.

Kaduna is left at 5.45 a.m., and 13 miles further on is Rigachikun, remembered as the former point of departure from the train for the tin fields. It was from Rigachikun the Government made a 12 feet wide roading for transport to the fields.

A further higher altitude is reached at Dumbi, 12 miles south of the station of that name. The native village is 6 miles nearer the station. From Dumbi there is again a descent. The land is open, with trees in some parts singly and occasionally in clusters, but never in the jungle density which flanks most of the line of another West African railway, the one from Secondee to Coomassie. The park-like appearance of this Province of Northern Nigeria makes the view indistinguishable from English scenery. The fields are in a bright, in fact brilliant, green from the overnight rain; the tall, waving grass brushes the carriages as they roll past. Sheep and herds of cattle are on the pasture land. One crowd of them merely gaze at the passing train; another batch, more apprehensive, scamper away. Their colours contrast with the uniformity of the green ground: brown, black, and a drove of about 30 all white. So the landscape continues until Zaria is reached. Here is a branch line—the Bauchi Light Railway—to the tin fields. To that I shall return for the Bauchi Plateau trek.

Proceeding northwards, after half-an-hour's stop at Zaria, 25 miles further on, for the third time since leaving Minna, there is a rise to over 2,400 feet above sea-level, at Anchou, and from here all the rivers and their tributaries flow into Lake Chad, those previously passed going to the Gulf of Guinea. Twelve miles south of Kano, which is 90 from

ZUNGERU TO KANO

Zaria, the Shallawa River—a broad, sandy stream—is spanned by the largest bridge on the Baro-Kano Railway. From Anchou there is a gradual fall, amounting to 700 feet, to Kano.

As one approaches the 50 miles radius from Kano City one sees evidence of close cultivation of the soil which marks that Province of Northern Nigeria. The land is flat, open, and in parts fairly well wooded. There appears to be no barren waste soil within sight. Plots, varying in size, are clearly marked off and separated by 2 feet high straw fences, close-growing grass of the same height, or neatly-trimmed bushes. The fields are green—freshened by recent light rains—and occasionally the bright colour merges into a fainter tint, whilst tracts are yellow with the ripened crops shortly to be harvested.

As the eye is cast across the level plains, now and again backgrounded by hills and small mountains, the scene might be taken for one in an English agricultural county. The illusion would the more readily be accepted, for the circular clumps in the fields might easily pass as small haystacks. They are native houses, and a fuller understanding of the situation is grasped as the busy figures hoeing the furrows look up and it is seen that they have black skins.

Are these busy groups of men industriously winning produce from the soil the "lazy negroes" in whom we—new-comers to the land—are to inculcate "the dignity of labour"? Can it be that we have as little to teach them in that respect as in several others?

The scenes of sowing, planting, reaping, gathering, are repeated in various forms as the train rolls on until, there in the distance, is a greyish line which must be the walls of famed Kano City. The engine heads straight for the wall, as though it would impatiently break down whatever should stand in the way of modern ideas of advancement; but as we draw nearer it would seem wiser councils prevail, and, bearing to the right, we swing past the city walls, showing that by tact, sympathy, imagination, and judgment the two civilisations can exist side by side.

Speed is being reduced, but a couple more miles are to be covered, and as we go slowly a clearer view of the stout encircling wall is discerned. First to relieve its evenness is the Dan Agundi Gate, and near that opening—between it and the railway—is the discarded mission house, where a few months ago poor Fox died. Next we pass the Nassarawa Gate, then the Mata Gate, and a few yards further on the train pulls up at the spot where Kano Station is to be built.

CHAPTER VI

ARRIVAL AT KANO

Plans and expectations—Small water-famine—The handy man—Change of quarters—Ants as sauce—Niger Company.

IT is well perhaps that things should not go too smoothly. It is well, probably, that though matters are thought out and plans made in advance they should crumble by no fault of the maker. It is as well, no doubt, that suffering the slings and arrows of outrageous fortune should befall one who until arriving in Kano had had a pleasure trip, not made less pleasurable by unremitting work, the joy of the journey enhanced rather than lessened by a few minor discomforts.

I had imagined that the previous enjoyment would be multiplied many fold at Kano, famous Kano. Everything possible had been done to prevent mishaps. The house had been engaged. It was one of those the Government has put up for travellers passing through. True it was a circular hut of mud and straw, but, I was told, two French officers were occupying a similar dwelling, so it was as good as I had any warrant to expect. The train by which I was to arrive had been notified to the quarter that had a right to know. Nothing seemed omitted from the preliminary arrangements.

No more forlorn figure landed on a foreign shore

than the writer of these lines presented, to himself at least, as he stood on the ground known as Kano Station. He knew only a single person in Kano, and, for what appeared justifiable cause, he would not humble himself by sending a message to that individual. No porters are at Kano, and there the fresh arrival stood, helpless to move, with a couple of dozen heavy boxes. He had not the slightest idea of the situation of the hut in which he was to live, and nobody present could inform him. It was a pretty predicament. Of course, there was a cause for the embarrassing situation, but it need not be explained.

An hour passed, and then someone saw who had a heart. As on several occasions in the course of this journey aid came from a Baro-Kano Railway man. Mr A. W. Brayscher, Traffic Assistant, the officer in charge of Kano terminus, came up and asked if he could be of service. Having told him, minus details, how badly stranded I was, he offered a mud and straw hut similar to the adjacent one in which he lived, belonging to the railway and used by engine-drivers. It was eagerly accepted and the impedimenta promptly transferred under its roof. Here I thought to settle down for a week, and, at all events, to be conscious of a spirit of independence.

But my troubles were not ended. Food now became a consideration. For that water was necessary. Where was it to be obtained? I learned, at a well "over there," the locality indicated being a field half-a-mile away. If, my reader, you desire to be satisfied with, if not thankful for, the high charges of your British Municipality or Metropolitan Water

Board, come to a place like Kano and prove what it is to be compelled to go out and find a well sunk in a spot unrevealed until you are actually at it. The humour (?) of the situation is the richer by your being conscious that you have been warned that the quality of the liquid is suspect.

Be the water whatever it might, it must be had. One has not necessarily to get desperate in order to have that frame of mind. One has only to be hungry and very thirsty, the thirst accompanied by a headache which produces a positive craving for a cup of tea.

It had become dark. Still, the blessed water must be got. I could not send Oje half-a-mile across strange grass country, with no sign of a path. The hurricane lamp had been lit, and I was about to start off with the faithful lad in search of the well when up walked Mr Brayscher holding out two pint bottles of water which had been boiled and filtered. Heaven knows whether I should have found the well, for the moon was not up, and there appeared to be nobody to act as guide. The search could now be deferred to morning.

I never had to attempt the task. Another dweller in a hut near by was Mr W. J. Marsh, who was a passenger on the ship by which I came out, but with whom I did not come into contact on board and who was practically a stranger, though he was in the saloon at a little entertainment on the voyage in which I took part. Hearing I had arrived in Kano, and knowing the water trouble, he very thoughtfully sent four pint bottles of the precious liquid, boiled and filtered. Mr Marsh, like Mr Brayscher, is on the Baro-Kano Railway. He is a First Grade

Foreman of Works, and is rated as a Second-Class Officer. Be his class what it may, I am proud to mention W. J. Marsh as a friend indeed.

As a matter of fact my indebtedness did not end with the indispensable water for breakfast. A week or so later the exceedingly intricate and delicate mechanism working the shutter of an expensive camera got out of order. After long and unsuccessful efforts to make it work the thing was given into the hands of Mr Marsh. I admit I had small hopes of his being able to accomplish anything. Had the matter been one of drawing an iron bolt or straightening the axle of a locomotive I would have been more trustful, but the elaborate springs of a photographic shutter resemble the interior of a Geneva watch.

However, the handy man at Kano Station, after a wrestle lasting not quite an hour with the fragile springs, sent the camera back in perfect working order. It was also the most natural thing in the world, when my Browning automatic pistol jammed, to call in Mr Marsh, who put it right in the proverbial jiffy.

The wealth of six pint bottles of filtered water, though seriously diminished after two meals, made the water question less urgent, and, therefore, I sallied forth the morning after arriving to buy a few utensils which had not been included in the domestic purchases down country. The walk brought me acquaintance with my greatest benefactor during the stay at Kano.

Entering the Niger Company's store to obtain the articles required, Mr Byrd, the Kano Agent—Manager he would be called in England—enquired if I was who I happened to be, and on my admitting the fact he said that the District Agent at Zaria, Mr Wilks (whom I saw there, but who I did not know intended taking the step), had wired him of my coming up, but that the telegram had only just been delivered, though handed in 24 hours earlier 90 miles away. It was subsequently ascertained that the native post office messenger had received the telegram for delivery in due time but had put it in his robe pocket and taken it home, judging that next day, on the way to his duties, would do just as well for the addressee. Mr Byrd, learning where I was living, offered the use of an unoccupied house in his compound. It was like the railway hut, made of mud and straw but had the great advantage of a cement, instead of an earth, floor. Although consisting of a single room, it was quite a mansion in its way. The change of quarters was speedily made and I at once settled down to write.

"You always speak well of the Niger Company," was the remark made by a man I met in the train. Certainly, I do. I have the best of reasons for doing so, for while journeying in these parts I have invariably received the utmost courtesy and aid from all members of the staff. This is evidently done on principle, for the few shillings spent at the stores must be of the smallest consequence. Nor can the attention be given me just because I happen to be Special Correspondent for a London journal. I have heard of similar help being rendered to other travellers who have passed over ground where the Niger Company are established. I have heard of it at Bassa, in the south of the Protectorate; I have heard of it at Yola, in the east; and I gladly testify to a large measure of appreciation in the north.

The superiority of my new residence over my former habitation was soon manifest. Whereas the white ants in my first resting-place were to be numbered in hundreds of thousands—at a modest computation—in the second they were a mere matter of hundreds, and with a hard floor the rendezvous they formed there could be swept clear periodically, which is not practicable where the floor of a hut is soft ground and the ants come upwards. In the new residence they descended from the walls and from above only. From the latter direction they dropped into the hot meals but seemed to make no difference to the flavour of the food. The best way was to look away from the table; then one could not be positive that ants accompanied the food in its transfer from platter to palate.

Still, the house is really comfortable. A mud wall encloses a verandah, level with the ground, round the house. The roof, of dried grass, is double. Between the lower and the upper ones a clear space provides excellent ventilation without interfering with the rainproof qualities.

CHAPTER VII

FASHIONS, GOVERNMENT, ADMINISTRATION

An Empire builder—The country and population—Hausa tribes—Moslem and Pagan—Sartorial distinctions—Ruling through natives—Election of their own rulers—Lugard's peaceful persuasion—A modern Earl of Warwick—The genius of Taubman Goldie and Lugard—Native administration—Residents—Taxation—Law Courts.

WHEN the British Government assumed control of the territories over which the Royal Niger Company had held its charter for governing and trading those lands were divided into the Protectorate of Southern Nigeria—since amalgamated with the Colony of Lagos—and the Protectorate of Northern Nigeria. Together they extended nearly half-a-million square miles. That has been the tangible contribution of the Royal Niger Company to the British possessions. Sir George Taubman Goldie, founder and head-and-front of the Company for a number of years, deserves the title of Empire builder, if ever man did.

Northern Nigeria is 255,700 square miles, with an estimated native population of 9,269,000. This population may be divided into Mohamedans and Pagans. The former are frequently spoken of as Hausas, although the term comprises the Fulani, the pure Hausa, the Beri-Beri, the Bornu, the Borgu, the Nupè, the Yorubu and others.

Apart from religion there is a marked sartorial distinction. Moslems when not at some heavy, laborious task usually display garments of ample size. Men above the poorest ranks wear flowing robes and trousers as close as a knickerbocker below the knee, above it very wide, the waist part sufficiently so to accommodate at least three persons if it were not folded and held in position by a broad strip of cloth. The women, who ignore foot covering of any kind, use cloths and wraps from the shoulders to within a few inches of the ankle.

Costume among Pagans varies from a loin-cloth for men who live on the belt of their area which adjoins Hausa country, where they have become what is called Hausaised to this extent, to the stage where ladies and gentlemen are in the simple condition of the guest at Hans Breitman's party.

Kano is the centre, the focus of the Moslem population.

A few brief words on the government of the Hausa Provinces. As stated in Chapter IV, we rule by and through the natives, leaving to them the selection who shall be their Kings—known as Emirs—subject to the approval of the Governor of the Protectorate. Although a Protectorate has been declared for a considerable period, previous to the assumption of power by the Crown a large part of the country was occupied only in name. The endeavour of Sir Frederick Lugard, the first Governor, was to bring those areas under influence without the use of troops if possible. No civilian could be more a man of peace than this ex-soldier. In one of his memoranda to the political officials he wrote: " Capable officers can do much more by

[*From the Painting by Herkomer.*

THE RIGHT HON. SIR GEORGE TAUBMAN GOLDIE,
Founder of Nigeria.

getting in touch with the people than can be effected by a series of punitive expeditions and bloodshed."

He acted on that principle himself. When eventually he had sufficient troops to impose his will he always held them back until amicable counsel, reasoning and argument became hopeless. Whereever an Emir, no matter what his former record, promised to rule his people fairly, justly, and not to war upon or raid tribes for slaves or other plunder, he was confirmed in his position and promised the moral and, if necessary, the material support of the suzerain Power.

Where Emirs persistently and defiantly continued evil practices they were deposed. When that had to be done Sir Frederick moved rapidly. He was up and down and across the country at remarkable speed and with marvellous energy, trekking all the time and covering wonderful distances in the hottest periods of the year, playing the part of the famous Earl of Warwick, unmaking and making Kings as he went along. Whenever the ruler had to be dethroned Sir Frederick called on the Chiefs of the people to select and elect the successor, whom he then ceremoniously installed, he representing the Great White King beyond the seas. Of the several thus put on thrones, I do not think a single one has had to be removed.

Even when military operations were imperative, it might appear astonishing how quickly the inhabitants acquiesced in the new order of things. That is to be largely attributed to the fact that in the old days of tribal warfare or raids the fruits of the fighting were gathered by the caste above, by the Emirs and their satellites and parasites; the commonalty had to be content with the husks. The readiness with which dwellers accepted the new Heads was to a great extent also due to the perception that the British hand was not to be on them but against the methods of an Emir whose weakness, and the consequent harshness of his hangers-on, pressed hardly on his own subjects.

Sir Frederick Lugard always made that clear, just as he endeavoured to obtain from the leading folks promises to amend crooked ways. In his first annual report to the Colonial Office he said: " I am anxious to prove to these people (the Fulani) that we have no hostility to them and only insist on good government and justice; and I am anxious to utilise, if possible, their wonderful intelligence, for they are born rulers and incomparably above the negroid races in ability."

It is to the genius first of Taubman Goldie then to that of Lugard that the faculty of the Moslem population of Northern Nigeria to govern has been utilised to the admirable extent in existence to-day. The former recognised and gave scope to the faculty in the time of the Royal Niger Company, when he was practically if not actually supreme ruler of as much of the country as control could be exercised over; the latter, on becoming Governor at the advent of the Crown, continued on, and extended, the same line. The result is that we have over hundreds of square miles a capable, efficient—one may say, in their own way a talented and gifted— civil service composed of natives of all grades who are doing duties which no number of Europeans could effect so well. Internal administration, maintenance of order, appointment of judges, punish-

FASHIONS, GOVERNMENT, ETC. 67

ment of criminals, assessment and collection of taxes are well carried out in the Hausa States by the Emirs of the various provinces and the men they select for the work, carried out in accordance with local tradition and still not violating the cardinal ideas of justice and humanity.

There are, therefore, more than 250,000 square miles, a population much over 9,000,000, many of whom were first-class fighting men in the shape of formidable cavalry, and 424 Englishmen officials. Most of these are in the political department and termed Residents. They advise the Emirs on matters which need assistance and they generally supervise, seeing that the Government is continued without those mischiefs and tragedies which stained the old rule of the Fulani, but interfering as little as can be in the routine of internal affairs.

In a narrative of this kind no more than an outline can be rendered of the singular system of native government. It is also referred to in Chapter XIII as I observed it in being.

I hope this part of the subject is not dwelt on unduly—it seems to me an intensely interesting study—by explaining how taxes are assessed, collected and allocated. The matter is stated pithily in the last annual report by the Governor of the Protectorate, then Sir Hesketh Bell, and his words, which cannot be bettered, are quoted. Possibly the statement does not make quite clear that the British official who fixes the assessment does so in conjunction with a representative of the Emir of the Province.

" In Sokoto Province each village is assessed,

after careful inquiries made on the spot by a British official as to the resources of the inhabitants, at a lump sum, and the apportionment of the amount payable by the individual is left to the village Head and his Council. They are directed to assess the individual in accordance with his wealth from whatever source it may be obtained. In Bassa the individual is assessed at a fixed and universal rate *per capita*."

These two systems represent the extremes of divergence which occur in methods of assessment and are each suited to the conditions existing in the Provinces where applied, which differ in a corresponding manner. In Bassa the village Heads could not apportion the tax proportionately amongst the individuals, whilst in Sokoto the native would disapprove of a system which compelled the poor to pay as much as the rich.

" The total amount of the taxes paid by a native unit are divided into four parts. Two of these form the Government share and are paid into the general revenue. The other two are paid into the Beit-el-Mal (native treasury). One is earmarked for the payment of fixed emoluments individually to the Emir, his councillors, his police, his official messengers, the officials told off by him to look after roads, buildings, sanitation, and public works generally, and to the payment of the native Judges (Alkalis). Also to defray the cost of public works such as markets, gaols, etc., road-making, well-making, of education, and of the subsistence of persons who according to Moslem tenets should receive State aid. Also towards establishing a

FASHIONS, GOVERNMENT, ETC. 69

reserve fund, in case at any time, owing to the failure of crops, it should be necessary to remit a portion of the taxes.

"The remaining fourth share is divided among the district and village Heads in proportion to the amounts of rents and taxes for the collection of which each is responsible. In some Provinces the district Heads have been placed on fixed salaries, notably Bornu, but it has not yet been decided as to whether this system should be adopted generally.

"The organisation described in the preceding paragraphs has not been entirely elaborated in the Pagan districts, but in every case efforts are being made, and in many with considerable success, to establish a common fund, administered on the lines described.

"Generally speaking, it has been found expedient to pay the native officials on a generous scale, and it must be said in justice to them that a marked improvement in his work has followed in every case where an official has been granted an assured income. The funds administered by the Beit-el-Mal throughout the Protectorate amounted to over £200,000 during the year under review."

TYPICAL DISTRIBUTION OF FUNDS ALLOCATED TO NATIVE TREASURIES, TAKING KANO AS AN EXAMPLE, A TERRITORY OF 28,600 SQUARE MILES AND WITH A POPULATION OF 3,500,000.

	£
Salaries, Central Administrations	6556
Salaries, District Administrations	20910
Salaries, Village Administrations	13940
Judicial	2760
Police	1769
Prisons	1438
Public Works Department	4836
Treasury	540

Education	£ 1240
Land Survey	600
Hospitals and Sanitation	1024
Special Grants for Economic Development	500
Charity and Entertaining	500
Miscellaneous Contingencies	1000
Balances and Reserves	12027
	£69640

From the same source I also take the constitution of the native law Courts:

"The effect of the payment of the native Judges deserves special notice. The improved position and growing efficiency of the native Judiciary has now been established. In former days the Judges had no fixed stipends and depended for their livelihood on the generosity of the reigning Emir, or on the fees collected through orders from their own Courts. In such circumstances it could hardly be expected that the Courts would be efficient or free from bribery and corruption. It is now generally conceded that the former weakness of the native Courts was caused rather by a radically bad system than by any real lack of men who could, if properly supported, efficiently administer justice.

"In Kano and Katsena a measure has been adopted which it is hoped it will be found possible to extend elsewhere. In these two Emirates the Courts do not execute their own judgments. The Court informs the Head of the district in which it is situated that an order has been given, and should this entail the payment of a judgment debt, the Beit-

FASHIONS, GOVERNMENT, ETC. 71

el-Mal is also informed by the Court. The district Head is responsible for the execution of the order, for the collection of any amount due and for its payment into the Beit-el-Mal. By this means a complete check on both the Judiciary and the Executive is established.

"At the present time in the Northern Provinces almost every district has a salaried Alkali's Court with considerable but limited powers. Minutes of every case tried in the district Courts are submitted monthly to the chief native Judges at the various Capitals of the Province. Serious cases are referred to the Courts in the Capitals of the Emirates. . . . Crimes of violence and robbery, which in the early years of the Protectorate were so regrettably numerous, have almost disappeared since the native Courts, with their corollary, native police (dogari), have been given a free hand."

In Kano Province last year the Alkalis' Courts tried 20,740 cases, of which 1,267 were criminal indictments and 19,473 civil actions. I grieve to think that the last category includes no less than 9,020 instances of the disturbance of connubial bliss under the heading of "Matrimonial." It is pleasant to learn that few of the assault cases were of a serious kind and still more gratifying to know that violence to women forms a small proportion.

An analysis shows that only ·07 of the population committed acts which brought the perpetrators within the law, whilst grave crime is so small in quantity that there is not a European nation which would gain by comparison with Kano Province, Northern Nigeria.

CHAPTER VIII

KANO PROVINCE AND CITY—BRITISH TRADE PROSPECTS

Town and country—Officials and traders—Belgravia and Bermondsey—A housekeeping budget—European stores—Buying and selling—A Syrian in the fold.

THE Province of Kano extends 28,600 square miles and has a population of 3,500,000 souls. Kano City and the settlement near it are, however, spoken of as Kano. Kano City accommodates a native population of more than 30,000 inhabitants. Outside the city there are an English official quarter and a few European stores. The latter are, roughly, two miles from the native city, and the official quarter is a corresponding stretch further on. Each centre is separate, distinct, isolated. Between the stores and the native city there is, however, constant communication, much coming and going for business purposes. Between the official quarter and the stores there is scarcely anything more than the most limited exchange of messages, verbal or written, stiff, formal and frigid.

There is not so much difference in London between Belgravia and Bermondsey as there is in Kano between the official and the traders' quarter. In London efforts are made to minimise and soften the extremes of existence, while at Kano, if there are extremes, the policy pursued has the effect of hardening, accentuating, emphasising them. Why this spirit should be necessary in Kano I do not know. It does not exist in Lagos or Zungeru.

I leave this part of the subject with the remark that I can say very little about the official quarter, as there was never any cause for me to enter it beyond a few yards when I had to go to the Post Office to despatch cables, for two visits to the Residency and one to the Treasury to obtain change of money. The place is no doubt comfortable enough. Reports say that it lacks little in that respect. But in Mandarin-like attempts to set up a caste apart from all other men, it reminds one of the Forbidden City of Pekin. Yet these matters are insignificant —I hope I ruffle nobody's sense of dignity by saying so—compared with the interest, the attraction, the fascination, and the importance of Kano City and its inhabitants.

First, however, some reference to the European stores which have been started at Kano. They belong respectively to the Niger Company, Lagos Stores, the Tin Areas of Nigeria, the French Company, and a Syrian trader. The latter has a house and does not live in a hut in the native quarter, as do nearly all his compatriots in West Africa. He approaches a great deal more than they to the European manner of carrying on business. Messrs John Holt have a site, but building has not been started.

All the stores adjoin one another. They are within a few feet of the railway. The sites were selected by Sir Hesketh Bell during his term as Governor. His policy of facilitating commerce in every colony of which he has had charge is recognised by merchants at home, and has been publicly acknowledged repeatedly. The Niger Company and the French Company do what is termed a canteen business—i.e., that of retailing tinned provisions, etc.—as well as dry goods, whilst the other firms confine themselves to the heavier class of articles, though a few of the former class are also disposed of over the counter. There is not sufficient demand to maintain even a single little store for Europeans. The number of white people, officials and traders, does not exceed 30, and all bring their requirements, except fresh food, for the term of service.

The stores started only a few months ago, when the railway was completed. They are not in working order and he is wise in his generation who does not rely on them. My stay in Kano has been longer than planned, with the result that for a week I had no bread; hard, thick biscuits—euphemistically called cabin bread—having to be a substitute. They were eaten with tea for which neither milk nor sugar was obtainable. Subsequently I learnt that I could buy fresh cow's milk from native farmers at 3d. a pint bottle. When the flour had been consumed, I again flourished on cabin bread.

On a supply of flour coming up—sold at 4s. 6d. for a 7 lb. tin—the always willing and useful Oje declared that he "fit to make bread," and quite a palatable quality he produced.

Fresh food retailed in Kano City is at low figures, though prices have greatly advanced recently. A chicken, furnishing a meal sufficient for two persons, is bought for 5d.; a guinea-fowl, larger than the chicken, costs 3d. or 4d. A duck is

KANO PROVINCE AND CITY

to be had at a corresponding figure. Eggs are purchased at 10 a penny. Sweet potatoes—long, thin, circular—are not disposed of by weight, but are retailed at sight; and fivepennyworth lasts four meals. Onions—larger than turnips, some of them scaling $1\frac{1}{2}$ lbs.—minus the strong flavour of the English variety—cost 4 a penny. By going two or three miles to the farms where they are grown, sufficient to fill an apple-barrel can be secured for 6d. A leg of mutton—flesh that is dearer than beef—sells at 5d., and is more than enough for four diners.

Man does not live by meat alone, and anybody coming here should bear in mind that he is entering a new country, from the European standpoint, where, although foodstuffs are raised, the population has quite a different standard of feeding from his; where railway communication has been merely a matter of months; that things which he probably considers necessary for his existence are just beginning to be sold and that they are of less importance and value to the firms selling them than other articles, which therefore are naturally given preference; and, further, that the articles referred to and others of the same character are occasionally sold out at the great port of Lagos. I had trouble there to buy two tins of sugar. Estimate, then, the position in Kano, distance of a week by railway.

With the exception of the Lagos Stores, all the establishments at Kano are in temporary buildings. The Niger Company has houses of mud and straw and one of corrugated iron. The Tin Areas Company has corrugated iron and also mud houses; whilst the French Company and the Syrian trader have confined themselves to the latter material. Each store stands in a compound. A section is 300 feet long by 100 feet wide. The Niger Company has four sections, the French Company four, the Tin Areas two, Lagos Stores two, the Syrian one. The buildings, of course, only cover a small portion of the ground occupied.

I have stated that the chief business of the stores is to buy, not sell. There are great quantities of native produce for which eager markets in your part of the world wait, and though a good profit should show between the prices here and those in Europe, there is strong competition in purchasing, and everyone will be able to gauge its effect on the vendors, who are keen and alert. They have sharpened the hereditary instinct in the course of generations. Therefore, it can be seen that it is no easy, certain course to sit down and deal for merchandise brought in. The principal articles are hides, skins (goats' and sheep), ground-nuts, gutta percha, beeswax, and ostrich feathers. I am only touching on articles brought out of Kano City in large quantities to the neighbouring stores, not to those on sale at the market there.

Sheep and goats' skins and ground-nuts form the main items in the former category. The skins are tanned and dyed red, yellow, and green. The dyeing process is kept secret, but I know that the ashes of dung burnt in open ovens near the entrances to Kano City—such spots being by no means attractive in an olfactory sense—I know that such ashes are used, and that the bright red colour much in favour is obtained from juice of the holcus.

I am unable to say at what price the skins are

KANO PROVINCE AND CITY

purchased. One cannot put such questions to buyers who, obviously, are averse from disclosing information which would be useful to rivals, but I believe the figure to be well under to slightly above 1s. each. The sound quality skins easily fetch 6s. or 7s. each in Europe. They are used for satchels, purses, bookbinding, and, within the last few years, slippers and boots have been made from them.

It is safe to state that the purchases of all the other stores together do not approach those of the Niger Company. One can see quite a string of dealers, accompanied by servants carrying skins on their heads, processions of camels and bullocks bearing large bales of skins, and hundreds of donkeys panniered with ground-nuts making their way to the compound of that Company.

It is no reflection on the men in charge of the other stores to say that they have a very difficult task indeed in competing with the Niger Company. In the first place, it is known, and was well known before its present competitors were heard of. Ask anybody in Kano of the Bature Company—the White Company—and, if he can, he will direct you to the Niger Company's store. European firms may comment as they will, the Niger Company is liked by the population. "In the days of the Company's rule," I was told in the southern part of the Protectorate, "we paid no taxes." That is not accurate, but it is believed, which is just as good as if it were. People, therefore, who have skins to sell naturally first think of the Niger Company, and as it has a name for fair dealing, undoubtedly a heavy preponderance is taken there. Everything is paid for by cash, on the spot.

But the Company depends not on its name alone. An elaborate organisation exists by which native merchants who are vendors are introduced by brokers —a better analogy is that of an outside clerk to a stockbroker—who help a transaction through. Some Arab and native local merchants have already established a branch in England, where skins and feathers are sent direct. To these men the Niger Company acts as forwarding agent, sending goods over the railway to Baro, thence by the river route to the sea for shipment.

Although the general canteen business of the stores—apart from the trade to Europeans—is small at present, it should extend. In Kano and the immediately surrounding districts there must be 50,000 to 60,000 inhabitants. Nearly all have some money to spend. The trade with these people will probably not be done in a direct manner, but by native retailers, who know their own folk best and with whom, as dealers, Europeans cannot compete. The trade, I think, will be a small wholesale one.

What can be done in that way is already clear from the six months' work of the Syrian previously referred to. In the six months he has been up here he has done business to the amount of £4,000 in English calico and beads. Doubtless the gentleman will be surprised to find that these figures are known to me. They have been obtained in no underhand manner.

No wonder he is about to open a place at Manchester to be used as a forwarding depôt. Though this Syrian, Farris George, is not to be compared to the large firms, his record demonstrates the field of trade that can be cultivated in Nigeria. A few years

ONE OF THE EMIR'S TRUMPETERS.

NATIVE SKIN-MERCHANTS WITH TRANSPORT, KANO.
(See page 76.)

ago he landed at Lagos and commenced trading in a street market in the smallest manner. Steadily he did more and more; was joined from time to time by members of his family; and eventually he became well-to-do. When, as the phrase goes, the railway opened up Kano to outside commerce, George was quickly on the spot, and he has improved his opportunities all the time. Although when the stores get into their stride his total will appear insignificant, I shall be surprised if he has not secured quite a respectable proportion of the whole, an amount not to be despised and very difficult indeed to lower.

CHAPTER IX

A GENTLEMAN ADVENTURER

The London and Kano Trading Company—The Captain intervenes—Army, Civil Service, Commerce—Discarding appearances—Contrast of mansions—The pleasure of business—"Traders" and others.

ALTHOUGH there is a law that no non-native of Nigeria may live permanently in Kano City, the London and Kano Trading Company has a large establishment there. That is because the firm took the step long before the present regulation was promulgated, or probably thought of.

The London and Kano Trading Company was started in 1903 by Mr Loder Donisthorpe and Mr White. Both were in the Northern Nigeria Government service, and they were so taken with the idea —and, I think I may add, with the prospect of making a fortune—that, not staying to finish their 12 months' term of duty, they resigned and commenced the new concern. But though chances were plentiful enough, the handicaps to utilising them formed a serious drawback, so serious that, at least once, abandonment of the enterprise was contemplated, or, at all events, considered.

Within the last year two events occurred which placed the L. and K.T.C. in an entirely superior position. One was the completion of the railway,

A GENTLEMAN ADVENTURER 81

which, forming a junction at Minna, connects Kano with the port of Lagos and with Baro, thus linking up the river route. The second occurrence was the advent of Captain J. J. Brocklebank on the directorate of the L. and K.T.C. That event proved the turning-point in the career of the concern.

Yet, it took place quite by chance, almost accidentally. Having acquired an interest in the company, he came to Northern Nigeria—not for the first time—for a short visit of 4 months, intending to dabble in the work and have some big game shooting; but, captivated by the first, he threw in his lot with the company and now largely directs its operations, which have since proceeded at express speed and have become greatly enlarged.

No more interesting or romantic figure—certainly among the Europeans—is to be found within 100 miles of Kano. Educated at Eton and Cambridge, Captain Brocklebank commenced soldiering by going on active service in the South African war, as a subaltern of the 8th Imperial Yeomanry, from which he was gazetted in 1900 Second Lieutenant in the King's Dragoon Guards and soon afterwards won the D.S.O. Seeing little chance of adventure with that regiment, he got seconded to serve with the Mounted Infantry of the Northern Nigeria Regiment, and in 1908 was promoted Captain in his own corps. The same year, at his request, he was transferred to the Political Branch of the Northern Nigeria Government, but in 1911 he resigned from that and from the Army, electing for leisure, travel and sport. The London and Kano Trading Company meeting him before he could formulate a scheme of jaunts, there he is. It is rumoured that he has a personal income which would enable him to pass life luxuriously and without effort. He evidently prefers to be in Kano.

He dresses with studied neglect. Sundays and week-days I have seen him in the same suit of clothes, which are not even of the style generally worn here in the bush country. They are made of tweed and are faded to the verge of shabbiness. The ends of the coat sleeves are usually covered by the turned-up cuffs of his shirt. Instead of riding boots, he wears low-cut shoes, like dancing pumps—of course, of dull leather. A first-rate horseman, he is never seen mounted; he goes hither and thither in a pair-horse buggy, the only horse-drawn vehicle in or about Kano. Colonials in hot climates have their hair cut close, but his would almost do for a Bohemian actor, musician, or artist. He is the only man I have seen for hundreds of miles who wears a beard that is more than stubble. Yet no one would mistake him for anything but what he is, a gentleman—gentleman from boyhood. Thinking of him, it strikes one as childish to painfully labour the point that the managers of the stores are merely "traders," as distinct and distant from the very superior persons who are not. Technically correct, the term trader is understood in these parts to apply to natives who sit in open places or who are peddlers.

Captain Brocklebank will occasionally say something stronger than a big D but always with the slight drawl which marks his intonation, never raising his voice, and with the smile which shows he is not angry. I have never seen him look so serious and solemn as he did when I was taking his photo-

CAPT. JOHN J. BROCKLEBANK, D.S.O.
(See page 81.)

THE PREMISES OF THE LONDON AND KANO TRADING COMPANY AT KANO.
(See page 80.)

graph. He speaks Hausa colloquially and will frequently make the natives laugh by his waggisms in that tongue. I have heard him switch off his conversation with an Arab merchant to discuss matters with a French officer who could talk only in his own language. He would probably strike you as being languid and indifferent, but no Arab merchant is more alert, mentally, to the turns in a business transaction, and I happen to know that there are few, if any, individuals who look further ahead in a commercial survey. He appears to take things easily, and never hustles; but no day's work ever overlaps another.

A man who in England is spick and span, keeps his high-power motor and dwells in a large town house and a country mansion, at Kano his domicile is a more or less dilapidated mud dwelling where white ants cause pieces from what must be called the ceiling to drop continually on the mosquito curtains over the camp-bed. The combined sitting and dining-room is, I warrant, not nearly as comfortable as the stable for his hunters in England. The "wine cellar" is a shelf in the mud wall furnished with one decanter and three other bottles. The wines are for his friends. He does not take any.

As we sat in this hovel, comparatively speaking, smoking cigarettes over a cup of tea, Captain Brocklebank leaned back in his folding chair and remarked laughingly, "I really don't know why I am here."

"Nor does anybody else," was my rejoinder. "I assume because you like it."

"Yes, that's the explanation, I suppose."

"But how came you to give up the Army, and

then the interesting occupation of the political branch of the Northern Nigerian Government?"

"Well, there did not seem much in humdrum soldiering. I might have reached command of my regiment, but there appeared to be nothing beyond. And with all its engrossing interest, the civil department in Northern Nigeria was a little monotonous."

"You wanted greater freedom?"

"Not quite that—opportunities for initiative. I felt that I wished to do something, to be going ahead, and going by my own efforts."

"Being your own master, as the phrase is?"

"Yes and no. I had not the slightest ground for complaint of any kind against the policy I was a humble unit in helping to carry on, nor against my colleagues, with whom I have always been on the best of terms. I simply wanted to do something fresh, and chance brought me here."

"Neither you nor your present associates regret the connection?"

The reply was a smile, followed by "I think not."

"Are you likely to remain?"

"Oh, certainly, unless there is an unexpected upheaval."

"That was not your original plan?"

"Quite so. I commenced by nibbling; now I have my teeth fairly locked in a grip of the things; and I have no inclination to lose them. I am going on."

In a compound near by Captain Brocklebank had 20 horses; his personal property. I asked whether they were kept for pleasure or for business purposes, and the answer was "For either, or rather for both." The cost of feeding such a stud by one who bought

A GENTLEMAN ADVENTURER 85

his guinea-corn in the fat period of the year is small. If his friends wish to borrow a horse for a day or so they can have it. If there is enquiry for something the London and Kano Company have not but which is worth getting, Captain Brocklebank sends half-a-dozen mounted messengers in as many directions to try and secure it. If anybody desires to purchase a horse he is pretty sure to see one at his figure among the batch; and if anyone desires to sell, then the Captain is ever a buyer. An animal more or less makes little odds.

The acquisition of a man of this kind by the London and Kano Company is of value beyond words. Well-to-do and helping the concern with "the sinews of war," he can assist in a commercial fight at every step. He has already reaped largely in the new sphere opened by the railway. Greatly liked by both the official element and the representatives of the merchants, he can probably do business easier than one of less ingratiating manners, and, being a principal in the firm, he can promptly say yea or nay to a proposition of any magnitude. A man of his education, means, family connection, and social status is surely the equal, to say the least of it, of anybody else in Kano Province, which shows still more clearly the absurdity of looking down on the commercial class as something beneath notice, or only to be noticed in curt, frigid form and sternly ignored in every other way.

CHAPTER X

KANO CITY

The founder—Hunter and prophet, too—The city wall—Warfare and slave hunts—Provocation and defiance to the British—The Emir's challenge—March on the city—First check—Renewed attempt—Entry—A new ruler.

KANO CITY seen from a distance of a couple of miles presents no special features to the eye. It is practically indistinguishable from the surrounding country, which is flat and sparsely wooded. Fields of tall guinea-corn and clusters of trees screen the houses of the town. In their midst, however, two oblong hills, side by side, with flat tops, stand against the sky-line. That to the left, looking westward, is named Goron Dutsi, and the one to the right Dalla. On this hill the founder of the city is said to have lived more than 1,000 years ago. He, Berbushay, legend credits with having killed an elephant single-handed with his spear and carried the carcase on his head to a spot near his house. The place where the burden was put down became Kano, and Berbushay was its first Chief. He was not so ambitious as the rulers of the Balkan States to-day and did not aspire to the kingly title. That was assumed by one David, forerunner of the several conquerors of Kano. His success had been foretold a generation earlier by Berbushay, who apparently besides being a mighty hunter was also a bit of a prophet.

Nearer approach to Kano discloses an encircling wall, with tall date-palm trees standing sentinel-like. A closer examination shows the wall to have a thickness of 40 feet at its lowest part, and to run to a height of 50 feet. The top has half-circles, at the backs of which bow-and-arrow men could shoot with ease, and elsewhere this opportunity for defence is varied by mud compartments—as hard as stone—fashioned into the top of the wall where men could stand and use muskets through loopholes in the solid wall. A deep ditch lies in front of the wall, which has thirteen gates for entrance. The road to each gate narrows, with heavy, low side walls, so that an attacking party would be crowded into a small space, allowing few to press forward together. Several of the gates were further protected by the wall turning at an angle outwards, allowing missiles to be poured on the flank of an advance party.

Inside this Kano, less than eleven years ago, a slave market flourished, although the country was then a British Protectorate, and out of these gates there issued forth from time to time the then Emir and his thousands of mounted spearmen, setting out on slave-hunting expeditions, cheered by the loud-sounding drums and trumpets, and encouraged by the cries of the women-folk, who yelled to their lords to bear themselves well. So the Emir's following rode on, raiding tracts of territory, carrying off the women and children, slaughtering male adults with never a second thought. When the dwellers in a village had wind of the coming onslaught and hid themselves, the raiders burnt the houses and crops to the ground, leaving the people to perish by exposure and starvation. Thus was the land being depopulated. In 50 years it had been decreased to less than a fifth.

In 1900 organised raids on a large scale, to keep up the supply of slaves, were brazenly carried on by the Emir of Bida and the Emir of Kontagora, almost within sight of the British administrative headquarters—then at Jebba—where the High Commissioner, Sir Frederick Lugard, sat impotent. It was as much as he could do to maintain his hold on the Provinces occupied, for the large contingent of troops—1,200—he had to supply for the Ashanti War had left Northern Nigeria helpless to stop the murder, plunder, and slave-hunting that was taking place from the north.

With the return of the native soldiers the subsidiary Emirs were dealt with separately, but Kano, the political centre, the strong place of Hausaland, stood out defiantly. Sir Frederick Lugard tried persuasion, for he realised that his resources were not on a scale to tackle the great fortress city of Kano unless at much risk.

The wall ran to a circumference of just over 11 miles, and the town had means of maintaining those within it indefinitely. Herds of cattle and sheep, and wide grazing grounds for raising more, acres on which were grown corn and wheat, gave a supply of food far in excess of requirements and made a siege, even were an army available for an investment, a futile proceeding.

Could Sir Frederick but bring the Emir to a peaceful frame of mind tremendous dangers would be avoided. But the Emir treated all overtures with

KANO CITY

contumely or open defiance and provocation. Still, the High Commissioner cultivated patience. An unsuccessful attack on Kano would be immediately followed by a rising of the most powerful Moslem Provinces. Some who had made their submission were suspect, and others were merely waiting to see whether Kano, to which their eyes were turned, and on which their hopes rested, would be able to defy the new Power which had established itself in the southern Provinces.

An event took place which brought the situation to a climax. The Magasi—Viceroy—of Keffi murdered a British Resident with his own hands and fled to Kano. The Emir challenged the High Commissioner, not only by giving the murderer refuge but by providing him with a house and according him the place of honour on the Emir's right hand in royal and public processions.

That was in 1902, and if there were any remaining doubts of the sentiments of the Emir they were swept away by his organising an expedition and marching at the head of it to attack the British garrison at Zaria, only 90 miles to the south, in November of the same year. Perhaps fortunately for us, the Emir and his armies turned back, on word reaching him that the Emir of Katsena refused to be drawn into the enterprise. But possibly others might, especially if they saw the now defiant, truculent Emir of Kano not only flouting the High Commissioner but actually taking steps to overrun a Province in which his representatives had been accepted and over which the British flag flew. Unless the whole country was to remain in a condition of ferment, unrest and apprehension, clearly there was only one course for the High Commissioner, and that was to strike, if he could. He determined to make the attempt.

As many troops as could be collected—as could be spared from other parts—were assembled at Zaria. They were exclusively Protectorate soldiers, for quickness in delivering the blow was a great factor towards the chance of success. The force was made up of 550 infantry, 101 mounted infantry, 71 artillerymen with 475 mm. guns and 4 Maxims, and the following Europeans: 24 officers, 2 doctors, 12 non-commissioned officers. Colonel Morland, D.S.O., was in command.

On the night of February 2 the column camped at the Shallawa River, 6 miles from Kano and next morning advanced on Kano, leaving the carriers in a zariba guarded by 2 officers and 75 men.

First an attempt was made to blow in the Dukawayia Gate, but it was so constructed that the guns could not be placed where their projectiles would strike. Then the guns were turned on the mud wall, in the endeavour to break it down or make a breach. The shells had absolutely no effect. Though of mud, the great thickness of the wall, baked by the sun's rays to the hardness of stone, remained intact.

The position was not a comforting one, in fact it was distinctly bad, for unless the city was taken, and taken quickly, the besiegers were likely to find themselves in the position of being besieged or of retiring, with Kano immensely enhanced in prestige by having driven off the English. The result would undoubtedly have been a general rebellion over the entire northern Provinces of the Protectorate, and possibly in the southern ones as well. Colonel Morland saw the impossibility of carrying the Dukawayia Gate and at the same time was impressed with the necessity of fulfilling Sir Frederick Lugard's plan. The town must be taken.

Although several of the gates had been built in the manner of the Dukawayia, the mounted infantry, which was commanded by Major Porter, reconnoitered and discovered a gate, the Kukabuga, where a gun could be trained without the gunners being under fire from the walls. A move was made to that point, the gate quickly breached, and a storming party, led by Lieutenants Dyer and Gascoyne and Sergeant Lefanu, rushed through. On a broad, open space a short distance ahead a large body of horsemen carrying spears were preparing to charge. A gun which was at the heels of the leading troops was quickly brought into action and a single shell discharged into the mass of horsemen scattered them. They never re-formed. The enemy manning the wall were easily driven off. As Colonel Morland's column moved into the city the defenders broke up and all real resistance had ended. There was some slight fighting on entry being made into the Emir's Palace. That was all.

The Emir had gone to Sokoto previous to the arrival of the British, taking 2,000 mounted fighting men with him. The force he had left to defend the city now streamed out with the intention of joining him. They were directed to surrender their arms, and, not doing so, Colonel Morland ordered them to be broken up, which was done by the mounted infantry.

Colonel Morland and his staff took up quarters

in the Emir's Palace, and so readily was the new order of things accepted by the inhabitants that a few hours later British officers were strolling about the streets, unattended, sightseeing. The very next day the market resumed most of its activities, and within three days from the entry was again in full swing, with a notable omission: the slave section had disappeared. The Headmen of the people were invited by Sir Frederick Lugard to elect the new Emir. Selection fell on the Wombai, the deposed Emir's brother, who had counselled him to submit to the British. He is on the throne to-day.

[Photo by Elliott & Fry.

SIR FREDERICK LUGARD, D.S.O.
First Governor of Northern Nigeria and now Governor-General of Nigerias Southern and Northern.

CHAPTER XI

KANO CITY—(*continued*)

Houses and rents—From 1s. 6d. to £5 a year—Mud mansions —No. 1 Kano—When to build and repair—Advice on building —A contract and a surprise.

THE residential parts of Kano are made up of irregular square mud houses, most of them with slightly domed flat roofs. That is the prevailing form of architecture. There are some round ones having thatched tops and a few made altogether from that material. They belong to the poor. The style is not favoured by reason of the danger from fire. The Emir allows the more flimsy product on an understanding that it be replaced by mud as soon as the worldly prospects of the dwellers warrant the improvement.

There is no private landlordism—or rather, according to the law, there is supposed to be none— in Kano. The State, in the person of the Emir, owns the ground. It is not his individually; it belongs to the people; he regulates occupation.

A ground rent is fixed according to the space covered by the compound—which may contain several buildings—at the fraction of a penny per square foot annually. This does not work out at an extravagant sum according to our ideas. You can, as a native of Northern Nigeria—none others are allowed to be occupiers—obtain a house if it be vacant or ground to build one at a rental of 1s. 6d. a year. These dwellings are not exactly palatial mansions.

The scale of rents rises by a few pence to 3s. 6d., at which quite a desirable residence may be secured. My very good friend Adamu Ch'Kardi, a man greatly respected by all classes, from the Emir to the beggars in the streets, pays 3s. 6d. a year, and as 34 persons live in his house and its annexe, and as Adamu is not a person to be content with piggish surroundings, the house will be estimated as pretty large. Those who desire to keep up greater style have full opportunity. Rents go as high as £1 a year or even £2, £3, £4, or £5, which is the scale for a palace with a large surrounding garden. The Prime Minister occupies a house of the kind in the corresponding Belgrave Square of Kano.

Though there are 30,000 inhabitants, streets are not named, but each house has a number. I do not know the top numerals; all my observations and investigations were made without official local assistance. Adamu's house is 4,032, and I have seen 6,249. So, whilst in the Cantonment at Zungeru you may live up to number 8 Zungeru—if I remember rightly that is the highest—here your address might be 6,242 Kano. I happened to pass number 1 and took a photograph of it. It struck me as distinctive—no. 1 Kano. But there was nothing distinctive about the house. The occupier's 9 olive branches came outside for the picture, but neither is that quantity of youngsters distinctive for a proud father in these parts.

The population is to some extent a floating one.

HOUSES IN KANO CITY.

The cheapest type of house. Rent, 1/6 a year. A detached dwelling. Rent, 1/9 a year. (See page 93.)

KANO CITY—*continued*

Many persons stay in Kano a matter of weeks or months, then journey eastwards or north for a similar period, alternating from Kano to the centres of commerce in the interior of Africa and on the shore of the Mediterranean. Certain of the Arab merchants keep their own houses in Kano. Others are boarded and lodged for a stipulated amount. The more general arrangement is for a man to be put up at no settled sum. He agrees to pay his host 1s. from each £5 worth of goods sold, and the host helps the guest by making enquiries respecting requirements in quarters where he will have better and more intimate knowledge than the stranger within the gates.

The mud habitation is characteristic of Hausaland. Persons in Europe may think of them as thin, weak structures, run up in a few hours and liable to be blown to bits by a strong wind. Nothing of the sort. A mud house which you folks at home would look upon as a mere hut, properly made may be the ideal form of domicile, away from the perfectly-constructed stone bungalow with scientific ventilation—punkahs, air-fans, etc., etc.—and electric light. And I am not at all sure that I do not prefer the mud dwelling. The principal advantage of the former is that a continuous draught clears winged insects, an exasperating torment when writing continuously. In the course of the last few weeks, days and nights have been passed in four mud houses each of which differed from the others. Two of them were as comfortable as one could wish to be, much more so than the ordinary house in England during the extremes of summer or winter.

But the mud house, as I have said, must be

properly built. There is a right and a wrong way, as in most things. They know the correct way in Kano. The time to erect your mud house is at the end of the wet season, when there is an abundance of water in the ponds and lakes of the city and the ground is soft, for you can obtain ample material gratis. But it must not be taken from the street; fields are set apart for the purpose, and there people draw supplies.

Bit by bit the walls are raised, the outcome of each day's work being plastered by hand into that of the preceding ones, and before the last layer has been laid on, the whole will be still susceptible to thumb pressure. Completed, the building is left to dry in the undiluted blaze of the burning African sun, which bakes all into the hardness of brick.

The wet season certainly puts mud houses to severe trial, and those of the jerry-built order sometimes succumb. Even the strongest, having walls two or three feet thick, have to be repaired and patched after continuous rain—as it rains in Northern Nigeria—and the time for general exterior overhauling is also at the close of the wet season, if the threatened habitation will stand so long.

Mud houses are quite common for Europeans near Kano City; in fact, with the exception of brick bungalows in the official element quarter, all whites have that type of dwelling. Part of this chapter has been written in one of recent erection which had not gone through the months of hardening process. It looked substantial enough, with its 24-inch stout walls, circular, from a distance resembling a Martello tower. One might have believed it to be proof

HOUSE IN KANO CITY.
Rent, 2/6 a year.

NO. I KANO.
The houses in the City are numbered to facilitate taxation. (See page 93.)

against any soaking. Five hours of much less than the standard tornado had caused a steady run of mud to drop with ominous sound on various parts of the floor. The wooden gutters that projected horizontally had been undermined and fallen, and the top of the wall on which they had rested was being steadily and in rather liquid form deposited around me. Still, the very centre of the room was, so far, clear of direct descent; and splashes of dirt, though persistently maintained, are a mere nothing in this country. Presently the owner of the house came in to warn me that I had better stop writing and move my bedding and boxes into his store. In his opinion it was not unlikely the walls would collapse. As he did not seem quite certain on the point I said I would chance it and remain. A journalist who desires to send an expected contribution to his paper must not be over-particular about falling walls around him. Nothing on this earth is so important to his mind as the thought that he must not miss the mail. So I rattled on.

Presently one of my boys ran in dripping, his face —as much as a black skin can be—pale. He gasped, " Massa, the wall he be fit for fall! " and at the same moment the friend who had placed the house at my disposal came and begged me in emphatic language not to make a fool of myself and to clear at once. I did, for the next worst thing to not doing his duty to his paper is for a Special Correspondent to get killed in trying to do it extra well. Sure enough, seen from outside, the thick wall had cracked from top to earth and the perpendicular had distinctly shifted from its original alignment.

The larger houses, in or out of Kano City, are

not home-made. There is a recognised trade of builders. If you are ordering a house do not fix the price by contract. You will probably be able, especially if you pride yourself on your astuteness, to beat the builder's estimate down to almost any figure you care to push it, but refrain from reflecting afterwards that you are an exceedingly clever fellow who has prevented somebody from making a fair profit, which you have saved for yourself. The builder will make the profit he calculated from the first. Your house, or rather you, will be the loser.

It is infinitely better to pay the contractor so much a day, or per week, as long as he and his assistants are building. He will certainly keep the job going as long as he can; it may run into months where days would easily cover from start to finish, but if you keep visiting the busy bees you can be satisfied that more and more is being added to the house, and when you feel content that it suffices for your purpose you cry out, " Hold! Enough! "

Should you, however, decide for a contract payment, be careful that it is comprehensive. Contracts are not sealed, signed, and settled portentous documents. They are verbal and made in the presence of an interpreter. What wonder that where Europeans are concerned misunderstandings arise, and naturally nobody is more surprised at them than the bland, ingenuous builder. He made sure everything was so perfectly clear.

I knew a European who contracted to have a house built, of course outside the city. He would leave no backway to any individual to get the better of him, so he carefully stipulated for every detail, and emphasised them all. He went to bed content that he had made a good bargain. No other Englishman, he was sure, had concluded so cute an agreement.

The walls grew, and as they did—the requisite thickness never lessening—his complacency rose in corresponding degree. The agreed height was reached, and the builder asked for payment.

"Pay you!" cried the indignant recipient of the request; "certainly not; not until the job is finished."

"It is finished," was the polite retort.

"Finished! How can it be finished with no roof? Put on the cement roof I said I wanted and you can have your money."

"Oh," explained the builder through the interpreter, "the cement roof is another man's work. Putting on a roof is never understood to be in our agreement. It is quite separate."

The householder withheld payment, and on the dispute coming before the Resident's Court—the tribunal which tries cases in which a white is complainant or defendant—the decision, based on local custom, was that the builder was right and that the other must pay.

CHAPTER XII

KANO MARKET

A cosmopolitan rendezvous—Arab merchants—The desert route and the iron-horse—War and commerce—Local industries—Arts and crafts—Skilled workers—Camels, cattle, sheep, horses—Pitiful brute suffering—An appeal.

KANO market is famed throughout Africa. To it pilgrims of commerce come east, north and a hundred and more directions between these points of the compass. It is said to be the largest market in the world, but a man who has also been to Timbuktu tells me that it is four times the size of Kano and has four times as many people frequenting it. Kano, however, need not bury its diminished head. If there be another Richmond in the field Kano shall not feel ashamed.

Various calculations have been made of the number of persons who congregate there on the busiest days of the week; 7,000, 8,000 have been figures given. I put it higher and estimate the crowds at 10,000 to 12,000 and one who probably knows Kano in this respect better than any other individual agrees with my rough-and-ready census.

What African cosmopolitan crowds they are! Not merely Fulanis, Hausas and Nupes, but Turegs—who gave the French so much trouble—Ansim men, Arabs from every part of North Africa on the Mediterranean—Tripoli, Morocco and Tunis—Arabs of every degree of colour, coal black to skins as white and clear as that of an English girl.

Fine-looking men most of them, and finely clothed: turbans of cambric and turbans of gold-like embroidered cloth. Vests—resembling an army officer's mess jacket—also of embroidered cloth, the edges set with valuable lace of rare make and exquisite quality. Beneath the full robe of white, blue or other colour, trousers on which fancy work of many designs have been wrought. Each of these garments costs a matter of sovereigns. I have handled vests for which the owners paid £7 each.

See these gaily-bedecked Arab magnates mounted. The native saddle with curved-up back displays the skill of yet another craftsman; saddle cloth of brilliant and varied hues—scarlet to yellow—girth straps picked out with designs woven in silver. Bridle and head-collar hidden behind tassels and hanging cords bearing more tints than the rainbow when the sun shines brilliantly after a summer shower. The running, horse-attendant completes the picture of men of affluence who omit nothing the absence of which would detract from their rank and dignity.

No Zaki salute—on the knees and with head to the ground—comes from these men. Meeting you when they are mounted, they may—one in a 100—raise the right hand from the elbow—tantamount to taking off the hat in Continental Europe—or, passing you on foot, they may, in the same proportion, render a slight token of military salute. As a rule they give no sign beyond a side scrutiny, as one does at an unusual visitor from another country

They convey to you that they know too much of the world to look upon you—you and each of you—as a great leader, a chief, a Zaki.

They are not as the Moslem who has never been out of Hausaland and who knows you only by the prowess and governing ability of your countrymen there. These cosmopolitan Arabs appraise differently. They tell you, by looks, that chance has given you the upper hand. So be it. They care not. Let them go on with their trading and they are utterly cold as to who rules. There is no common, fellow-feeling between these men and those among whom they move. No feeling of patriotism unites them. There is a link, however, stronger, more potent, one that would draw as a magnet millions of Moslems in Africa and beyond. It is their religion. Let us beware.

You may not like these Arab merchants from the north and from the east. You may regard them as prepared to trade in anything for gain. You may believe them to have been the moving spirit of the former slave-hunting days. But they are picturesque, and if you are not satiated with sightseeing you must turn and look at them.

These Arabs, who are principally from Morocco, from Algeria and from Tripoli, bring European goods—wools, cloths, beads, scents—and take back chiefly skins and ostrich feathers. They formerly came, and some still do, by camel caravan from the north, traversing the sandy wastes of the Sahara. The journey occupies 6 months in the wet season and 4 months in the dry.

It was inevitable that the extension of the railway from Lagos would draw the life out of the desert

AN ARAB MERCHANT
Who trades from the shores of the Mediterranean to Kano.
(See page 101.)

EX-SERGT.-MAJOR DOWDU.
A Beri-Beri from Bornu.

route. This process of travel is dying of inanition. It might still have lasted years, for trading was to be done en route and people naturally conservative in habit do not readily change their methods. But the Morocco trouble and the Tripoli war have given the desert route the happy despatch. It is already practically dead. Healthy commerce and warfare cannot exist together, and the desert route has been abandoned by the majority of the Arab traders.

They are coming and going by the sea service from Europe to Lagos or Forcados and thence either by train all the way from the former port or from the latter one by boat up the Niger to Baro and then by rail to Kano. These plans have been accompanied by other advantages, for the continental goods previously brought by the Arabs from the Mediterranean ports have to a considerable extent been replaced by British manufactures. Moreover, several of the Arab merchants are establishing branches in Manchester and Liverpool. If they can obtain in England the articles wanted the men will not incur the expense of going to the Continent to buy.

The Arabs from North and from Central Africa form a very small proportion of the crowds in Kano market. How are these crowds to be described? Not at all, unless at tabulated length. Buyers and sellers come in from districts 100 miles away and intermediately. There are markets and markets, near and far, large and small, and Kano is the hub, the receiving and the distributing centre of them all. Sokoto, Katsina, and their surrounding districts send horses and cattle. Villages near weave cloth, plait straw into mats, basins and a dozen other forms, and place the article in Kano market. Kano itself and a wide radius around supply hides and skins, and Kano tans and dyes them. It is the combined Lancashire and London of West Central Africa; manufactures and the centre of exchange. But there are no large factories. Tanning, dyeing, weaving, the basket industry, leather work, all and much else are done by individual families or by men employing half-a-dozen employees.

Do not conclude that Kano market is only for big transactions. You can buy anything there, from flocks and herds to native-grown cotton, ginned or unginned, or less than a handful of ground-nuts—known in English fruit shops as monkey-nuts—for a few cowries, of which 280 are the local rate of exchange for a penny.

Arts and crafts flourish in Kano market. Yes, arts and crafts essentially. Note the skill of the fancy leather worker: satchels of many kinds; long, flat purses wherein a double compartment slips perpendicularly into another—a favourite form of keeping money or documents—slippers and covered sandals of brightly-dyed leather carrying devices in still brighter contrast; cushion covers looking as though a dozen chess-boards had been interwoven; large and small bags; whips and many other articles fancily formed of leather, and strips of it decorate spurs and anything where art or ornament can be used with effect. Nothing is more noticeable than the riding boots reaching above the knees and bearing in front brilliant figuring fit for a Claude Duval.

There is the wood carver, handling a small, crude blade and fashioning on calabashes, large and small, curves and lines and flowers, symmetrically shaped and arranged, and selling the whole thing, according to the size of the vessel, for 1d., 2d., 3d., or 4d.

In the blacksmith's shop only implements of utility are being produced, principally the hoe, which, used by hand, takes the place of our plough in forming a furrow for planting. It consists of a short handle—about 18 to 24 inches—and a small shovel blade set at right angle at the end.

Although not made in the market, there you may see knives and swords of diverse quality, always encased in a leather sheath. The knives, which are of the dagger type, are mostly worn for show. A common way of carrying is at the elbow, the lower part of wearer's arm passing through a broad ring of leather. Swords nowadays are not regarded as to be drawn for offensive or defensive purposes. But every gentleman of quality wears one. And in Hausaland a gentleman of quality may be a man of poverty with his robe in rags. For ordinary walks abroad the sword will be held by a length of lamp wick or several strips of discoloured linen passing over the shoulder. On State occasions—for processions of the Emir—the sling will be wool, plaited to thick tubular form, the ends finished by large tassels. Green, yellow, red are the colours of slings, some combining the three.

These swords are remarkable evidence of the ability of the metal workers. The blades are occasionally made from high quality steel previously used in a similar capacity, but most have been iron which bound packing-cases, and to this iron is added odd bits of other iron—nails or whatever of the kind comes to hand—the whole welded by hand hammering.

It is astonishing to take some of these swords and, placing the point in the ground, bend them to a half-circle, so finely tempered has the metal been brought by the simple process. The handles are dulled and set with pieces of brass cut from used cartridge-cases and fitted artistically. The leather scabbards are also daintily picked out with small corners of the same metal alternating with polished tin. The swords range in price from 1s. 6d. to 35s.

A number of used cartridge cases will be hammer-beaten by hand into one sheet which is made into a fairly deep dish to hold food or the takings at a stall.

The locksmith's stall has ordinary shaped padlocks of iron, copied from European patterns and commonplace in make and finish. At this stall I bought a couple of native-made padlocks—all that were in stock—very rough in shape but, I think, quite unique in form. Each was an oblong box, and at an end a screw, having a ring top, was wound. When the screw was inserted and turned to the left it went along the threads, closed the bolt and came out: it was the key. When the screw was again inserted and turned righthandwards it released the bolt and returned.

Native-grown cotton can be seen being drawn into thread by hand, and although, as just stated, most of the straw work—flat, dish-shape and baskets with covers, like a lady's house receptacle for needles, cotton, thimbles, etc.—is done in the outlying villages, men and women are also practising the industry in the market.

Guinea corn is another feature of the market, though little is to be seen. Sales of large quantities mostly take place with the article stored. Outlying markets, however, send supplies to Kano, where at present more than 10 times the quantity available would be bought as food for labourers on the tin fields.

The Government at Zungeru has recognised the situation, and a few days ago I met by chance my old friend, Mr J. E. Selander, lately Engineer-in-Charge of Construction of the Jebba-Zungeru section of the railway, who since August, when the line was handed over as completed, has been detailed to make a survey for motor roads in various parts of Kano Province.

Most valuable of all would be one from Katsina, about 120 miles north-west of Kano. Katsina is a great centre for horses, cattle and grain produce. Motor roads would be practicable for 9 months in the year, and impossible only during the heavy rains. The country is flat, with no necessity for bridging. Cost of labour should be low, about 1d. a day per man, and when the road was finished motor lorries could be run in conjunction with the train service from Kano. Transportation from railhead to many of the tin fields could be made easy for mechanical means.

Just off the centre of the market is an Alkali's Court, placed there specially to adjudicate on quarrels arising on the spot. Persons get to loggerheads over some deal. There is no long-drawn wrangle and subsequent exchange of solicitors' letters followed by briefing of counsel. The parties and their overlooking witnesses, with the evidence fresh and red-hot, simply step across to the Alkali's Court and he judges and settles the dispute out of hand. It is justice whilst you wait.

We turn to the cattle section of the market. There are camels, bullocks, sheep, donkeys and goats. Horses stand in an adjoining street. Few camels are bought and sold. Ansim, near Lake Chad, seems to be the country for that business; £7 each is the average price at Kano. A bullock fat for the butcher is worth £4, whilst his brother to be used for transport, in nearly every case with panniers, will realise from 35s. to 45s. The price of sheep has a longer scale, comparatively, than any other animal. The value is from 3s. 6d. to 18s. each. Goats are sold from 3s. to 4s. 6d. each.

A donkey figures at an average of 30s., which is double the price of a few years ago, due to the demand for transport to and from the tin fields.

A horse, or rather pony, useful for riding is worth £5. An animal of corresponding kind in England would change owners for from £15 to £25. A polo pony should be obtained in Kano for something between £8 and £12. The English figure is £40 to £60. Kano is not a horse-breeding district. Sokoto and Katsina are the principal districts whence they come. Kano is the chief market for that stock.

The horses are generally small, I should say, from 13½ hands to 15 hands. One of 17 hands towers over nearly all it will pass in the course of a month. The animals have not the stamina of the British horse and are slower. They are entire. An experiment was made to have 17 geldings in the

THE MAGISTRATE'S COURT IN THE MARKET.
His Worship is on the steps. (See page 107.)

A DETACHMENT OF THE EMIR'S POLICE.
(See page 68.)

mounted infantry, but the animals proved dull and spiritless and were discarded as useless.

Horses are unshod and mercifully their tails are not cut short, for flies around Kano are a perpetual torment to man and beast. The rest-house (!) in which I was sentenced to live, but to which I did not go, would have been a torture in that respect. It stood in a field near where herds of cattle passed accompanied by swarms of winged insects. An ideal place, truly, to put anybody who was writing hours daily. Knowing what I now do of Kano ways, it is just what might have been looked for from one quarter.

The bit used by natives is similar to that seen in North Africa and other Arab towns. The pace of the horse is checked by the rein bearing on the bit, as a person would press a lever, the action causing the bit to press on the palate, and as the iron bar has two prongs which rise as the rein is tightened, the result is extremely painful. At times blood will trickle from the animals' mouths, the palate having been pierced by the prongs on the bit bar. It is right to say that this bleeding will occasionally be caused by champing and not by misuse.

Horses ridden by natives are, as a rule, never thoroughly groomed. They are given a rub down about once a week. I have heard that once a year represents a nearer estimate on the period when the operation is performed.

Of course, horses belonging to Englishmen have the pattern bit in use at home, and the doki boy—as the groom is styled, doki being horse in Hausa language—is soon initiated into the use of curry-comb and brush. The weekly cost of having a horse is small: 3s. for guinea corn and 3s. 6d. the doki boy's wages.

The pain from the native bit is nothing to the unutterable suffering endured by camels and donkeys engaged in bringing loads to Kano City and taking them thence to places around. It is too terrible for words to express adequately one's sense of shame and anger that such a state of things should exist. I am given to understand that the folks at the Residency are so frightfully busy, but I do wish the Resident would find a few minutes to make representations to the Emir. I am certain an immediate improvement could be brought about and probably a permanently better condition effected in the course of a few months.

Camels have large patches of flesh raw and open and on these places the wooden saddle holding heavy packages will rest. At times the blood can be seen running from under it, as fresh skin is rubbed off. When the load remains on the beast for a long journey the heat of the body will dry the liquid part and a sore forms which becomes glued to the load. When this is taken off strips of flesh are torn away and into these exposed parts stinging and other flies cluster in swarms. As the animals have the packs removed from their backs the cries and groans go to one's heart. It is awful.

One of the worst sights I saw was that of a camel with flesh exposed and festering for about 6 inches long and 2 inches wide between the eyes and the nostrils, and the whole of this skin-bare flesh was practically covered with flies, which the beast was unable to shake off, as it was tied to a string of other

KANO MARKET

camels. A pennyworth of shea butter mixed with minesam would have kept the insects away effectively. I do most earnestly plead to the British Resident at Kano to have such distressing occurrences remedied.

A man from Lagos up at Kano was with me me when a file of camels were approaching their destination. He rubbed his hands gleefully. "This is quite Eastern," he exclaimed, as the animals swung along towards us.

Presently they were halted and made to go down and then was commenced the unloading. The beasts wailed piteously.

The visitor asked me, "Why do they make this painful, crying noise?"

I said nothing, clenching my teeth.

As the loads were removed and the bleeding flesh exposed my friend said, "Good God! This is terrible. Now I am sorry I came." He turned away. The sight was more than he could bear.

The poor, patient little donkeys also suffer shockingly. No notice is taken by most natives of sore backs and flanks when placing loads pannier fashion, so heavy that a donkey may have difficulty to walk, and when standing puts its legs wider apart to prevent the topheaviness overbalancing.

Oh! how I wish the King and Queen, with their solicitude for all sufferers, human and animal, would go to Kano. If they saw one thousandth part of what I witnessed I am certain a new era would open for the silent victims of the brute creation in this part of the world.

A more pleasant topic is that of the people of Kano.

CHAPTER XIII

KANO MARKET AND CITY

Deference to the Englishman—A sagacious policy—Administration of justice—An Alkali's judgment—The native Treasury—Kano municipality—Money matters.

REFERENCE has been made to the Arab merchants. They, however, constitute only a small number of the multitude who frequent the market and the adjoining streets. You will see them at their stalls or continually passing along in the afternoon, the thoroughfares crowded with them: Fulanis, Hausas, Nupes, Beri-Beris, male and female, many carrying in hands or on head cotton goods, native and imported, for sale. It is a busy multitude and few there are not intent on business.

The men are tall and bear themselves well, in turban and robe wide and ample, of blue or plain white or white figured with green or whatever may be the decorative colour. Respectful, nearly every one of them. They invariably give the salute which is regarded as due to the Englishman in Northern Nigeria: removal of sandals and kneeling on the ground, though, of course, where persons are thickly gathered only the semblance of the compliment can be performed.

Where instead of the turban a kind of white fez is worn, as is frequently the case with young men, it is lifted in courteous salute. An Englishman may

A CORNER OF KANO MARKET.
Note the Stocks. (See page 112.)

A SECTION OF THE MARKET WITH OPEN-AIR STALLS.
(See page 104.)

well feel proud whilst walking in the streets of Kano, not because his vanity is ministered to by the repeated deference, but that he may reflect and remember the courageous pioneers of only a dozen years ago who with resources improvised in the country won the land for Great Britain and placed the name of Englishmen highest in the land.

Going through the streets the white man is gazed at as an unusual sight, but the people did not look at me with more interest than I at them, wondering how we, a mere handful, overthrew their rulers and the large armies of mounted, trained fighting-men and captured their strong towns. However, one need not wonder long. Knowledge of contemporary events gives the answer. Still more to admire—for, after all, conquering is only a feat of arms—is the sagacity which produced the policy in full operation to-day, that of the people ruled by those whom they have selected, and rulers and people thoroughly co-operating with the governing Power in administering the affairs of the country. History furnishes no example where that has been done with anything like the same material in a similar period.

A peculiar thing struck me in connection with this general salutation. In Zungeru, esteeming the excellent feeling shown by the native population to the English, I was told I would find it still better in Kano. That is just what I did not find. In Kano City, yes, and, to an extent, at the despised British traders' stores, but the nearer one goes to the Residency quarter the less general is the salute given an Englishman. Apparently, estimating from such signs and tokens, he is respected most in the native area. Strange, this.

Not alone the city but the entire Province of Kano is ruled by the Emir, who appoints native Judges, and from him subsidiary Chiefs and village Headmen, through Chiefs of districts, take instructions and render reports. We rule through the native rulers, the leaders of the people. A very brief survey of its operation in Kano City may not be out of place.

The entire administration of justice has been placed in native hands, except where a European is involved. The Alkali, as the Judge is called, decides cases civil and criminal, framing his decisions on custom and usage based on the Koranic law. That, purged as it has been of corruption and inhumanity, is approved by the population, who are overwhelmingly Mohamedan, as being right and just, much more than would any application of English forms and methods. The Alkali is paid a fixed salary from the public Treasury and no longer, as formerly, has a share of the monetary penalties exacted.

Moreover, although acting under the general administration of the Emir, the Alkali is irremovable, as Judges are in England. These features of a regularly-paid, ample salary and fixity of office give the Alkali—and other Alkalis as well—an independence of judgment uninfluenced by temptation of bribery. The Governor can, of course, remove an Alkali, and though there is no formal appeal from an Alkali's Court, which at Kano is empowered to deliver death s ‘ence in a case of murder, all the decisions can be ltered by the Resident or revised by the English Chief Justice attached to the Governor's headqu   er staff.

THE PRINCIPAL MOSQUE.

AN ENTRANCE TO THE COURTYARD OF THE

KANO MARKET AND CITY 115

Judicial and administrative functions are separate. The Alkali decides punishment and the Emir's officers carry it out, just as in England, though Nigeria practice is the outcome of native usage.

A single decision of the Alkali is selected as an example. A young constable complained that his wife—who looked his senior by several years—entrusted with some cattle for sale had appropriated the proceeds and transferred her affections to another married man with whom she had dissipated the money claimed by her rightful lord. The woman admitted the action but put in as defence that what she had sold had been purchased with her own earnings and was her individual belonging. She proved that to the Alkali, who thereupon dismissed the charge of theft but held that if the woman did not promptly return to her husband the new domestic partner she had taken unto herself must monetarily recompense the original one for the loss of connubial felicity and to the extent of the wedding portion he paid for the angel on the hearth, minus a proportion for the years of married life.

The Married Women's Property Act may not be embodied in clauses and sections; statutes of Parliament are not codified and docketed; jurisprudence is not packed in dusty volumes, one contradicting another; but the principles of justice and commonsense, blended with the outlook of the people on what is right and proper and fair, mark the judgments of the men set up to decide among them.

Assessment and collection of taxes have been explained in Chapter VII. I went to the Beit-el-Mal and saw the accumulated revenue in boxes holding copper and nickel penny coins, bags of guinea corn—taxes paid in kind—neatly piled and stored to be sold at suitable opportunity—and boxes containing silver coins, which were interned in an inner chamber, locked and dark.

Hanging up ready for inspection at any moment by those empowered to examine were satchels in which had been put counterfoil receipts, all numbered and in regulated order, and suspended near was the book specifying what should be in the building and the general total. The descriptions were written in Hausa, but with Roman characters and figures. The intelligent Fulani and Hausa people have been trained by British officials to modify their former system to this extent.

I was also formally invited by the Resident to accompany the Acting Governor of the Protectorate on his visit to the native prison and on that occasion peeped round the corner inside for a few seconds. Though I believe the prison is excellently kept, I should have liked to have gone more privately when there would have been opportunity for asking questions.

Quite a different place, outside the city, which I should also have been glad to look over was the school for Mallamai (Mohamedan scholars) and Chief's sons at Nassarawa. But for some reason the aid to general investigation at Kano, which I had a right to expect, was proffered in such a way that nobody with self-respect could use it, and having to set about seeing things by other means, so much time was occupied that the Nassarawa school was one of the places which had to be cut from the programme. The establishment is based on the lines

THE ROYAL COURTS OF JUSTICE.
(See page 114.)

THE NATIVE TREASURY, KNOWN AS THE BEIT-EL-MAL.
(See page 115.)

of that at Bo, Sierra Leone, which was copied from the one in French Senegal.

Besides the central, native Government, Kano City has also a rough form of municipality. It is divided into wards, each under a Wardmaster, responsible to the Emir. The streets are kept scrupulously clean from refuse. That must be placed in stated spots and is removed daily.

As a matter of fact, there is little. The people waste nothing that can by any possibility be utilised. Cattle are killed in the open market by the Mohamedan priest, and nearly every part goes to a useful purpose: some of the internals are made into strings for musical instruments and from the bones praying beads and other articles are fashioned. Small portions of offal thrown in the appointed places are disputed for by ownerless dogs who wander about and by vultures.

Do not shudder at the word vulture and conjure up scenes of battle and men dead and dying. The vulture is quite a useful institution here. In the compound where I live two will perform the office of minor scavengers. So much are the birds esteemed that you kill one at a penalty of £5.

Even the clearings where cattle stand is removed by arrangement with the city authorities by persons who buy it either to use in the preparation of cloth dyes or for field manure.

To persons going up to Kano—or, for the matter of that, to any part of Northern Nigeria—small money will be a considerable convenience and probably saving. No gold coins circulate although legal tender. A two-shilling piece is rare. If a shilling is given in the market-place for a purchase, more likely than not that the stallkeeper will have to ask several of his neighbours to change it. The threepenny bit and pennies and halfpennies are best for one's exchequer. The "dash"—i.e., tip—is not the disease it has grown to be in Sierra Leone and Lagos, but tangible recognition of little services rendered is not wasted at Kano, any more than it is elsewhere. Visitors may, however, be reminded that a "dash" is not looked for in Northern Nigeria to the extent it is in Coast towns.

For everyday transactions nothing equals the threepenny bit for convenience. It is preferred by sellers. A good supply should be brought up from the bank at Lagos or Forcados. I am now in possession of my second £10 worth. Persons must not rely on obtaining the coin to any extent here nor on the way.

Of £25 drawn from the Bank of British West Africa at Zaria, no threepenny bits could be spared for that amount, £50 being the minimum with which they were given and then only to the extent of 2½ per cent. of the sum drawn. I could be given no more than £1 in sixpences, the remaining £24 was in shillings. Both the Manager, Mr Fenn, and the Cashier, Mr Cameron, are always willing to accommodate clients as much as possible, but request for smallest money and for nickel pieces are so many that a scale of proportions has to regulate drawings.

A STREET IN KANO.

DOCTOR'S SHOP IN THE MARKET.

CHAPTER XIV

SOME ASPECTS OF SOCIAL LIFE

Wives of the upper-class—Women and the mosques—Polygamy —Its difficulties in the home-circle—How to maintain peace— —Hints on management of the feminine character—A domestic diplomat—Slavery—The former and the present position—Status of a slave.

WIVES of men not well-to-do have stalls in public places, peddle or trade by travelling fairly long distances. When the women are their own capitalists the money earned is by no means handed over to the husband. He, too, must work and pay towards the housekeeping. Women of the Hausa and kindred tribes have decided wills of their own. The profits from their trading go to maintain aged relatives or to obtain for themselves cloths and other articles of adornment which the husband's wages will not procure.

Wives of what may be styled the upper-class do not trade. Nor do they perform housework. That is done by hired servants or by domestic slaves. These wives are not kept in seclusion, but they seldom go out of the compound adjoining the husband's house except on Fridays—the Mohamedan Sabbath—and then only to visit intimate female friends.

Although many women have affixed to the head,

suspended round the neck or attached to the arm little leather cases containing selections from the Koran, unless advanced in years, they do not attend a mosque for prayers. Their religious worship is fulfilled at home. Why only elderly ladies at the mosque?. Because, say the Mallamai—teachers; literally, wise men—presence of the younger feminine element would be likely to deflect the thoughts of the male portion of the congregation from the sacred purpose for which they go to a mosque.

Polygamy is general, as with all Mohamedans. Among the native friends made in the course of the journey I count Abigah one of the most illuminating on domestic problems. Abigah's father, also that name, is King of Lokoja. Abigah junior speaks English fluently. For 12 years he was an attentive pupil at the Church Missionary Society school at Lokoja, becoming a teacher there in secular subjects. Outside the school strong pressure was put upon him by an official then high in the public service of the Protectorate to forswear Mohamedanism. Immediate reward and alluring prospects were offered. The young man was firm. He would not, as he expressed himself to me, " be false to the faith of my people." He is now at full manhood, and, like all his brothers, has been sent by the father to learn the world in the best manner of tuition, namely, by having to earn a livelihood away from home.

Abigah junior has two wives. Now, there are tribes much lower in the scale of civilisation than the Mohamedans of Northern Nigeria when the more wives a man has the prouder each of them is

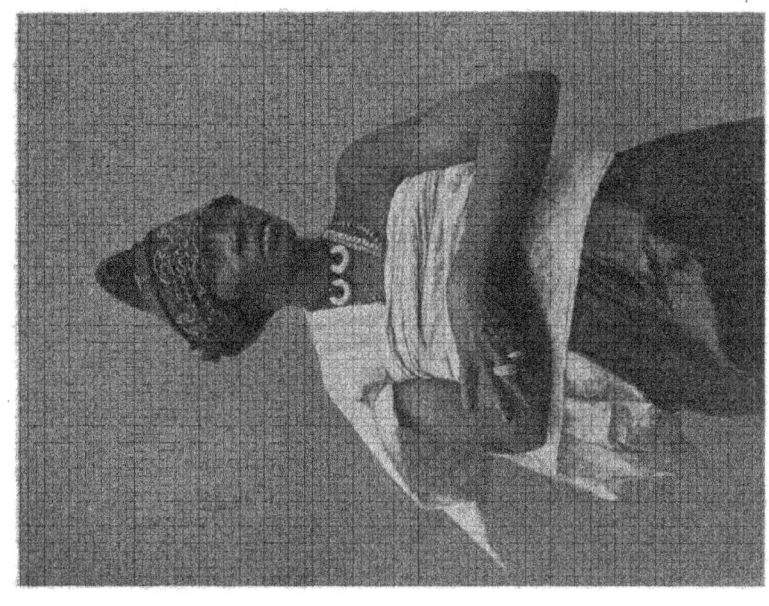

A HAUSA BELLE.

HAUSA WOMAN TRADER.
Her clothes are silk and her rings silver.

to be one, as the larger the number the greater the husband's importance. They are not reciprocally jealous. It is different with the Fulani, the Hausa, the Beri-Beri and cognate folk. A man has to be both tactful and firm to maintain peace in the domestic circle. Abigah told me he determined to start with that object in view, and therefore directly he put on double matrimonial harness he informed his spouses, in kindly but decisive tones, " Remember, there must be no wrangling. If either of you want to quarrel, quarrel with me." His admonition has been effective.

In the higher castes wives do not sit at meals with the husband, though in some cases they cook for him. It would not be considered dignified for him to be seen by them eating. The food is carried to him by a male servant. Where wives are on good terms together the husband's cooking is done co-operatively. When strained relations make that course impracticable, wives take in turns culinary duty two or three days each.

" Never," Abigah warned me, " tell one she is a better cook than the other in the hearing of that other."

" Why? " I innocently asked.

" Because," he replied, " there is nothing so likely to make a woman bad-tempered and spiteful to her own sex than being inferentially belittled by praise of someone she knows well."

At times Abigah has to leave on business for weeks. He takes one wife. I enquired, " But is there no rivalry as to which shall be with you? "

" Oh, yes," he exclaimed, " and I manage it in this way. For several days previous to going I am very soothing to the one to be left, reminding her she is to go next and promising to bring her a present of a fine piece of cloth."

" You keep your promise? "

" Certainly."

" Does the wife who has been your companion regard your company as preferable to a length of cloth? "

"Well," said Abigah, confidentially, " I give her a little present, too; something small, so as to make matters as nearly equal as possible to both. Never," he added, advising as though I were about to plunge into polygamy, " let any wife believe you like another better. Make each think she is *the* one." A domestic diplomat is Abigah.

Reference has just been made to domestic slaves. As the subject may not be fully understood at home a short explanation is offered. Under British suzerainty the capture of any person as a slave, as well as sale, exchange or gift of a slave have been prohibited; and all children born of slave parents after the promulgation of that declaration were to be free. It may be asked by worthy individuals at home, who only England know, why Great Britain should assent to the status of slavery in any shape or degree?

The answer is, first, that in Northern Nigeria slavery was a recognised and integral part of the social organism, and had an enactment been put into effect that all slaves were forthwith at liberty to discard control there would have been crowds of workless, loafing gangs roaming over the country, a misery to themselves and a danger to peaceable, industrious inhabitants. Secondly, such an enact-

TUREG TRADERS FROM LAKE CHAD.
They are reformed robbers. (See page 100.)

ABIGAH (SEATED) AND HIS TWO WIVES.
(See page 120.)

ment would have brought to ruin many rich and middle-class families whose herds, farms, and businesses were carried on by slaves.

That would inevitably have created an uprising which local troops would not have resisted. Even had England herself found money to remunerate owners, the first-mentioned peril would have occurred and the entire basis of society and commerce thrown out of gear.

What the British Governors did, in addition to what has been stated, was to get the Emirs to agree that any slave might claim his freedom by payment to the master. The roads, the railway and other public works then being put in hand by means of the grant-in-aid from Imperial funds enabled a slave by exertion of his muscle to gain the wherewithal for complete independence.

The method was a simple one. He would go to an Alkali's Court and make his desire known. The Alkali gave a certificate which enabled the man to move without restraint and at the same time intimated the position to the department under which the man wished to serve. The department deducted in weekly amounts from the man's earnings the recoupment to his former master, which was remitted through the Alkali.

The fact should not be overlooked that domestic slavery—i.e., slaves born in a household and remaining there with parents—is a very different thing to the barbarous raiding, with its attendant bloodshed, which was in full swing previous to British influence making itself felt.

Even in the earlier period a man could be prosecuted for ill-treating a slave, who by law was entitled to food, housing, care in sickness and release from all control for several days in the year. That the practice of domestic slavery did not bear hardly is shown by the large number who voluntarily remained, notwithstanding the facilities for independent employment. There is generally mutual trust and confidence between master and domestic slaves. It is not unusual for the former to supply the latter with goods for trading and to send him or her on a journey of several days' duration. On returning and handing over the takings the slave will be given a proportion of the profits. Were slavery the servitude which some folks view it, nothing would be easier than the oppressed to go off with sufficient endowment of the master's property to give a sound start in an unreined career.

CHAPTER XV

THE MISSIONARY QUESTION

Missions and Moslems—Strong comments—Bearings of the situation—Present practice—The British solemn promise—The alternative.

I SHOULD have preferred passing over the question of religion in connection with politics, but the matter is of supreme importance in Nigeria and therefore I shall not mince words in dealing with the subject.

An English friend in Nigeria has sent me a copy of the *Birmingham Weekly Post* in which a letter appeared from a missionary, stating, apropos of the prohibition of conversionist activity among the Moslems of Kano Province:

". . . It will now be generally known that the Government have shown themselves in their true colours, and not only England but the whole Christian world will now see that the English Government in Africa, Egypt and West Africa especially is distinctly anti-Christian and pro-Mohamedan. In all the large towns in Northern Nigeria schools are to be opened by the Government, in which Mohamedanism is to be taught and fostered. We hear, too, that in Bauchi the Pagan tribes are being put under Mohamedan Emirs, which practically means that the Government intend to force Mohamedanism on the Pagans and compel their law Courts to be based on Mohamedan law."

My friend has asked me to write him what I think of the communication. As I have no time for private correspondence I sent a postcard saying, as comment on the missionary testimony, "The 9th Commandment." It is distressing to find a gentleman who is a teacher of religion and an exponent of ethics delivering himself of half-truths mixed with facts in a way to give an entirely wrong impression.*

Let the public at home understand the situation in all its bearings. Mohamedanism may sit lightly on a section of the population, but once allow the idea to take root with the inhabitants that this faith of theirs is being menaced and you produce the cohesive influence which will bind the population together in a resisting, very likely an aggressive, mass. Now the Government does no more than leave the people and their religion alone.

There is perfect freedom of thought and practice. The native clerks and artisans from Sierra Leone, the Gold Coast and Lagos who are Christians can, and do, have their churches and chapels and worship as they please. To admit active propagandist methods in such a Moslem centre as Kano would be tantamount to waving a lighted torch in a magazine.

Do not speak of its being done tactfully and without ruffling the susceptibilities of a population

* Since this was written I have met the writer of the letter on the journey down the Niger. The matter was discussed and he told me the letter was sent to a relative without intention of its subsequent appearance in print. Publicity having been given to the assertions, I think it right the above comment on them should be made, notwithstanding my cordial relations with the writer.

THE MISSIONARY QUESTION 127

ever suspicious of interference with its national faith, the faith on which its laws are based. Picture the result of projecting among such a population a fanatic of the type of some missionaries. No doubt their intentions are good enough. These intentions put into practice at Kano would pave the way to making it correspond to a place the way to which, a proverb says, is also paved with good intentions.

Further, a solemn promise would be violated by allowing missionaries in Kano against the expressed wish of the native rulers, who are opposed to the intrusion on the ground that it would be a danger to peace. When Sir Frederick Lugard formally extended the authority of Great Britain over the territory he pledged his word that no interference should ensue to the religion of the people.

It shows a total absence of knowledge of local circumstances to argue that there is no interference by allowing missionaries to come in, the native being free to listen or not, as he desired. The native of Northern Nigeria looks upon every Englishman as above himself, as one to whom he must listen and obey. A missionary would be regarded by many in the same light, but the strain on the loyalty of others —of the great majority of the leaders and thinkers— would be too great. They would likely resent it with as much fanaticism as that which the missionary advocate shows in his epistolary fighting, with this difference, we should realise in their case that the sword was a more practical protest than the pen.

Of course, if the British nation is prepared to impose missionaries on its Moslem fellow-subjects of Kano against the advice of every disinterested native and European whose word is worth anything

—opinion I found unanimous, even among devout Churchmen—then do so; but count the cost. You will need a considerable force of white troops permanently stationed in a distant tropical land where preservation of health is a serious thought for each European living there. You must have the little army in a country where at present it is not necessary to maintain a single white soldier, except for a term as instructor to native troops. If the British public are prepared for all this and the attendant danger, to please those who agree with the gentleman whose letter was published, by all means do it. But count the cost.

There are a number of other aspects of life in and around Kano upon which a great deal could be written, but a message is to hand stating that the long-expected transport carriers from Rahama to the Bauchi Plateau will be ready by the time I arrive at the former spot.

I must not, however, close this chapter without short acknowledgment of assistance I have received here from two men among several others. If I were to mention at every place the courtesy and aid received I should have to tabulate a list and give the names of almost all with whom I came into repeated contact. At Kano, however, the early difficulties in being in a position to acquire full information were as unexpected as they have been exceptional. The task has been fulfilled, thanks in particular to Mr. W. P. Byrd, Agent of the Niger Company, and Captain J. J. Brocklebank, of the London and Kano Trading Company. The facilities for moving about which they gave me, especially Mr Byrd in that respect, and the channels of information which I was

"ZAKI! ZAKI!"
Natives giving the usual salutation to a white man.

RESPECT TO THE AGED IS SHOWN BY REMOVING THE SHOES
AND CURTSEYING.

enabled to reach by the help of both allowed me to carry out my duty almost as well as if I had gone forth arrayed in local, exalted patronage. My indebtedness for much interesting knowledge is also due to my excellent native friends, Adamu Ch'Kardi, of Kano, and to Suly, of Fuggi, the adjoining village. With sincere regret I take leave of them and of others whom I frequently met.

CHAPTER XVI

THE BAUCHI LIGHT RAILWAY

Zaria and other stations—The two gauges—Through new country—Second-hand rails—A new post for Sir Frederick Lugard—A relic of tribal warfare—Sport for the gun—A derailment—Blend of tongues—Smart re-railing work.

GOING down the railway from Kano the traveller opens his eyes widely at Zaria Station. At Kano there is no platform and no station. Time had not been sufficient to build either. Passengers climb into the train from the rails. For 90 miles southwards—to Zaria—the same conditions exist, with this difference, that there are not so many people to see the engine and carriages and their human freight as at the terminus. At Kano a small corrugated iron shed for the telegraph instruments, a mud house for the office, and a board indicating the place are all that mark the spot. You thoroughly realise you are in a country only recently opened.

But, arriving at Zaria, instead of a single track there are seven wide gauge—3 feet 6 inches—four narrow gauge—2 feet 6 inches—tracks and commodious engine sheds, a large building being put up to warehouse the increasing quantities of tin which the Government expects from the tin fields.

White railway officials hurry hither and thither with an air of bustle, hustle and business, and, most

THE BAUCHI LIGHT RAILWAY

striking of all at first sight, a station with an upper story for the administration staff. As you look nearer you notice that the roof is merely of iron and that the ornamented woodwork appears somewhat crude in its first coating of green paint. But, coming from where there are none of these adjuncts, the general appearance of Zaria Station is imposing, and, although tiny by comparison, the thought occurs of Euston, Paddington or Waterloo. Men coming upwards from the Coast may not be impressed by these things, for they have recently been where larger dimensions rule.

Bound for Bauchi, at Zaria Station the traveller takes the first turning to the right, literally so, as he walks from one side to the other of the island platform for the continuation of his journey. But the continued progress is not quite so promptly accomplished as may be imagined from this description.

The boat train from Lagos, which should leave on the previous Friday evening, is due at Zaria 11 a.m. on Tuesdays. The traveller must wait till next morning, as it is not possible to transfer luggage, etc., from the boat train to the one going to the foot of the Bauchi Plateau in time to reach that destination the same day, and, as the Bauchi line is fresh and unballasted, the service cannot safely be carried on during darkness. The night is therefore spent in a rest-house, for which a charge of 2s. is made. Next morning at 7 a.m., the train starts from Zaria Station for Rahama, turning eastwards and forming an angle to the main line.

I will not work myself into a state of uncontrollable excitement and frenzy over the Bauchi Light

Railway having been laid down a narrower gauge than the line of which it is a branch, nor will I belch forth fire and fury, in the shape of epithets of stupidity and ignorance, against whoever decided on the gauge. I will content myself with saying that it would have been better to have had the uniform gauge and thus avoid the delay and expense of breaking bulk on transfer. The line was laid down at a time of emergency and was largely an experiment, for then the exact direction of the main tin deposits had not been determined. The prime object was to have rail transport for the tin as quickly as possible and for as long a distance as the £200,000 given by the Home Government would cover.

There is no need to weep and wail and tear one's hair about the thing, for it is merely temporary. Embankment and bridges have been built to take the wider gauge and the rolling stock is easily convertible to use on that measurement.

You in England, as many do here, may laugh at this little line, which needs a day to traverse 88¼ miles, sometimes not doing it in that period. You may call it ironically, as people do here, the Bauchi Express or the Bauchi Flyer, but I must admit I was never so thrilled at any mechanical means of traction, never so impressed by any trial trip of a gigantic ocean liner, never so moved by participating in the initial run of a train at home embodying some new feature intended to make the public admire, I was never so thrilled by any one of such many departures in which I have taken part as I was when the train started round the iron curve from Zaria for Rahama.

THE BAUCHI LIGHT RAILWAY

One must indeed possess a dulled imagination not to have one's feelings stirred by contemplation of this line running through quite new country where it seems but yesterday a white man had scarcely trod. Who can go over this line and omit to think of John Eaglesome and his staff for having given them in the course of a few months means of transportation on a course where everybody is feverishly eager to get to his destination at the earliest possible moment, for nowhere more than in mineral prospecting is time, every minute of it, money.

You may rate me too ecstatic. But trek 90 miles along unmade paths in the extreme hot season or in the excessively wet season. Then say what you would give for a railway lift from starting-point to finish.

The first $14\frac{1}{2}$ miles of rails are second-hand. They are taken from the old tramway which ran from Barijuko, on the Kaduna River, to Zungeru previous to the advent of the Lagos Railway. The remaining $5\frac{1}{2}$ miles of rails of the tramway are being used for the trollies which take the refuse from Zungeru every morning. The old tramway station is re-erected as the central market shed in Zungeru native village. That is the way they administer in Northern Nigeria. Nothing is wasted. Lugard had left when that was done, but his spirit and methods remained. Complaints are heard in England of extravagance and wastefulness by public departments. I wonder whether the appointment of Sir Frederick Lugard to control the spending departments in London would effect a remedy.

Passengers on the Bauchi Light Railway have a plain van with a sliding door the height of the coach.

A van serves for two men, who must bring chairs and, in case of the train being detained overnight en route, beds, and also make their own arrangements for cooking. The demand for accommodation frequently exceeds the supply; and that men be not delayed, the traffic staff provides a similar van but one usually used for goods. Such a van will not have the cooling, protecting matchboard under the iron roof, and persons using a van of that kind should therefore remember that a helmet, or at least some headcovering, is a wise provision against sun troubles.

Vans have a small compartment at each end for native servants, but there are no stoves. Should, however, there be a delay during the journey, passengers' cooks get out and kindle a fire on or near the track. That is the chance for a hot meal. There are seven stations: Awai, Soba, Duchi-n-Wai (for the Berrida and neighbouring tin mines), Karre, Kudara (for the Wassaku Concessions), Worroko and Rahama.

The first 10 miles passed are open, flat country, having slight bush, with sections here and there under cultivation for guinea corn. Near Awai, 17 miles from Zaria, can be seen the remains of a walled town. The wall, now quite thin, has been worn away by the weather to a few feet in height, broken and irregular at top, and within it thick trees of many years' growth and wild grass demonstrate that where thousands of souls lived and where their children might be dwelling to-day has been destroyed utterly, the dead fruit of fierce tribal warfare. A few straw, circular huts belong to recent comers who are tilling bits of the desolate city.

THE BAUCHI LIGHT RAILWAY 185

At 10 o'clock, whilst at Soba Station, word came that the heavy rain of the night had caused a wash-out of the line some miles ahead. Questions were asked whether we should have to tramp the remaining distance to Rahama. "Oh, no; it would only mean a stay of about four hours."

Now, you folks at home, delayed at a tiny village station would probably exhaust the interest of the place in a few minutes and relieve the tedium of waiting by gloomy maledictions or settle down to fitful and impatient reading. Not so out here. We are all philosophers at such trifles. We know that a day's set programme may at any moment be completely upset by the elements. One of the passengers, Mr D. Bannerman, of the Northern Nigeria (Bauchi) Tin Mines, complacently unlocked his gun case, shouldered a rifle and, accompanied by a little party, sallied forth in the bush to look for sport and perchance bring something fresh back for the dinner pot, arranging with the engine-driver that a long loud whistle should notify that telegraphic word had come that that washout was near being remedied. Mr Bannerman was back well before a start was made, at 2.45.

Thiry-five miles from Zaria the Duchi-n-Wai hills loom in front, only the tips of them, above the dark green of trees, now much closer, which on both sides have closed in the view to a mile or so. They soon give way left and right to fields less freely timbered, with an occasional acre bearing guinea corn.

It had been clear when we left Soba that the journey could not be completed that day, so on reaching Duchi-n-Wai, at 4.15, a stop was made for the night. Cooks cut wood for fires from trees near and commenced preparations for dinner.

With two camp-beds up and mosquito curtains there is not much room for other furniture in a van. Folding chairs and tables are therefore brought and put on the rails, and along the side of the train they are ranged, each with its hurricane lamp amidst plates and dishes.

The native servants make their fires the other side of the train, sit round them and join together in song, sleeping on the ground, in the open, which they prefer to inside the carriages.

Six o'clock next morning another start was made. At Bibin, between the 60 and 61 miles' boards, high, rocky hills are within a few hundred yards of the line. As the engine stops for water and you glance backwards, it looks as though the train had entered a very narrow opening. In front is a similar view. Going out of this gorge there is again grassy plains studded with trees.

We had left Kudara Station, 66 miles from Zaria, and were thinking of an easy, plain spin for the rest of the journey, when occurred a sudden severe jolting, the more pronounced as the sleepers are of metal and not covered by gravel: we were derailed. There was just a semblance of panic among some of the passengers and one rather excitedly jumped from the train. We had been going round a curve and doing it slowly, at 6 miles an hour, so there was not much danger of being upset. The train was quickly stopped. The driver gave the double whistle which is a distress signal and tells all who know railway language that there is a mishap.

It happened that near by was the hut of Mr

THE BAUCHI LIGHT RAILWAY

Robert Brown, Bridging Foreman, who had gone in to read a letter from his wife, in England, which the train had dropped a few minutes earlier. Running out and seeing what had occurred he had a trolly put on the line and sent word to the temporary workshed at Kudara Station for hydraulic jacks and other implements. The double whistle had also brought hurrying to the spot Richard Brown, driver of a ballast train a quarter-of-a-mile away. Never have I seen men work with more energy than these two and the driver of the train, J. Swainson, did on that tropically hot morning. Swainson had ordinary jacks on the engine, and a start was made with them. Of the seven coaches, three had been derailed, each 26 feet long and weighing about 8 tons.

Everyone who has duties keeping him in this country speaks some Hausa. It is especially necessary for persons who are in constant direction of natives. A large gang at work on construction— for the line is not nearly finished, and is only open unofficially for the convenience and assistance of transport to and from the tin fields—had been summoned and Robert Brown disclosed his linguistic acquirement as his men ran to and fro at his orders.

But there are some words for which the Hausa tongue has no equivalent, and these words have become incorporated in their pristine freshness into local vocabularies. Thus, it sounded amusing to hear, "Kow jack; Muzza muzza." ("Bring the jack, quickly, quickly.") Sharply also were called the orders to "Kow crowbar," "Kow slewing bar" and "Kow" half-a-dozen other things given their English names.

By the exertions of the two Browns and Swainson (who had all along been obliging in every way he could to the passengers) the three derailed coaches were lifted back on the rails, and in an hour-and-a-half from the time of the accident the train was again running. As it moved off we gave a hearty cheer for the Browns and for Swainson.

No further incidents marked the trip.

At 88 miles the train glides round a headland, and a little in front there are several straw huts and a crowd of figures—there have been scarcely any at the intermediate stations—diminutive in the distance but distinct, white-robed, indicating that that is Rahama; and in a few minutes the train pulls up in a shallow cutting which is the present railhead.

You climb up from the track by steps cut into the clayey earth, and shortly after rain it is all a chance whether you maintain your balance whilst making the ascent. Having got to the higher ground you are at the jumping-off point for trekking.

THE RELIGION OF THE MOHAMEDAN FORBIDS THE USE OF SOAP, AS IT CONTAINS FAT.
Shaving is therefore done with the aid of water only.

SPECIMEN OF THE BARBER'S ART.

CHAPTER XVII

AT RAHAMA RAILHEAD

Engaging carriers—How to facilitate getting away—Hausa horse coupers and political economy—Bullock transport—Donkey carriage—The man who belies a fable.

AT Rahama one says good-bye to the railway. Henceforth locomotion must be of the animal or the human kind. The whole of the transport onwards is in the hands of the Niger Company, and everybody who desires to progress must go there.

Perhaps I should not say "must." All are free to make their own arrangements, but it will be found impossible to engage carriers direct, for every man-Jack available is constantly employed by the Niger Company, who could do with hundreds, if not thousands, more. Had the Company, or someone else, not organised transport there would have been such scramble and chaos in the endeavour to get carriers for the tin fields that the Government would have been compelled to itself organise the service, for the confusion would have been intolerable. As matters are, everything goes much easier and is a great deal more reliable than if carriers were hired casually.

The Niger Company is sharply, even bitterly, criticised for the time occupied in goods reaching consignees in the tin fields' area. The fact should be remembered and counted as an element of consideration that not only is the country new but that the tin-mining industry has come unexpectedly and with a rush and no public or private concern in the land which is actively involved can cope with the mountain of requirements which have arisen. Railways, roads—where there were not so much as bush paths —and transfer of thousands of men from one occupation to another are not evolved in a day, or a year, by the mere want of them. They cannot be produced by a Governor's proclamation, the most potent document in Northern Nigeria. They take time; and attempts to do things too hastily, regardless of special local difficulties, mean courting a complete breakdown.

Decidedly it would not do for men to come to railhead and bid against one another for carriers. That would mean the individual with the longest purse would always be first, and the cost to everyone would be more than it is. If the Niger Company at Rahama is advised well in advance of a person's wants he is seldom, if ever, kept waiting. Goods cannot be forwarded at once. A man and his immediate belongings are. Of course, people must not expect 300 carriers apiece. The plan is to allow sufficient for personal requirements—I think 30 carriers to an individual is the present limit—and an ample margin beyond. Engaging and taking away a large number of carriers might be a trick to keep other persons back.

Above everything, I am informed, is it necessary to let the officer in charge at Rahama know as long as possible in advance. Whilst I was there a man who had not given previous notice of his requirements offered to pay more than anybody else, and was willing to put the money down on the spot, if he could be immediately supplied with carriers. His offer was declined. The transport officer acted on the principle of the Company, that having taken in hand persons' needs it was morally bound to comply with them, as though there had been a contract. It seems to me that the work at Rahama is regulated by a sense of responsibility and fairness.

In obtaining a pony for trekking there is a broader choice. It can be bought from or through the Niger Company or purchased direct from a dealer in Rahama Town, near by. I should not advise the latter way. The horse dealer here is not far removed in instinct from his counterpart in England. He takes stock of his client and acts accordingly. "He savvy plenty he be Bako Bature"—"He recognises that the buyer is a stranger white man," as a Hausa interpreter expressed the situation to me—and therefore fair game. Although the horse merchant has not been a deep or diligent student of the works of Adam Smith and John Stuart Mill, and probably cannot read or write a word in any language, he estimates to a nicety the extreme doctrine of political economy, and nobody knows better how to hold the market and shape his bargains after that preliminary.

A horse for which £12 is asked in Rahama Town can be bought through the Niger Company for £8, 10s. I will not give my own experience as it might be thought I was favoured. I will relate two cases of fellow-passengers which came under my notice, as each showed me his mount for an opinion. One went direct to a Rahama dealer and paid £8, 5s. for an object on four legs, which, poor beast, seemed innured against the persuasion of reins or whip

Another passenger had from the Niger Company a black Katsena pony—next to the Pagan horse, the best type for trekking in a country of broken roads and stone-stepping spruits—at £8.

One must not expect at Rahama a fiery, untamed, prancing Arab. Untamed, possibly yes; more probably, utterly broken in spirit and with a mouth as firm as granite. No novice need fear getting on top, and if he does roll off there is not far to fall, for the average height appears to be from 12 to 14 hands.

Should a horse be wanted for settled use in the country it ought to be obtained at Zaria or Kano, the latter greatly for preference.

A further word of advice. Bring saddle and bridle from England. Any for sale here are immediately snapped up. Owing to the competition a man will likely have to pay more for an English bridle and saddle falling to pieces than the cost of a new one at home plus the expense of carriage out.

The Niger Company bullock transport for the tin fields keeps 150 animals going, worked when necessary in teams of 16. Thirty oxen will draw 12 two-wheeled carts of half-a-ton carrying capacity at an average speed of 10 to 12 miles a day. The men who drive were taken over from the old cart transport between Zungeru and Kano, instituted by Sir Frederick Lugard previous to the railway being laid. The training on the road was done by drivers from India, many of whom had passed through the military transport service there, to which no doubt is to be traced some of the words used. The bullocks shamble off hearing " Tashi! " the Hausa word for " Start! " and stop at the sound of " Halt! "

Besides bullock carts and wagons, donkeys are

also used in the dry season for the tin fields' work, not in traction but in pannier style. They are cheaper than human carriers. A donkey will take the load of two of them, and one man—the owner of the animals hired—looks after three. The donkeys have not to be supplied with provender. They fend for themselves on the march, feeding on the dry stalk of the guinea corn—in some cases an inch in diameter—after the ear has been garnered.

The Rahama branch of the Niger Company is in charge of Mr Percy Garrard, who had Government experience in South Africa, East Africa and India. His post is far from being an enviable one, especially on the arrival of a train, when perhaps several men who have given no notice of their coming want to be horsed, equipped with carriers and away in a twinkling. Though his position is one where many of us would turn savagely on folks harassing us to death, or at least to distraction, Mr Garrard does nothing of the sort. He just does the best he can for everybody, giving precedence for those for whom he has prepared and fitting up the others as quickly as he is able. He works rapidly, as he must or he would be overwhelmed by the continuous stream of matters claiming attention.

He is one of the most remarkable individuals to be met with in Northern Nigeria. Not alone that he is incessantly occupied, doing things at lightning speed and yet never becomes flurried nor loses his temper, it seems incredible that the whole of the transport work at Rahama is directed by him with only one European to assist in the multifarious duties, which commence at high pressure at 6 a.m., and continue at an equal rate throughout the day.

Nobody has so many pressing requests from impatient travellers. Everybody who arrives from the Coast of course wants carriers at once, probably needs a horse, and, more likely than not, wishes to take with him more packages than there are carriers to bear them.

All these desires are urged on Mr Garrard, and, naturally, each person believes his own business to be more urgent than that of anybody else. The wonderful thing is that Garrard not only tries to please everyone, but, notwithstanding the tragic fate of he who in fable attempted a similar result, Garrard succeeds, although it is seldom possible to do all that is asked. He has an infinite capacity for what is known as getting on with people. All speak well of him; in fact, that is putting the position too mildly; they speak of him enthusiastically. A couple of men who were out for their second year and had been through Rahama four times said to me, " If you write a book on your travels you should include Garrard's photograph. We would cut out the picture and carry it with us, and whenever we happened to be annoyed at not having forwarded things we wanted, whilst we were miles away in the bush, we could look at Garrard's portrait and that would give us pleasurable recollections and tone down anger at the delay."

The offices and stores of the Company are corrugated iron sheets, not fixed together to form a wall, but merely touching one another, leaning on bamboo frames and covered by a dried-grass roof. The whole thing is taken to pieces and carried forward as the railway line advances and is put together at each new railhead.

AT RAHAMA RAILHEAD

Rahama is also the clearing centre outwards. To it, from different districts, comes tin, which is sent by the Bauchi Light Railway to Zaria, then transferred to the Baro-Kano Line and taken to Baro, where it is carried down the River Niger and shipped to England.

CHAPTER XVIII

ON TREK—RAHAMA TO JUGA

Heavyweight and overweight—The white barred—Collective displeasure—Getting off—A doki boy—Tin-mine pilgrims—A scion of royalty—The rest-house—Village elders—Acrobatic horsemanship—The carriers—Headman Hanza—Over the edge of the Pagan belt.

BE sure no package exceeds 60 lbs. That is the first thing to govern preparation for the trek. If parcels are heavier carriers may refuse to take them. Do not talk about "making" the men do so. You who have had experience with carriers on the Coast, in other parts of Africa, or in the Far East, must not think of putting into operation methods which obtain there. You will find that the natives here are entirely different, have different ideas, and require different handling. You must begin learning knowledge of carriers and other labour afresh. That is not the product of my own philosophy. The words were said by a man who had been mining all over the world and whose years of observation probably doubled those of anybody now actively engaged in Northern Nigeria. The carrier here is, however, one of the best fellows on the face of the globe. He needs to be understood. That accomplished, you can get him to do anything in reason. Such is my conclusion and testimony. I

ON TREK—RAHAMA TO JUGA

am referring to men who are carriers from choice, not to those taken from other occupation, more or less against their wish.

Though it is essential your loads shall not exceed 60 lbs. each, to avoid opening and redistributing the contents of trunks in the open ground there is no reason to inconvenience yourself by placing more in boxes than you desire. The golden rule is not to have any above the specified standard. Below it does not mean increase in the number of carriers. The procedure at Rahama is this. All packages are set in a line. Mr Garrard looks at each and quickly weighs them up mentally, testing by lifting. A load of, say, 20 lbs. is placed with another or more and all securely tied to equalise every load to about 60 lbs. The carriers do their own roping, according to the individual manner of bearing a package, which is on the head.

For the first day an early start is out of the question. A number of little things have to be done which cannot be effected in advance. Nor should a long stretch be decided upon for the initial stopping-place. The men like a near one in order that they may settle down and become accustomed to their loads before the journey is entered upon in real earnest. You will lose nothing in the end by humouring these feelings of the carriers. Give way to them in small things, which do not matter, and you will be able to have your way in larger ones that do matter.

My packages were paraded in the way prescribed, and the carriers stood behind them ready for Mr Garrard's directions. Just then I walked up, and as soon as it was seen that I was to accompany the party two of the men showed restiveness and said they did not wish to go. Now, I do not think I am a very fearsome-looking personage, and I failed to understand why a glance at me at once deterred otherwise willing workers. It was subsequently elicited that the two men had previously marched with a European who had hurried, harried and bullied them, and whilst they were quite ready to take any load and go anywhere, they desired to do it only with their fellows. When a party of that kind travels the men usually do very short distances in the preliminary part and select their own stopping-places, generally near a market that suits them, but whatever time be lost by these deviations they are sure to make it up and to arrive at a destination at the stipulated hour. They merely like to do things in their own way.

Mr Garrard simply dismissed the gang and called up the next in waiting. All these carriers working for the Niger Company receive a fixed wage, with additions for the journeys carried out. I asked whether any reprimand or punishment would be given to the two refractory carriers. Mr Garrard replied, not by him. The gang would be put last of those in waiting and might not be sent out that day. The members of it would, therefore, lose their "extra," and those of them who were willing would be sure to lead the couple of recalcitrant ones to a suitable place and there administer the measure of their displeasure at being baulked of the earnings.

The fresh carriers were soon apportioned their loads and streamed away towards Gidan Gombo, the first stopping-place, 11 miles. They left at 11 a.m. The caravan consists of 20 carriers and a Headman, two doki boys and three boys for domestic service.

ON TREK—RAHAMA TO JUGA

The last department is made up of a steward, a cook and a small boy as general help.

I did not ride out until 4 p.m., staying to write and send off *African World* despatches, as after leaving Rahama I would not be near a post office for at least nine days. Kogini Rahama—Rahama Brook—a narrow river, had a bridge made of rails and sleepers thrown across it by the railway survey people, but it had met the fate of many bridges at this season; it had been broken by the storms and floods. Mr Garrard has an arrangement with the owner of a canoe to take across any traveller and his carriers at a charge of 2s.

A few hours previous to my starting heavy rain had fallen, and the first miles were over ground so slippery for the horse that I found it quicker to walk. Where the road was firm I rode hard, in the endeavour to get to Gidan Gombo before dark. Mr Garrard's own doki boy, who was to bring a parcel back, came with me, and however quickly I rode he remained running in front, carrying a rather heavy writing satchel all the time. (Doki is the Hausa word for horse, and all servants, no matter their age, are styled boys.) Among those for whom I shall take away a very kindly feeling, and also one of admiration, is the best type of doki boy.

The portions of greasy road were so long that, following the brief twilight of the tropics, though darkness had set in by 7 o'clock I was still jogging along. The doki boy, however, knew the route, and there was no drawback except that of going over strange ground with no moon. About a quarter-of-an-hour later there was the unpleasant sound under these circumstances of breaking water ahead.

Nobody had passed us for some time. During the day it is easy to learn if a stream across the high road is fordable. Persons coming from the direction on the tramp have evidently crossed the water, but at night, after a recent downfall, streams which might have been walked over on stones prior to the deluge are impassable.

I was nearing the place and debating in mind whether to chance trying to go over—there seemed no alternative, unless I was either to ride back and so put twenty miles on the journey, or stay at the spot all night—when a light swung ahead. A little party from the rest-house had brought a lantern to obviate the difficulty of crossing and by its light stepping-stones were clearly visible. The rest-house was only a mile further on, and into the compound I passed at 7.40.

An example of willingness on the part of good carriers was furnished. One had been overtaken by a mounted messenger when nearly half-way with an order to return. He was bearing a steel trunk not less than 60 lbs., and awkward to hold. It contained papers which should have been shown at Rahama. The man turned back, set out again, and although walking alone and going over the same ground on which I found it not easy to keep a horse up, and the latter part over which the pony went at a fair pace, still the carrier, who only had two hours' start, came in at 8 o'clock, with no more stimulus than 1s. given at Rahama.

The rest-house compound at Gidan Gombo had within it quite an assemblage of natives who were tramping to Naraguta district attracted by the expectation of employment at the tin fields. Not labourers

—they sleep in villages—but Coast mechanics and similar workmen and interpreters. In a rest-house compound are a number of smaller mud huts for the carriers, and in these shelters coloured men pass the night. There was a lad among them said to be son of the former Emir of Kano. If so, the scion of royalty had been much reduced in position. He—who whether the story be true or not was evidently of a superior caste—had been servant to Captain Maclaverty, of Zungeru, and was walking to Naraguta with a friend of the family—an interpreter—to enter the service of an Englishman there.

These rest-houses are put up by the Government. But for them one must perforce carry a tent or go to a native village, not an ideal place in which to sleep, from the health or any other point of view. The rest-house usually consists of a fairly stout circular mud wall, round which is a lower one, the intervening space covered by the sloping roof and forming a verandah. Rest-houses are in charge of the Headman of an adjacent village. He collects, for the Government, 2s. per night from each occupant, the payment including a supply of wood and water. If required, he has to sell for himself, at fixed rates, fowls and guinea corn for horses.

It is quite a little ceremony at some places where the Headman, accompanied by one or two village elders, pays his respects to the white visitor by coming to the rest-house, and there on knees saluting, by bowing the head and exclaiming several times, "Zaki! Zaki! Zaki!"—literally "Lion" —corresponding to "Sir" or "Your Honour" or "Your Lordship." The visitor gravely replies "Agaisheka!" ("Hail to you!") and then proceeds to business by stating his requirements in the matter of supplies and asking how much he has to pay. After the evening meal prepared by his servants in a cook-house in the compound, bed is the usual order of procedure.

The start next morning was at 6.30. I did not accompany the carriers but turned back to look for a Swan fountain pen jerked out of my pocket the previous afternoon and immensely valued not so much for its great convenience on a journey of this kind, when writing must be done at odd moments anywhere, but still more prized at being the gift from former colleagues. Nearly an hour's search along the road failed to discover the article, so the forlorn hope was abandoned, and I turned round to overtake the carriers.* They would be, of course, about two hours in advance.

I had long repassed Gidan Gombo and, relying on the horse's reputation for being sure-footed, was galloping him along a ridge on the road, each side cut into a ditch by further heavy rains of the early morning, when, a slip to the right, he involuntarily bent his head and over it I went, as cleanly as if I had been an acrobat. As is my practice when dismounting in this manner, I retained hold of the reins, but it was well the doki knew his manners and pulled up, for the bridle came off completely. A mud bath and a few slight bruises constituted the

* On discovering the loss the previous evening at the rest-house I sent a note to Mr Garrard, by his doki boy, offering £1 reward to any individual or body of men who found the pen. Next morning Mr Garrard sent out a party of six, notifying that 10s. would be paid to he who recovered the article. Although the night rain had displaced portions of the road, one of the men brought back the pen, which was handed to me on the return journey, some months later.

casualties, for the pony did not even go on his knees. He looked rather forlorn standing in the road with naked head, and as I went up to replace the bit he appeared to say, with a half-apologetic, sorrowful air, " Well, upon my soul! Who would have thought it?"

The sun had come out strongly, removing the dampness and leaving a caking of earth and mud on breeches and shirt as I cantered along to Gussum, 14 miles from Gidan Gombo, reaching it some time after the carriers.

Everybody having now settled down to their work, I decided on a 5 a.m. start for next morning, but at that hour the night rain was still falling, and you will seldom induce carriers to step out into a storm. If one comes whilst they are on the march they sturdily go on. A wetting from above is the most severe minor discomfort a native can suffer. It was 7 o'clock before the air had cleared, and we set forth. The Naraguta pilgrims continued towards their goal along the road that has been made southwards, whereas we, after going back a few hundred yards, left the road and struck southeast.

It was the first day I had ridden with the carriers, and within a couple of hours, without having spoken to any, I seemed to be on good terms with each. A more buoyant, light-spirited, smiling set nobody would wish to march with. One, Amadu, had suspended round his neck a kind of shepherd's pipe roughly fashioned of wood, which, with a line of airholes along it, yielded shrill tunes. We set out with this pipe sounding a cheery note that stimulated all of us more for the day's work.

Another leading figure of the party is the Headman Hanza, a fine type of Hausa, the kind of man whom nature has indicated should be above his fellows. His control of the men is thorough yet easy, and exercised with an entire absence of anger or high words. When he has to speak to any of them reprovingly, which is only called for when getting them to make more haste for the early morning assembly, it is never done by shouting. A few words in a deliberate, slow tone are all that is necessary. His articulation through a perfect set of teeth is so clear that a stranger to his language could catch every syllable.

It is on the Bauchi Light Railway that the Pagan belt of land is first touched, but there they are a very mild variety, a kind of Hausa-Pagan, the two having largely mingled and intermarried. Along the route we are now crossing there is a nearer approach to the real article, but nothing approaching the wild tribes on the further stages on the plateau. Men and women in the Gussum-Juga direction wear scarcely any clothing—males, a narrow loin-cloth; females, a bunch of leaves in front and another at the back—and keep themselves rather apart from the other population. The men turn from their work in the fields to bow to the white men. The Hausa villages and Fulani farms are not far from the dwelling-places of their aforetime prey, for slaves, and sworn enemies. Cultivation of the land, though not general, is fairly frequent. Pagan villages, instead of always being made in rocky heights where they were safe from the raiding Fulani horsemen, are now seen pitched lower, and not infrequently in the valleys. The British power ensures them protection and peace. Raiding for slaves is over, in these parts.

From Rahama the ascent to the plateau of Bauchi Province is an imperceptible slope. After leaving Gussum towards Juga there is a gentle down-grade for half the distance, carrying and concentrating rain from the hills and mountains, and in the course of a few hours making dry river beds and shallow streams into rushing, dangerous waters. This we experienced.

CHAPTER XIX

RAHAMA TO JUGA—(*continued*)

Stopped by a stream—A volunteer—Amadu the carrier—Sun heat —Across the river—" Kow abinshi "—The doki boy's experiment—The climate and granite—Domestic details on trek—A chilling downpour—Mark Tapleys—Sun and warmth —Hanza's command—A dignified procession.

HALF-A-DOZEN men who had come from the opposite direction, and who were some distance to the right, shouted in a warning tone as we passed, " Rau " (" Water "). The reason we soon understood. A few minutes later we were at the edge of a steep bank below which a swift, swirling river was being impelled from rapids quite near. The sound of the torrent as it fell on the rocks made one feel utterly insignificant, a mere twig if within such force and power.

It was clear that the water was not to be crossed lightly, and the first thing was to ascertain whether the depth was above a man's shoulders. Under the direction of Hanza several of the carriers threw aside their loin-cloths and waded in. Almost at once they were off their feet, swimming, splashing, laughing, shouting with joy at the cool bath. The bends of the bank enabled them to get back without distress. Evidently, however, the river was impassable, for some of the carriers could not swim,

RAHAMA TO JUGA—continued

and even if all could the question of taking over heavy loads had to be solved.

Hanza considered the best course would be to send the horses across and to instruct one of the doki boys to ride to a village a few miles distant and bring a man who had a boat. The "boat" I subsequently found out was a large calabash ball with a stake through it, the upper part grasped by a passenger who sat on the calabash. This floated whilst the voyager was carried along by the stream; if he were able, paddling with feet until he was across, and if he had not confidence to do that then carried by the current until a turn of the bank on the other side intercepted him. Such a "boat" was lying near. When discovered, the question of conveying boxes over remained a difficulty.

The horses were unsaddled, taken to a point where it was calculated the current would not bear them past the part on the opposite bank where they could get out of the water, and swum across. We saw one of the doki boys mount and ride away. There was nothing for it but to sit down and wait.

We had arrived at 10.20, and after an hour's delay and no sign of the doki boy, Hanza told me that one of the carriers thought he knew where the bed of the river rose somewhat, and had volunteered, if I would consent, to try and carry the loads across one by one. Glancing at the strongly-running stream, I said I would first prefer to see the man go over unencumbered. Hanza answered that the test was whether the man could keep on his feet bearing a load against the pressure of water. I appreciated the argument and looked along the line of packages for something easy. In order to cover the ground as quickly as possible I travel lightly. It seemed rather hard to decide what, if a sacrifice had to be made, should go. The photographic equipment was the lightest, but that was the most precious, more precious than the food. Scanning the boxes, I selected a case containing a tin of kerosene as being the article the loss of which would cause least inconvenience. Hoisting it on his head, Amadu—for he was the volunteer—went down the bank and entered the water.

Gingerly he stepped out, for the current went hard and the ridge along which he walked was not too broad. Fortunately it curved leftwards, so he was able to give ground to some degree to the pressure of water on his right. But as he went deeper his efforts, it was distinctly visible, were more severe, and by the time he was in the middle of the stream—at its widest point—I had become very anxious. The river was up to his shoulders and beating across him ominously.

He went on, with the eyes of all his fellows following him intently. My gaze fixed intently on the now slowly-moving figure, which seemed to be struggling to maintain its upright position. I saw he was treading into deeper water. It was washing round his ears, and in a moment more had reached to the top of them. Still he pushed forward, and as the level of his eyes was reached and he painfully struggled on, his arms stiffened in the endeavour to raise the heavy load pressing on his head, and to bring his face above water to breathe. I could stand the sight no longer, and, breaking the spell of silence, shouted "Adja kasa! Adja kasa!" ("Throw it down! Throw it down!")

RAHAMA TO JUGA—continued

Amadu either could not hear or would not heed. He stopped, and not once but thrice or more he tried to bring his face above the water. No, it could not be done there. Would he wear out his remaining strength and drop? A score of pairs of arms must have involuntarily twitched in the desire to help the brave carrier whose endurance was at breaking-point. His feet felt their way by inches, and whilst I stood, both sick and fascinated, more of his head seemed to show, and, sure enough, he was on the upward slope, and in a few moments again stood still, now his mouth and nostrils above water, and drew several long breaths.

Lifting the load two or three times in playful manner, as a signal to his comrades that he was all right, he strode on into the shallower flow and putting the box down on the bank scrambled up. I gave a volley of hand-clapping as vigorous and hearty as I ever rendered to actor or singer, and the carriers also broke out into loud " Ah's " in token of admiration. Without waiting for a question from Hanza, I told him that I would not think of consenting to any further experiment of the sort. The risk was far too much for the man, without a thought of the safety of the things he was willing to carry over.

Amadu swam back, and all stretched themselves at ease to await the boat. Ground-nuts bought at a small village earlier in the morning were roasted and eaten by the happy, light-hearted carriers. A fire was easily made by gathering leaves. Notwithstanding the downpour of the night, the sun had dried them to tinder.

So powerful were the sun's rays that my chest,

exposed for the coolness, was as though a strong mustard plaster had been administered. When the blistering and peeling process ensued I had some bad five minutes. My arms, the skin now quite dark and hardened by three months' daily exposure on horseback to wind and sun, also blistered. The camera, of polished teak and with brass binding, specially made for the tropics, gave a tendency to stiffness of the joints due to warping, but the excellence of the wood and workmanship stood the test without impairing the apparatus for usefulness. A closed tin of butter, protected in a thick wooden box, melted and percolated through. I afterwards learnt that the temperature had been 139 degrees. So fresh is the atmosphere on the Bauchi Plateau that although I had given up my horse to another at half-past eight, and had, therefore, tramped with the carriers for two hours, I was not in the least fatigued, in spite of the heat.

At 1.15 the doki boy was seen coming back. He was accompanied by three villagers who called that there was an easy ford a little higher up. Pointing, they made towards it, and Hanza and a couple of men went to verify the information. Pushing our way through grass higher than the tallest among us, we came to a clearance a few hundred yards above the falls where the stream had narrowed considerably, and here the villagers demonstrated by wading to the middle breast-high and holding up their arms. The carriers were brought round, and by 1.45 we were over, I going pick-a-back. And very cool and comforting the muddy water felt as it made its way between the leather riding leggings and through the laced boots.

RAHAMA TO JUGA—*continued*

It then transpired there were two further streams near by to be got over. The next was a little deeper than the place just crossed, but presented no serious bar.

The third, however, though not so deep as the first, was quite as broad, about 300 feet, and proved to be only just fordable. Some of the carriers would not venture with loads, which were, therefore, taken over by a few making double journeys, and I sailed across "flying-angel" fashion, the sturdy Amadu being the craft. Instead of the water going deeper by degrees, almost at once the furthest point down was touched and lasted half-way. Balanced aloft, it was not too pleasant feeling the moving foundation gently and tentatively feeling his foothold, suddenly immersed to the chin, and to be conscious of a fairly hard current washing over your knees. However, nothing worse than a ducking was possible, and that was avoided.

When all the traps had been gathered it was 2.30, and Hanza enquired whether I would stay for the night at a village near by or go on to Badiko, which was three hours' march. Personally, I would have preferred pushing on, but the men had been out $7\frac{1}{2}$ hours in great heat, had not stopped at any place where they could get a meal, and had three high stream crossings, so after a little consideration I elected to stay at the village overnight.

There were notes of gratification at the announcement, and at once we struck inwards, passing, left and right, a plantation set with yams; then between guinea-corn 10 feet high, the stems bending and providing a shaded avenue; ground-nuts just in leaf, set at right-angles to the path and growing on ridges, the furrows as neatly weeded as any kitchen garden in England.

As we went across the open fields Hanza called to some people in the distance "Kow abinshi" ("Bring food"), and the cry was gladly repeated by the carriers—"Kow abinshi, Kow abinshi." The hearers proceeded to carry out the request and to obtain the articles necessary for a little business, which to the Hausa women is second nature.

The tiny village into which we stepped was surrounded by guinea-corn taller than I had seen anywhere. The stems were 12 feet from the ground, completely hiding the mud houses. A roomy, circular one, not arranged by the Government—for the place is off the main bush track—but one belonging to the Headman of the village, a Fulani, was placed at my disposal. He brought fowls, a pumpkin, and had yams dug up. The inclusive charge for the house as well was 4s. He explained that no guinea-corn could be spared for the horses, so the doki boys were sent to cut grass.

Next morning came the villagers who had shown the river crossing. They were given 6d. each. As I came out of the house the second doki boy appeared. He wanted a "dash" for having swum his horse across the river the previous day. I asked him for what he thought I paid him wages; he shrugged his shoulders and smiled. Then I said that any "dash" I might give him would be at the end, not the beginning of his services, when I knew how he had done his work. Again a broad smile. Finally, I told the gentleman that the next time he asked for a "dash" I would discharge him instantly. A bow, and a "To, Zaki"—("Very good, sir")—

was the acknowledgment. The ". To "—pronounced " Taw "—was repeated by the circle of carriers who had come, doubtless at his invitation, to see the result of the doki boy's experiment with the new master. It had failed.

To get to Juga that day was not within the range of trekking at this season, so Badiko, where I had calculated to be more than 40 hours earlier, was selected for the day's halt. The village Headman led the way from the village—the name of which I gathered phonetically as Lafee Sala—through a maze of growing guinea-corn to open country. At the edge of the plantation, land formerly cultivated had reverted to a wild state.

Traversing a few miles of bush country, we pass hills of rock, showing, with uneven tops, one line behind another. Occasionally 15 feet boulders are at the side of the path, rolled down from the mountains, cut and severed by perpetual rain wearing away this hardest of granite until it breaks and tumbles below. Mountains hundreds of feet high have huge slabs resting on the solid hill. Intense heat has expanded, and sharp cold the same day has contracted, the rock, splitting it into slabs and dome-shaped crags. All around, on the rocky hill and over the earthy soil, there are the grass, trees, and the low bush of Northern Nigeria, with patches here and there of guinea-corn, sweet potatoes, groundnuts and yams. The entire acreage is cultivatable.

Small Hausa villages are passed. At one, native-grown cotton is being drawn into thread by the naked fingers. Badiko is reached at 9.45 a.m. and a stop made until the following morning. Water and wood are brought by a little maiden and her small brother, both bearing the necessaries on their heads in the orthodox fashion.

The first hour or so at a rest-house are occupied by attending to the domestic details, when one has to superintend them oneself. The cook receives his instructions for the day and perhaps is sent to market for articles not provided by the village Headman. The horse must be looked after. It is a sound precaution to always have him fed within sight; otherwise the doki boy will take the "chop" for his own larder and the pony be in the plight of the "poor little dog" in the nursery rhyme of Mother Hubbard. The amount of guinea-corn I give out is 2 lbs. before starting in the early morning, 2 lbs. on arrival at the day's destination, and 4 lbs. about 5.30 p.m. after watering, with plenty of dry cut grass. Two lbs. can be gauged as two double handsful. A full day with the pen will find you quite ready for bed at 7 o'clock.

I fixed 5 as the hour for starting next morning. Four o'clock is my favourite time to commence trekking, 3.30 is still better; but, for either, a clearly-seen roadway or a full moon is required, and as at this period the nights are quite dark and we are mostly on bush paths, it is desirable not to set out until at least the approach of daybreak. The early start enables 18 miles, which is as much as carriers will cover, except in emergency, to be done by 9 or 10 o'clock; allows marching in the coolest hours, and gives a full day for work.

It is remarkable how a reliable Headman, without watch, moon, or sun, will wake up and rouse his men at any hour. But if I can avoid doing so I never rely entirely upon anybody. My watch had been rather erratic and was not quite sure at the end of a day whether to be 20 minutes fast or 20 minutes slow. It refrained from registering the happy mean. In order to run no risk of being late next morning, the night at Badiko I put it on an hour, there being, of course, no clock to check by. I had not met a European since leaving Rahama. As might have been expected, it was eventually discovered that before the alteration the watch had been 20 minutes ahead of meridian time, so instead of rising at 4 o'clock as intended, I turned out at 2.30 a.m. and within an hour had finished breakfast. When the fact became clear that I had anticipated the time of assembly, I sat down to an hour-and-a-half of writing by a hurricane lamp. At 4.45, not waiting for Hanza's whistle, I sounded my own. He, however, was ready; repeated the sound; and we sallied out just as a thin streak of dawn appeared across the eastward sky.

As the sun rose we wound round great hills of rock, circular, oblong, pointed, and flat topped, the liquid deposit of past ages now gneissose and hegmatite. Here and there the face had been washed by recent floods to a brightness which in the distance looked like a mirror of running water.

At 7.45 a halt was made in the market-place of Magama village for the carriers to have breakfast. Ground-nuts, maize, and milk made up the meal, Hanza having a rather superior course of milk mixed with powdered millet and taken from a calabash by a wooden spoon. When they had finished eating every man washed his mouth and teeth at a stream, and one good-looking young Hausa completed his toilet by placing antimony on his eyelids. Another had utilised a few spare minutes by bringing needle and cotton and mending a garment: scarcely an indication of "the lazy black."

At 8.30 Hanza's whistle caused the loads to be hoisted and five minutes later the chilling wind gave sign of rain, which presently came in torrents. Mr F. G. Graham, in charge of Lucky Chance Polchi Mine, hearing I was in the neighbouring village and noting signs of the coming downpour, had ridden out and left an invitation with the head of the little column for me to shelter at his house, near by. At the path leading to the haven of hospitality Mr Graham's servant waited to direct me. But what the carriers, my own servants, and the doki boys had to endure without any protection was quite good enough for me, in oilskin and mounted, so, with a message of thanks to Mr Graham, I went on with the men, who were being drenched.

I am sure I would not have been happier in the dry house eating a welcome second breakfast, for the heavier the rain beat on them the merrier the carriers became, shouting and singing. In spite of the discomfort they would not be downhearted. At each gust of wind, enough to shiver them, they shouted the louder. Amadu's musical pipe was brought into vigorous use, and when from sheer lack of breath it slackened for his lungs to be replenished, the men broke into a chorus, the notable part of which seemed to me to be a series of hurrahs. It made one's heart glad to be with a party determined not to be cast down by trying circumstances. Somehow, although it is known not to generally last long, tropical rain in the daytime is usually distinctly depressing. I suppose the feeling is induced by the sudden fall in temperature. Little more than half-an-hour and the rain had ceased; the sun shone, and soon we were all dry again.

Meantime, there was evidence we had entered the tin country, not merely where it was being prospected, but where it was in being. A board announced "Nigeria Tin Corporation," and as we went along men, singly and in twos and threes, were met carrying shovels. Further certainty we were nearing the goal was a piece of wood on low posts notifying "Juga, $5\frac{1}{2}$ miles." That was probably fixed before distances were understood and when a few miles understated made no difference to anybody.

Passing the board we entered the nearest resemblance to African forest hitherto touched. Trees were more thickly clustered and bordered closer to the path, which led to the long narrow valley of South Juga, the Juga Hills towering to the left. From a rise in the ground, we saw below a village and small market. Hanza halted his command, took from his head the pail he had used inverted to keep off the rain, and replaced his turban and a long robe. Telling the men to maintain even distance between each other, and, seeing that I was close behind him, he gave the word to go forward and we did, with quite an appearance of dignity. It was pleasant to see this esprit-de-corps and pride in a leader, and responded to by men who might be supposed to belong to the casual labourer class. As though we were a regiment of regulars, we went through the village, and in less than half-a-mile more swung round the path into the compound of houses which are the administrative headquarters of the Juga properties. In the middle and at the sides were flower beds of zinnias, red, pink, yellow, and white, and another bed of large sunflowers. The fair face of an English girl would have made one fancy oneself at home again.

CARRIERS READY TO START.
(See page 153.)

A BRIDGE WHICH IS SWEPT AWAY BY THE STREAM DURING THE WET SEASON AND REGULARLY REPLACED.

CHAPTER XX

JUGA TO NARAGUTA

Native feminality and the cavalry spirit—Scarcity and economy—A house of straw—Carriers, professional and other—Diversified panorama—Parting with the first carriers.

THE journey between Juga and Naraguta, 35 miles, is mapped into three stages of a day each. I wished to push through in two days. Headman Hanza was for the easier form of covering the ground, but on the intimation being conveyed to him that the quicker programme must be carried out and that the night would be passed at Toro he at once acquiesced, with "To, Zaki," and we moved off.

Passing through the native village of Juga, where the carriers had put up for the last few days, it was clear that, true to their reputation, they had improved the occasion by ingratiating themselves into the good graces of the ladies, and many were the partings verbally exchanged as we marched away. Pre-eminent in receiving these attentions was my first doki boy—a gambling thriftless rascal—for the reason, I suppose, that the cavalry spirit always has a charm for the other sex.

Seven-and-a-half miles out, at the market-place of Kadaura, the carriers halted for their first meal. I also had arranged the plan of having breakfast en route instead of disposing of that necessity before starting, as is my usual practice. Perhaps there is some pleasure in an open-air table, but it does not facilitate one hurrying. Nearly half-an-hour elapsed before Oje and his assistant presented the porridge. They were not to blame. The ground was wet from the overnight rain, and still more so the twigs collected for a fire. Oje was equal to the drawback, which he overcame by pouring kerosene over the wood, a method not to be encouraged in a part of the country where a tank of the oil which can be purchased in England for 2s. 8d. costs 18s. 6d. and in some places is not to be obtained at any price. Living in a land where there is scarcity of certain essentials, habits of economy become imperative.

The country traversed resembles that previously described, with the exception that the path draws further from the mountains.

Toro was reached at midday. The Government rest-house is on the slope of a low hill, and on riding up to the building I found it occupied by an official engaged in telegraph construction. He was good enough to offer to share with me the one-roomed dwelling, but as I wished to have a few hours' work I thought better to pitch my tent elsewhere.

There was a rest-house 3 or 4 miles further on. To have gone there would not have materially saved time on the journey. I therefore elected to have a house at the bottom of the hill, a house belonging to the village Headman which was kept, so he informed me with many bows, for distinguished visitors. It was of straw throughout, and as I looked at the flimsy structure I bethought the mud walls of recent residences as quite mansions.

There was a kind of entrance-hall, also of straw, which gave an extra apartment. The floor was ordinary earth. It had not been hardened in any way.

As the boxes were about to be taken in up rode Mr F. L. Bensusan, of Juga Mine, who had overtaken me on the road and from whom I had parted a few minutes earlier when he was to turn off to Tilde Fulani. Seeing me returning down the hill he cantered forward to ascertain what was amiss. He remarked that the house was all right in the absence of two visitations: one was a strong wind, which would throw it down, and the other rain, which would come through the roof on the bed.

I replied I intended to slumber in the hope neither would come and I trusted that that night would be different from all other nights of late. He, however, insisted on lending me his waterproof ground-sheet, which he rigged up as a second roof, sloping one side so that the rain would run off to the side of the bed instead of weighing down the sheet, water and all, on to the occupant.

We had tea and biscuits and then he instructed his steward boy to tell his carriers to go on to Tilde Fulani and he would follow. The steward boy took the instruction and returned with the message that "The carriers say they no fit.* They fit stay at Toro and go Tilde Fulani to-morrow."

"No fit!" exclaimed Mr Bensusan; "you go and bring me the carrier who say he no fit."

There is usually a ringleader and spokesman in these little mutinies.

---

* Fit is used in pidgin English expressions to mean either willing, desirous or able.

The answer which came back turned pressure from an individual. "The carriers say," reported the steward boy, "no one say he no fit. They all say they no fit!"

"Oh, do they," observed Mr Bensusan; and he put on his helmet to go and make his recalcitrant servants toe the line. I followed to support his action.

"Who say he no fit to go for Tilde Fulani?" demanded Mr Bensusan, as he faced the half-dozen men. No words; only scowls.

"You take up your load, and you, and you, and you," was the order given along the line. The men did, and they had not gone 500 yards when they were laughing among themselves as though nothing had happened. The essay had failed, as did the one on me in the village of Laffe Sala. Doubtless the men reflected, at least they had tried.

These men were not professional carriers, men who had taken to the calling from choice. They were labourers on the mine called upon for the special service. As a rule the labourer does not accept kindly the work of a carrier, and the carrier can seldom be prevailed upon to keep to any other occupation.

Soon after daybreak next morning Hanza's whistle and Amadu's musical pipe roused the carriers, who had been sleeping in the scattered huts, near my own, on the small tableland of grass on which the village stood.

For the last time in this stage of trekking they headed their loads and we were off towards Naraguta.

There are no fresh features of the country, which, however, is rather more open and flat. The tall hills

JUGA TO NARAGUTA

on the left are of irregular height, and towards Naraguta they bend inwards to the path to a point where the way, after a short climb, is through a gorge. That leads to another broad expanse of country, also edged by a series of unconnected hills which in their turn bend inwards. Swerving round the end of them one rides on to the sub plateau which contains Naraguta.

A wide panorama is unfolded, circled by hills clearly and sharply defined against the sky background, and beyond these hills, showing between them, are others, fainter by the blue haze covering them as though it were gauze, giving the effect of what artists term " distance."

Across this panorama of verdure there are, perhaps three or four miles away, clusters of little brown circular objects, which look as though they were mushrooms on the plain. A telescope or field-glasses would disclose them as mud huts, the settlement of natives drawn to Naraguta for employment of one kind or another, whilst further evidence of human occupation is a squarely-cornered bungalow, nearly as small as the huts but distinct.

This sub plateau, slightly sloping to the middle, where runs the Deleme River, and fringed by hills which rise gradually, is covered with green. So are the hills. They give a dozen or more tints as the grass is fresh or dry and as the sun shines directly or as its rays are modified in varying degrees by passing clouds that render patches of shade and contrasting brightness.

The atmosphere is clear and affords full vision all round the plateau, and a picture so long round that the clouds in some parts are quite different to those in others. It can be seen, as we survey the scene, that whilst in one district against the hills there is a clear sky, adjoining that area rain is evidently falling. A ride of about three miles with all this enchanting scenery and we are near the centre of the plateau.

It was within half-an-hour of completing our journey that the weather, which had behaved splendidly, altered. The rainstorm which had been witnessed from afar was coming towards us and in a few minutes the poor carriers were cold and dripping. They had to stand through the downpour whilst I went forward to find the correct one of several paths, and when I came back to lead them to the bungalow placed at my disposal by Mr Frank D. Bourke, Manager of Naraguta Tin Mine, none felt more miserable at their condition than I.

Probably the dullness of spirits we all felt was due not so much to the rain as to the knowledge that we had reached the place where we were to part company, as my stay at Naraguta would be long enough not to justify retaining 20 carriers. All through the marches we had been on such excellent terms with each other that severance of association was welcomed by neither side. However, it had to be.

The rain had ceased and the men stood in line in front of the bungalow. I thanked them for the way they had worked and handed to each a tangible token of recognition. They gave the equivalent to a cheer several times as they went across the compound towards Jos village, Hanza staying to the last and repeatedly turning to wave a farewell.

A GOVERNMENT REST HOUSE.
(See page 151.)

THE HEADMAN'S HOUSE AT TORO, WHERE THE AUTHOR SLEPT.
(See page 170.)

CHAPTER XXI

TWO SHORT JOURNEYS

Man proposes—A narrow river barrier—Travellers this side of the stream; beds, the other side—Pagan cultivation—A postal description—Headmen and Headmen—Gotum Karo.

THIS narrative may be made easier to follow if explanation is given of the outline of movement. That is based, not on a series of consecutive marches, but of making Naraguta a centre of operations and working from there in two directions, of a few days each, until the final trek is entered upon, which is to be across and off the Bauchi Plateau, then over it again and back to railhead.

He is wise who travelling at this period of the year—October—does not make sure in the morning where he will sleep that night. Man proposes; a set of unexpected circumstances disposes. I formed this plan. To leave Naraguta at 11 a.m.; lunch at Gurum—a bad 10 miles of road—afterwards covering the seven miles to Bugi.

Gurum was reached in an hour-and-a-half. I set out for Bugi with, as guide, Mr Leighton, of Gurum Camp, which is the headquarters in Nigeria of the Anglo-Continental Mines.

A five miles' ride through pleasant, open, bush country took us to the Gurum River ford. Though a narrow crossing, the merest glance showed that visual bearings must be taken before entering the water. The morning's downpour had deepened and quickened the current, which swirled and rushed in a menacing manner, as to say, "I forbid anybody touching me whilst in my present mood." One of the Gurum Camp doki boys who frequently acts as guide across the stream declared himself "No fit" to try and get over. He declined to step from the bank.

We turned off the path to try another point, near the rapids, about half-a-mile away. That was at once seen to be utterly impossible. Not only had the water risen considerably; the surface showed that it covered holes and rocks, and in the shallow sections were flat granite faces so polished by the running water that it was evident no horse or man could maintain foothold. Going over at that point or at the ford was out of the question. But there was this difficulty to turning back and staying the night at Gurum: the camp-beds were doubtless on the other side. They had been sent by carriers in advance of our start and as we had not overtaken the men they must have got over. It was easy to conjecture where; it must have been by a narrow bridge of tree-trunks much higher up, over which horses could not be taken and where the river did not allow them to be swum or otherwise led.

Gurum Camp has a name for hospitality to persons on trek, but, like most places, it possesses no spare sleeping equipment. What was to be done? Our hope rested in the trust that we were earlier than the carriers, whose way was along a path near the other side of the ford. How we devoutly wished they had not struck a different direction!

Still, they were not likely to look for us and we might not see them, hidden by the long grass. Standing at the edge of the river, we therefore took turns in shouting and sounding a whistle. The performance had become a trifle monotonous and trying when we were gladdened by the sight of the loads moving along our front a few hundred yards distant. The whistle drew attention, and on the men coming to the brink of the river they were made to understand that they were to return to Gurum Camp, and we also retraced our course.

Next morning, little rain having fallen during the night, I determined to again try the ford of the Gurum River. The stream had greatly abated and the doki boy now quite " fit " to lead the way over. The necessity for a guide may be explained by the fact that although the crossing is a narrow one it is hazardous to go over without a competent guide after a storm, as the action of the water, pouring along, frequently works deep holes in the bed, and a horse stumbling into one might readily break a leg. Should the guide step over such a cavity he could swim away. Taking a zigzag line, with the water up to the horses' girths we went across.

A little way past there is a patch of cultivation by Pagans who live up in the neighbouring hills. It is a good example of their skilled agriculture. Yams, sweet potatoes and ground-nuts are planted on ridges of earth straight, wavy and forked shaped; and on low circular mounds enclosed by a six-inch higher layer of soil to keep the rain from running off the ground.

Another system of miniature irrigation practised on the patch is that of rings of earth, about three feet

M

in diameter on the top of which—three inches wide—ground-nuts grow, the cup-like interior retaining rain. Narrow, shallow ditches intersect the field and are instrumental in fertilising it.

The lines between the early-growing crops are scrupulously weeded. Notwithstanding continuous alternating showers and sunshine, there was not a blade of parasitical growth. I estimated the Hausas of Kano Province to be scrupulously clean farmers, unexcelled until I came to this Pagan country. Yet the people, who are also workers in metal and have a love of music, are, I suppose, to be ruled outside civilisation because they wear practically no clothes. How horrible! Wait until they learn the graces of the silk hat and the unnaturally tight-lacing, then they will be our brothers and sisters, especially if they do the proper thing religiously. Now they have their ju-jus, their harmless superstitions. How awful! I hope we on the continents of Europe and America have no ju-jus.

Having returned to Naraguta the next short journey was to Fedderi, for the purpose of seeing the tin-mining there. Fedderi is 24 miles southeast, two days' trek. It is postally described as "near Naraguta."

There are Headmen and Headmen; I mean of working gangs or carriers, not village Headmen. Many of the former are thoroughly reliable; some, speaking a few words of English, I fear cannot be given that character. They mislead both sides between whom they are a link of conversation, the white man and the labourers or carriers.

Hearing I wished to visit the tin-winning opera-

TWO SHORT JOURNEYS 179

tions at Fedderi, Mr S. A. Molyneux, the Manager, offered the use as carriers of his labourers who were bringing tin for transport. They presented themselves, in charge of a Headman named Gotum Karo. He at once favourably impressed me as having thorough control over his men, who promptly moved as he ordered. Instead of allowing them to pick up and, as is sometimes done, to an extent scramble in selecting their respective loads, he partly lifted each to try its weight and sharply told off a carrier for the duty. I subsequently heard that Gotum Karo had been in the Northern Nigeria Regiment. He had evidently taken away with his service the facility of giving the word of command. I soon discovered he had also acquired some of the evil cunning of " the old soldier."

As the labourers stood in line, the packages laid in front of them, Gotum Karo advanced towards me and proceeded to several salaams and " Zaki " repeatedly. Becoming impatient to get on the road, I interrupted the salutations by asking severely what he was seeking and why he did not move off. He came to the point immediately. " They," he said, pointing over his shoulder to the labourers, " want chop money," i.e., money for food allowance.

Oh, that was it. During the performance of Mr Gotum Karo's prolonged politeness I had become suspicious and therefore was not taken unawares. Knowing that Mr Molyneux would not have sent his men without the wherewithal for sustenance, I answered, " Tell them they will have no chop money from me. If they no fit to carry loads, you take them back to Bombature (the important white man) Molyneux." After a pause I added, "Any dash (tip) I give be at Fedderi."

Gotum Karo did not deliver the message. He simply told the men to lift the boxes and to march. This little omission of his involuntarily disclosed that the scheme to obtain money was his own idea, not theirs. He would have had the lion's share; probably all.

But Gotum Karo had imbibed the British characteristic of not knowing when he was beaten, though his application of the doctrine was not to be admired.

When we had arrived at the rest-house at Tilde Fulani, where the night was to be spent, Gotum came and spun a story of having lost 12s. and of the labourers owing him money. I cut him short by enquiring what he expected me to do, and he then put the request into the form of "Lend me 2s." until the following day, when he would recover his debts and pay. This style of a loan is a common manner of extortion, as it is realised that the white man will not ask for a shilling or so due to him. The fellow declared—a palpable untruth—he had had no food for 24 hours. I gave him 6d. and told him that if he did not clear out of the house I would kick him through a doorway, indicating the one. He retired.

It may be matter for wonder that such tricks should be tried on persons who are practically, if not actually, guests of the delinquent's employer. Yet they are frequently, probably with knowledge of the reluctance on the part of a visitor to complain.

CHAPTER XXII

THE NIGER COMPANY'S JOS CENTRE

Jos and St Peter's—A wet and dry object—Fashion in stationery—Smoking and writing materials—The cost of money—Coin in transit—Tin-mine labourers and food—Inception of European transport—Linguistic stimulus and aptitude—Donkey caravans—The animals' acumen—Double-distilled philosophy.

FOUR miles from Naraguta is Jos. You have never heard of Jos? Were you however distantly connected with the tin fields Jos would loom very large in your thoughts. Comparing very small things with great ones, you can no more go to Naraguta and avoid Jos than anyone would think of going to Rome and not visiting St Peter's. At Jos is the store of the Niger Company. Similar places, or rather places resembling it, can be found in other parts of Northern Nigeria, but Jos is essentially the store for the tin fields, albeit most of the mines are several days' journey. The nearest store in one direction is Zaria, about four days away, and on the opposite side a small one at Jemaa, about five days distant.

Many things have been said about this Niger Company's store at Jos. Some of them were stated to me before I went out from England. They were to the effect that there would be no need to carry things on the voyage or to buy them on the Coast as "everything" could be obtained at Jos. When I reached what may be termed the Jos radius several men told me that the Jos store contained "nothing," or that it only contained those things which I should not need. Put in practically the exact way uttered, the matter was presented that whatever was asked for at Jos would sure not to be in stock. Now, as in most extreme assertions, the truth was found between the two.

I was rather a pitiful-looking object on reaching Naraguta. My boots were literally falling to pieces. They had showed signs of distress weeks earlier, and I had tried to buy a suitable pair both at Kano and at Zaria. Kano had no such article for sale, and the only pair to be purchased at Zaria was at least 5 sizes too large. Oje had tried his hand at keeping the soles from parting from the uppers, by driving nails, extracted from small packing-cases, through the top of the welts. Faithful Oje! He had mended my brown bush-shirt, worn and torn to rags by pushing through thick growth; and, as long as they would hold together, he had sewn my tattered socks. He still "fit," as he told me, to keep going at the boots. But they had been too severely tried. Riding across streams that reached to the knees, soaking the boots, and the next minute into a blazing sun had as effectually disintegrated the parts as a hydraulicing jet performs similar office on soil and tin. Had readers seen me in the condition at home I am sure they would have compassionately dropped a copper in my hand.

At Jos I was shod in a twinkling. Among further requirements, one was as far off from boots as a fountain pen, and that I also obtained. The pen cost no more than 6s. and has been in continual use. But there were a number of things between the two which I was unable to obtain. The Jos store, like every other institution on the tin fields, has been unable to cope with the demands made upon it. The demands have grown at a greater ratio than supplies could be forwarded.

The store is an immense convenience. No matter how well equipped a man's belongings may be when he brings out the hundred-and-one things necessary for a fairly-long residence in a new country where food is only obtainable in limited quantities, it is certain that he will have made some miscalculation of needs. Thus Jos sets the fashion in many things.

There is a shortage of stationery, and you receive envelopes made by your correspondents in the country: crude and awkward and very inartistic, but the best that can be done under the circumstances. Suddenly comes along an ordinary envelope, and then, whoever sends you a letter, you will find using this identical kind of envelope. The Jos store has had a stock of stationery!

So with smoking requisites. There have been times when men have had no alternative between either using the Contrabanda cigarettes sent out for natives and sold in boxes at 1s. 9d. a 100 or smoking nothing at all. Then, day after day, whoever you meet has between his lips a Three Castle cigarette, or it may be a Gold Flake cigarette, or, perchance, a State Express. Everybody is sporting the same brand, whatever it be. Answer why: Jos has received a consignment.

It is peculiar how shortage of articles affects different people. Unto me, who had come from England to learn all about the country, were brought many complaints and expostulations.

"Is it not bad," said one, "that I can buy no flour?"

"What do you think?" remarks another. "I can get no biscuits."

"Here none of us can buy a cigarette anywhere," is the agonised wail of a third. And so on, almost indefinitely.

To each and all I replied that I felt I was a greater sufferer than any. To every tale of woe, I represented my own plight and endeavoured, I must admit unsuccessfully, to play the martyr by setting forth the pathetic tale that " I cannot obtain either ink or paper."

The Finance Department is specially interesting. There is no bank nearer than Zaria, and were it not for this Finance Department of the Niger Company the mines would have to keep very large sums of money for the labourers' wages. It is not a banking business; money is only paid on demand. Of course, there has been a preliminary arrangement between the mining concern and the Niger Company in London by which the former guarantees to meet the cheques presented to the latter up to a stipulated sum.

That arrangement having been settled, the mine manager sends to Jos—maybe a distance of four miles, maybe a five days' journey—for the money with which to pay his labourers weekly, presenting a cheque for the amount. The money is charged at a rateage according to where the cheque may be payable. Supposing it is drawn on the bank at Zaria, then 1½ per cent. is the rate; if it be drawn on the bank at Lokoja, which is further away, 2½ per cent. is charged.

Why this difference? In England we are not charged a larger rate for a cheque drawn on a bank at Newcastle than we do for one drawn on Birmingham. No; but in England transport charges do not enter into the question as finely as they do in Northern Nigeria. It all relates to the cost of getting up specie, which works out on the river at the rate of 1d. per £200 per mile; and, of course, land carriage adds to the expense. Cost of transport regulates the price of everything in the country, even of money.

Specie is made up into boxes, each containing £300, weighing 80 lbs. This is in silver coins, gold having practically no circulation in the country. A mine manager makes his personal provision for taking the money from the Finance Department to his own place. The usual plan is for the manager or one of his principal assistants, carrying firearms, to travel with his own carriers, who bear the money on their heads.

The Niger Company's plan differs. A European accompanies the specie and has as a guard for it four dogarie, i.e., policemen belonging to one of the native rulers. Then, besides each carrier bearing a load, there is another between each of them as a relief. So if any of the men fall out his relief takes the load, which prevents the gang stopping or a box passing from the direct view of the European. When long journeys are undertaken stops must be made sometimes overnight, but the method of working is to get the men over the ground as quickly as can be done with as few stops as possible.

Although the Finance Department was established for the mines it is of very great service to anybody travelling through the country who may require cash. All that is necessary is a telegram from the bank where the traveller has a deposit to the Niger Company's Finance Department authorising payment of the sum asked for. And a feature of the department is the patience and courtesy of the one in charge, Mr E. B. Simmonds, in dealing with the many matters, occasionally novel ones, which come before him from men strange to the country.

Another Niger Company department at Jos, separate from the others, is that of Transport.

Than transport no matter is of greater importance to the mines. Everything depends upon it. By "everything" is meant the primary items of food and machinery, on which all else rests. Even were the soil capable of being cultivated to an extent which would yield food for the labourers brought from other parts of the Protectorate, at least some years would have to pass before the process was in operation. Food must, therefore, be imported from the districts where it is grown.

It has been said there is not sufficient food in the country to satisfy the requirements of the 12,000 or so labourers on the mines. As, with insignificant exceptions, these labourers are all natives of Northern Nigeria, and no foodstuff to speak of crosses the border inwards, it is obvious that previous to coming on the tin fields they must have eaten indigenous products. I am sure that any difficulty in obtaining sufficient labour is largely, if not wholly, a question of food supply, and that supply cannot flow unless there are efficient channels for its passage: transport.

There is the general problem of labour on the mines and the rate of payment by the owning companies, but consideration of that aspect of the question does not come within the scope of this chapter, which is to deal wholly with the matter of supply. The same means, on the return journey, are employed to take the tin towards its destination. Transport from railhead at Rahama and also at the terminus of the trunk line at Kano is wholly in the hands of the Niger Company, except in the case of one or two mines that have partially made their own arrangements.

To survey the situation thoroughly it is necessary to hark back to the time when the railway was being pushed up as extensions of the Lagos line and had only reached Rigachikun, 585 miles from the sea. That marked the old route to the Bauchi Plateau tin fields. From that point a road was made. As the line was laid further up, Zaria, 622 miles, was touched. That had all along been recognised as the most suitable place for direct access to the foot of the Plateau, in the direction where the main tin deposits had been located. There was, however, about 100 miles between the railway and the foot of the Plateau, to the south-west of the line.

At this time the Niger Company was doing all transport to and from the mines. Twelve to 14 days were occupied on the Rigachikun road, and a fair proportion of goods was sent up and tin brought down along the Loko-Keffi route, on the opposite side of the Plateau, for shipment on the Benue

River, thence down the Niger to the sea. But in looking into this important matter of road transport, perhaps it will be best to start at the inception.

It began between five and six years ago, when the Niger Company commenced regular prospecting for tin. Before that time the only whites up-country were the Government officials, and as they were few and far between there was no call for transport, even of the primitive and limited kind in operation to-day. The Niger Company's prospecting camps needed supplies, both of food for the squads of natives employed and of material for the engineers, as well as edibles for their tables. So small caravans of carriers were sent up to the camps. The route was then what is known as the Loko-Keffi one; that is to say, from the sea by river to Loko, from which point the overland line was taken to Keffi, almost due east.

At that time the amount despatched, inwards and outwards, was probably 5 tons monthly. Now by rail to Rahama, and from there distributed via the Niger Company's Jos centre, it must average 500 tons monthly, with about 14 tons still going over the old Loko-Keffi route.

As the various tin-mine companies were formed and proceeded with their operations, transport became a first-value consideration. You have only to plant yourself in a virgin country and depend upon outside supplies for sustenance to realise that. Folks in England, with everything brought to their doors—parcel post and carrying agencies playing the part of universal provider—can scarcely appreciate what it means to have a single slender source of supply, and that necessarily an uncertain one.

Try the real simple life under these conditions, not a few hours from the railway or navigable river, but five to seven days' journey. Then you will understand how much gratitude you can feel towards people whom you are glad to pay at their own figure for what they bring; and you are also sure to discover what a wealth of strong language you can employ without an effort when you are disappointed in such small items as kerosene, or flour for bread-making. You may afterwards wonder at your linguistic aptitude, you who at home never uttered an expletive under normal annoyances and disappointments; yet in most instances the tongue accomplishment comes in the easiest and most natural manner possible. I marvel at my own deficiency in that respect.

It was the Niger Company's organisation which supplied the indispensable adjunct of lines of communication to the various mining camps. The Company had all the human machinery working. There was none other, and therefore the system which was wanted and that available adjusted themselves accordingly. It only had to be expanded. True, the expansion could not be made on a scale commensurate with the needs of the hour. But what would have occurred had that organisation not been available? Each camp would have had to make its own transport arrangements. That would have resulted in confusion, if not chaos. The competition for labour has been bad enough. Imagine what it would have meant for the mining concerns to have scrambled for carriers as well, whose services were in more urgent demand than ordinary labourers.

I am no special pleader for the Niger Company, but I do consider it due to that body to state that the tin-mining industry would have been in a much more backward state had the Company not taken the part it has in the development of the fields. I have been told that if the Niger Company had not —in the matter of transport and its Finance Department—somebody else would. Possibly. That does not alter the principle of merit being given where earned. Were I not here writing these despatches probably someone else would; and there is no doubt scores would be glad to do it. Yet surely that would be a poor argument against awarding any reward there might be due to the individual who did the work.

So, too, it has been said that the Niger Company was actuated by self-interest; that it was not philanthropic. Who is, in business? If the Niger Company has profited by its enterprise it deserved to. It at the same time helped—or, at all events, enabled—others to thrive. I am free to admit that occasionally it has among the employees a member whose manner leaves something to be desired. Any more than elsewhere, there is no monopoly of boorishness and rudeness by any class in Northern Nigeria. It is quite the exception, though here and there are bad examples. I found it in the case of a mining engineer whom I met on horseback—an awfully important personage whose silly pomposity made me laugh, where he looked for my being impressed—and, whisper it not in Gath, I have even come across one or two Government officials whom you would not recognise for gentlemen, though they would have you think they were far from the

NIGER COMPANY'S JOS CENTRE

common clay. Yea, in a certain place, no doubt taking their cue from the head of it, there is a small collection of such freaks, with a few men among them who must not be so labelled.

The Niger Company looms so large in the acquisition and in the industry of the country that, like the Government at home, it is a big object at which to have a shy; and, I cannot avoid thinking, blamed at times as unreasonably as is the London Cabinet whatever its political complexion.

I have said the road and bush transport began on a regular scale between five and six years ago. Then it was confined to human head carriage. After a while donkeys were tried on a small scale, and their use has been extended during the dry seasons. Two years ago 10 two-wheeled bullock transport carts were put on to connect Loko and Keffi, and since then others, and also four-wheeled wagons, with teams of 8 and 16 oxen, have been working between Rahama and Jos.

A few camels were formerly employed, but not continued, as the animals are not obtained without difficulty in Nigeria; the nearest market for them on anything but a small scale is over the French border, though some are still utilised for transport from Kano to the Ninghi district. Now, I hear, the long-expected motor lorries have arrived at Baro and are to be running on the road in the course of the next few weeks. I am informed that Mr. Kendall, the Niger Company's chief transport officer at Jos, is considering whether bullocks, which need extreme care to keep in a condition, cannot be superseded by horses. In no part of Nigeria are they used in any other way than for riding, with the exception of a pair Captain Brocklebank has trained to draw a buggy at Kano.

The relative values of the given forms of transport are: Head carriage, one man bears a 60-lb. load; a donkey takes a 120-lb. load; each bullock in a two-wheeled cart draws a 500-lb. load; one camel bears a 420-lb. load; one motor lorry carries a 4,400-lb. load.

Donkeys are not bought outright. The animals and their owners are hired. Each man has three donkeys under his personal supervision on the march. These quadrupeds are generally spoken of as a synonym for stupidity. In Nigeria they develop acumen which puts the human controller in a quandary where he perceives a divided duty. The load, placed pannier fashion, is not tied on. Its weight keeps it in position. But the four-footed bearer will take into his head to ease the task by walking close against a tree in a way that throws the entire load to the ground.

The donkey owner has to catch the erring beast, which, light-hearted at its sudden buoyant condition, has likely run on ahead. Brought back after a chase, the man has then to lift the 120 lbs. to the original position. You may be sure that in the meantime the companion pair of donkeys have improved the shining hour by roaming around, usually in opposite directions; or, if they do go together, it will probably be back on the path along which they came. The combined trio performance may be coincidental; it may be arrant conspiracy.

Whatever it be, the donkey owner and the white man in charge of a caravan numbering hundreds of the patient little brutes must be endowed with a large and double-distilled philosophic temperament not to exhibit loss of a calm exterior.

I must bear testimony to a measure that is being taken to add to the comfort of the human transport carriers. The Niger Company is forming at eight-mile stages rest camps of huts, with caretakers and women to cook the carriers' food. The carriers will thus be able to rely on having meals, and a day's march not arbitrarily fixed by the position of villages from one another.

A few words on recruiting for carriers. The labour is obtained in the open markets. Men from the mines are not accepted knowingly, so as to avoid dislocating local conditions. Gangs who have been working on a mine and who present themselves at Jos must bring from the manager under whom they served his permission to enter the Niger Company's service before they are enrolled. Forty labourers and Headmen who had been on the Bisichi mine applied and were declined for the reason indicated. Remembering how strong is the demand for carriers, this is " playing the game " as it should be played, and it deserves recognition.

CHAPTER XXIII

MINES—MEDICAL

Tin-mining—First Exclusive Prospecting Licence—Early tin-winning—Mr Law's work—Health and economics—Feminine nursing—The medical service.

ALTHOUGH Jos is chiefly known for the Niger Company's trading store and Finance Department, there are two other phases which should not be omitted. They are the Company's Mining Department and the headquarters of the medical officer, who is supposed to be engaged by most, if not all, the mines, whereas he is really the officer of only a few. The Mining Department, is, to an extent, explained by its title. There may, however, be people in England who are not acquainted with the part the Niger Company has taken in development of the tin fields, and it is for these persons that this short story is given; not in any tone of exaltation, simply an unvarnished tale with tone and shade to present what seems to me a true picture. Nothing like a complete history of the movement is being rendered; merely a thin outline for better understanding of how the position of to-day has been reached.

In 1901 Mr Walter Watts, Agent-General—a West African title corresponding to General Manager—of the Niger Company asked Sir Frederick Lugard, High Commissioner—Governor

—of Northern Nigeria for a concession to send prospectors for tin. The High Commissioner refused, on the ground that there was no mining law to regulate the situation. The position was altered the following year by the promulgation of the Mining Proclamation, and on Sir Frederick returning from furlough in England Mr Watts followed him to Jebba and obtained the first issued Exclusive Prospecting Licence, which related to 1,000 square miles with Badiko as centre. The same day Mr George Macdonald was granted a similar E.P.L. for 3,000 square miles surrounding that ground.

On receipt of information from Mr Watts that he had secured a Licence, the London office of the Niger Company despatched Mr G. Nicolaus to test the existence of tin. He located the Deleme River deposits at Tildi Fulani as a payable portion. Mr Nicolaus was on the tin areas only a few weeks, but his reports led the Niger Company to send Mr H. W. Laws to ascertain definitely whether the areas were of commercial value.

In 1902 Mr Macdonald commissioned Mr Probis to test the land the former had acquired. The resultant report on the prospects generally induced Macdonald not to proceed with the work.

The investigations of both Nicolaus and Probis were confined to the north of the Plateau.

Meanwhile, in the early part of 1902 Mr, now Sir, William Wallace, then in the service of the Niger Company as Political Agent, accompanied the expedition against the Emir of Bauchi. At the close of operations, by means of messengers he obtained about a quarter-of-a-hundredweight specimens of tin from the Deleme River, at Naraguta, which is six days' journey from the place whence Mr Wallace had sent his emissaries. That, apparently, was the first tin obtained by a European in Northern Nigeria, although about the same time Mr George Macdonald led a prospecting party into Bauchi territory and brought back tin.

Mr Laws arrived towards the end of 1903 and formed his principal camp between the present Naraguta Mine and Naraguta Extended, in fact where Naraguta village now stands. His expeditions practically discovered the configuration of the Plateau and located tin at Jos, in the neighbourhood of Bukuru and at N'Gell. At the close of 1905 Mr Laws took out plant and commenced systematic tin-winning at Naraguta.

Having discovered ore, the next question to be decided was what should be done with the acquisition? Whilst the Niger Company had every wish and interest to see the tin fields, and the country generally, grow and flourish, it had no desire—so I gather—to add to its commercial responsibilities that of mining on a large scale. It preferred that should be done by people who could concentrate on that form of activity.

There was, however, this difficulty, that scarcely any outside attention was given to the subject. No notice seemed to be taken of what was being done. The Company was, therefore, faced with the alternative of itself working the mineral deposits or abandoning them. The latter course would have been a criminal one—speaking in a figurative sense —against the shareholders, to whom the discoveries belonged, and steps were taken for Mr Laws to demonstrate what was in the ground; in other words, for the mining staff to indefinitely work the centres where tin had been found in payable conditions. Still, scant notice was taken by outside bodies, notwithstanding the results. In March, 1907, Lord Scarbrough, Chairman of the Niger Company, told the shareholders that during the previous 15 months 240 tons of tin oxide, of £30,000 value, had been obtained from the Naraguta property, and the following year a corresponding amount was won. It was effected without machinery, by the antiquated methods of ground sluicing and calabashing.

Not until 1910 did the possibilities of the tin fields attract the consideration which has since given them so much prominence. At this point the wider question is left for future treatment, as I do not purpose now writing a full account of the short history of tin-mining in Northern Nigeria.

The policy of the Niger Company appears to have been only to develop a mine until other people saw the thing " good enough " to take up. That is the rôle of its mining staff, which have headquarters at Jos, quite distinct and some little distance from the trading store. I believe that all the earlier properties have been disposed of, but the further potentialities of the country are still being tested in various directions.

It may be asked why the Niger Company gives to second parties, even by sale, the opportunity of making a profit which it might itself reap. Whilst I am no more empowered than any other investigator to speak for the Company, I should say that the reason is the one stated above. No doubt the Company is only on the threshold of the advance to be made in trading development—trading in agricultural, sylvan, and other produce—in Southern and Northern Nigeria, and to do that adequately is, to use an inelegant but expressive term, to bite off as much as it can chew. The fact should be remembered that it gains by everyone's prosperity.

On surrendering the Charter, the Government agreed to give the Company half of its 5 per cent. royalty on the export of all minerals. Besides the river and road transport, prosperous communities, white and black, mean increased trade for the stores, for although there are a number of such new arrivals in Northern Nigeria the Niger Company maintains an incalculably premier position.

Present regulations for mining are explained in the next chapter.

The health of every white man on a mine in Northern Nigeria is a serious matter for each owning company. Flesh and blood is not as cheap as in some parts of industrial Britain; it cannot be replaced at a day's notice and to an illimitable extent. A man, whether he be manager or in any intermediate grade to the most junior rank, is brought out at no little expense. If he becomes altogether incapacitated at an early stage of his service the persons in whose engagement he is lose what the double journey costs, for he will probably not have rendered sufficient work to recoup them; whilst if he goes temporarily on the sick list as long as he remains there he, of course, is not earning anything for the firm which has paid his expenses. Men of use in Northern Nigeria are therefore valuable, as horses are where it costs money to replace them, though perhaps in the same place there is so great a supply of human animals that *their* living or dying is of no economic consequence.

The question is put at its lowest commercial basis so that the importance of health may be seen from every point of view, and in setting the position in that light I rely on my meaning not being misinterpreted to read that men in the service of mines are only rated as horses. I desire to show that a mine—or, for the matter of that, any other employing concern—in most cases loses by the breakdown of a member of the staff. Here the mines' employees are alone being dealt with.

Were the tin fields camps clustered in one or two small areas the problem would be easy of solution. They are not. They are scattered over the country, in some instances more than a week's journey by road from one another. Special medical provision for the mining staff is therefore not an easy programme to carry out unless a fairly large number of doctors were appointed, and at present the quantity of men who might require their attention is too few to justify that course. There are the Government medical officers, but they are stationed where they can be of most use to officials, and that may be 30 miles or more from a mine camp.

Under all these circumstances some of the mining companies, and the Niger Company as the only European trading firm in that part of the country, decided to provide special medical facilities for their employees in the Bauchi tin fields region. There are two doctors: Dr Watson, who is stationed near Juga, and Dr Arthur Emlyn, who is at Jos, regarded as the headquarters and within range of more mines than any other situation would be.

I have looked over the hospital at Jos. Previous to it being built patients were accommodated in tents and in small but comfortable huts. The hospital was put up by Dr Emlyn, and, except for two weeks when he was ill and his assistant, Dr Watson, supervised the native workmen, the whole scheme was effected by the former, who combined the parts of builder, nurse, housekeeper, and medical attendant. I find that during the two years the hospital has been in existence there have been 65 European patients, of whom two have died. The official records show that one was in hospital two days and the other two-and-a-half hours. The cases may therefore be regarded as having reached a critical stage before coming to the hospital. I have not had time to obtain the total visits of European out-patients, nor of natives, which far exceed those of the whites.

Strengthening the medical service in Northern Nigeria is a measure which should be well pondered over by the Government at Zungeru. The value of a hospital can be gauged from what is done by the establishment at the Capital of the Protectorate. The necessity of a hospital is not to be estimated by the fatal cases which come under its roof. An overwhelming majority of sickness am ng whites is that of fever. The great chance of a cure is taking the indisposition in time and nursing, and no nursing on this earth equals the nursing of a sympathetic woman. A nurse of the best kind is the nearest picture we can imagine of one of God's angels. The light, feminine movement; the exquisite solicitude for suffering; the sisterly soothing influence on a pain-racked brain; the gentle, yet not tiresome, attention to unexpressed wants, all these seem almost divine qualities which appeal to even my dull, unimaginative mind. They impress me, who had never needed them; they are qualities not possessed by one man in two millions; they are qualities to be found in several places in West Africa; they have counted in many recoveries to health.

The Zungeru hospital is spoken of as a sanatorium. That is because men go there when early symptoms of malaria declare themselves, and frequently after a few days' treatment—which may be described as rest, change, and the inestimable frequent medical examination and attendant nursing—the aforetime invalid returns to his duties thoroughly well. There must have been hundreds of lives saved by hospital treatment in West Africa, lives which would have been lost but for prompt entry into a hospital.

Those of us who have seen men stricken with fever in some out-of-the-way spot in the bush, lying on a camp-bed in a mud hut many miles from the reach of a doctor, ourselves doing in a rough way all the nursing we could, we know what a relief it would have been to welcome the appearance of a skilled man versed in the art of healing.

In Nigeria, North and South, most of the Government medical officers are as splendid fellows as you would wish to meet. In Southern Nigeria some of the cherished personal friendships I have made in the course of journeys are among that profession; and in Northern Nigeria if I have not come in contact with so many they have been sufficient to show that the same spirit prevails. I gladly remember two who went out of their way to render me acts of kindness: Dr Johnson, of Zaria, and Dr Costello, of Naraguta.

CHAPTER XXIV

A MURDER TRIAL

Mining licences and leases—The Government Inspector of Mines—Nine years without doors—Two Residents—Poisoned arrow welcome—A murder trial.

PREVIOUS to leaving the subject of the tin fields it is appropriate a few words are said on the Government administration of that territory controlled from Naragutu.

Leave to prospect in the area known as the tin fields has been suspended, pending a regular survey of the properties pegged out, and as the suspension is temporary, and, moreover, does not apply to other parts of Northern Nigeria, it may not be out of place if the conditions under which minerals can be sought are stated.

The first requisite for anybody who wishes to go prospecting is to obtain permission from the Governor or whoever may be acting for him. If not received before arriving in the country, it can be asked for at Zungeru, the Capital of the Protectorate, or at Lokoja. The former is on the railway journey and the latter on the river route, which are the only avenues by which one can enter. In order not to entail delay of waiting at either place, permission is also to be obtained at Naraguta, after the application has been forwarded to Zungeru from

Lokoja, which would be done by telegraph if not made previous to the applicant's arrival there.

The Governor's assent is given in the form of a general prospecting right. That costs £5, and the applicant must show he has available locally not less than £100. That done, he has to get a permit from the Resident in each Province where he seeks to prospect. The Resident only withholds a permit if the district is in an unsettled state.

An Exclusive Prospecting Licence comes next. The cost is £5 per square mile, and the prospector must have satisfied the Crown Agents that he possesses £500 in money for every square mile applied for. Whilst he holds the Exclusive Prospecting Licence he has the sole right to have a mining lease of the ground. Before, however, it is taken out, he must submit plans, which have to be passed by the Government Inspector of Mines and the Advisory Committee associated with him, which consists of three or four Government officials, who have power to co-opt non-officials.

Everything being in order and satisfactory, the applicant is granted an Exclusive Prospecting Lease. Following the Exclusive Prospecting Lease comes a Mining Lease. For that he must show he has at command £10 for every acre applied for. A lease is given for any period up to 21 years.

It is incumbent on a man coming out for a company that he shall have a properly-executed Power of Attorney. That is stipulated so as to fix direct responsibility and to avoid disavowal by the man's principals of steps he might take in their name.

Anybody holding an Exclusive Prospecting

Licence cannot sell or transfer it without the consent of the Governor. Should he, the Licence can be cancelled. The object of this measure is to prevent hawking or peddling of Licences and is an endeavour to protect the public against persons who might try to exploit uncertain or valueless land.

Whilst, of course, there is a Mines Department at Zungeru—really a section of the Secretariat that specially deals with mining matters—the office of the Government Inspector of Mines, Mr E. A. Langslow-Cock, at Naraguta. A few facts of the duties he has to perform will not be out of place here. Upon him is focussed most, if not all, dissatisfaction at the mining law and impatience that things are not done or decisions given. Langslow-Cock is too good an official, too loyal a subordinate, to even suggest or infer that he should not be blamed for what he has to carry out or for that at which he must hold his hand. If people blame him let them, he seems to say mentally. His temperament enables him to receive the slings and arrows of criticism with equanimity, and his personal popularity stops marksmen from dipping the points of their shafts into bitterness.

The work of the office has been said to be in a state of chaos. A greater misapplication of words could scarcely be used. If statements of that kind are not completely denied there usually is a suspicion that there is some ground for the indictment. As the term is understood, I say there is none. With the staff the Government Inspector of Mines has, the duties have been expeditiously and well performed. With the exception of the railways, where it is a question of safety of life, there is hardly a department of the public service not undermanned. Until this year the Protectorate has been allowed an Imperial grant-in-aid. Whether on that account or for any other, expenditure on salaries has, in most cases, been kept as low as possible—in many instances much lower than they should be—and too few men in receipt of them for the extent of country occupied. This does not apply specifically to the Government Inspector of Mines staff, but generally.

Naraguta is the centre of administration for the Central, formerly the Bauchi, Province. Naraguta bulks so largely in men's minds that some persons who have not seen the place regard it as a small town. Nothing of the kind. Except for the scattered houses and offices, all but two of mud, for the half-dozen or so English officials, there is nothing, beyond the alluvial tin operations a few miles round and the native village which has sprung up in consequence, to mark the country from the virgin land it was 10 years ago.

"The office of the Government Inspector of Mines" sounds imposing. That building Mr Langslow-Cock had to have put up by his native servants. No windows or doors are fitted to the mud structure; only openings. I have seen him drawing a Government map whilst rain came through the roof, dropping at the side of the table at which he worked.

The Resident, Mr F. Beckles Gall, has the luxury of a three-roomed stone bungalow. He deserves it. For nine months, when stationed here, which included the wet season of 1911, his dwelling consisted of two circular mud huts, both having merely holes in the walls for light and ventilation, and through them the rain swept night and day. I learnt by chance conversation that his present abode is the first with doors he has lived in for 8 years.

The Naraguta Resident has the attributes which help to make the best form of administrator in a high position: the qualities of open-mindedness, a capacity for taking any amount of trouble in order to fully understand every view-point of a question, and, not least, a sympathetic temperament which inclines him to help people instead of baffling them or putting difficulties in their way in an effort to enhance his own importance.

I think the Government are fortunate in having at Naraguta a man of the type of Mr Beckles Gall, for however indifferent a Resident may be to irritating or causing resentment among people who are not in his coterie, the Government at Zungeru, certainly the Colonial Office at home have no wish to see the resultant friction, bad feeling, and public comments in England. It is bad enough for a person to plume himself on being superior to all mankind; it is infinitely worse to parade belief of that superiority and to try and enforce it by contemptuous acts to those who, though not within his circle, by reason of his position must communicate with him from time to time. The supercilious attitude which I saw to an offensive extent towards non-officials at another place—I cannot help concluding, bearing seeds of possible mischief in the event of trouble with the natives—is altogether absent at Naraguta.

Besides being the chief centre of the mines administration away from Zungeru, Naraguta is the

A MURDER TRIAL

headquarters of the Hill Division, which is that section of the political service which deals with the Pagan tribes of the Province. The department is in charge of Mr C. L. Migeod, who in the course of his service has had two horses killed under him by poisoned arrows aimed at the rider. Those occurrences did not take place whilst hostile measures were being taken against the wild people of the hills. That is a step which every Governor of the Protectorate has frowned upon. Political officers are expected to allay, not aggravate, any resentment natives may feel towards the white man's presence and to get recalcitrant tribes round to a spirit of sweet reasonableness and an accommodating manner without necessitating the use of troops. Mr Migeod was endeavouring to carry out this policy, and whilst riding up a hill to a village on the top for the purpose of more fully explaining a message he had sent pointing out how nice it would be for the villagers to pay taxes, he received the welcome stated. He was a passenger on the ship by which I left England, but though we spoke freely on board he mentioned no word of what is now related. I only heard of the matter when I came to live in the district.

In a subsequent chapter the method and manner of ruling these Pagan tribes is explained. They, unlike the Fulani, the Hausa and cognate people, have no corporate life.

A single instance is rendered to show the spirit which animates the Government of Northern Nigeria in dealing with the inhabitants of the country.

A native was charged with murdering another and the case came before the Resident at Naraguta for trial. The prisoner, who had been brought in from some distance, was taciturn, but pleaded "Guilty," that is to say, he declared, "I did kill him." He repeated the phrase, but would say nothing more. He remained obstinately silent when pressed why he did it. The witnesses could explain no cause. The only reason they knew was that the prisoner and the man killed had quarrelled. Mr Gall did not forthwith sentence the prisoner to death. He reflected that no individual takes the life of another unless there is a strong motive, and he remembered that the poor wretch on the ground in front of his table was, after all, like the rest of us, a human being, though black and friendless.

Although prompt justice is generally esteemed in Northern Nigeria, Mr Gall put the case back and sent one of his native political officers to make enquiries in the district where the crime took place. Those enquiries showed the prisoner to have been provoked and wronged to such an extent that instead of being sent for execution he was given a month's imprisonment.

I learnt these particulars, not from Mr Gall, but since I have left him, and from a non-Government man, who, as is the way in this country, had not been sufficiently interested in the incident to be able to tell me what was the provocation. "I have my own business to attend to and cannot bother about such details, like you journalists who want to know all of everything; in fact, it was Gall's splendid fairness to the poor devil that made me notice the thing at all. And good luck to you for putting it down." So spoke my informant.

CHAPTER XXV

TROUBLES OF THE TREK

Philosophers' test—At the back of white men's minds—Human calculations—Blows to plans—Oje leaves—The servant problem—Short, severe rations—Doki boy Kolo—A Pagan pony—Its performances—Injury to insult—Human and equine elements.

If anybody endowed with an unflinching philosophic spirit wishes to have that spirit tried to the utmost, if anyone desires to test whether his heart will break at unexpected, unavoidable, exasperating delays and disappointments, then let him come to Northern Nigeria under such conditions and limitations as I and endeavour to carry out a time-table of moving through the country. Nobody I had met in England seemed to have any idea of the difficulties, each appearing small in itself, yet, accumulating, presenting an absolute bar to progression, a bar that no will could overcome.

A Governor, Resident or other high official in the public service is able to bend the resources of each district to his requirements. Rightly so, for matters of high importance may depend on the celerity of his movements. A Director of a large company or a member of a mine staff finds everything arranged. Horses and servants, previously provided, meet him at railhead and an ample supply of food boxes is sure to be included in his equipment by those who made the arrangements on this side. The sooner a good-salaried man gets to his task the quicker his employers are likely to turn dead outlay into a living profit.

But in the case of the journalist whom nobody knows, a stranger within the gates, nobody's child, perhaps misled by well-meaning folks in England who, in full belief, assured him there would be no special trouble in getting about; one who has to work out one's own salvation almost from stage to stage. Him, my readers, bear with in his efforts, wearing efforts, more wearing than any physical exertion, bear with him in delays which to you may seem inexplicable. You in that other part of the globe, away from this West Africa where transport and movement are distant from railroad or river, you can go from place to place by probably half-a-dozen alternatives should one fail.

Here there is no alternative; you must wait. You must depend on yourself absolutely. A man whose property you visit may give you some help to get on the way; it were unreasonable to look for anybody to do more.

Here as in other parts of the globe one must not expect too much just because one is a journalist. The journalist may at considerable outlay go to a country for the purpose of making the work of the men there known to the larger world outside. The men may care nothing for that knowledge being propagated nor for the opinions and judgments of the larger world—in which case, if I dare say so, they are foolish and make a gigantic mistake—or they may live in a little world of their own which takes count of little beyond. Their all-in-all is bound up in the place where their lives are spent, and nothing else matters. A visitor from abroad may be more an object of curiosity than of interest. In the course of pilgrimages through lands as Special Correspondent for the *African World* I have met some peculiar characters but never, I think, more—or as peculiar—as in Northern Nigeria. Certainly they are the exceptions. I make no complaint personally. These reflections are simply put down as observations on the workings of minds so unusual that they must be noted. There are frequent speculations as to what is at the back of the black man's mind. I have occasionally wondered what moulds ideas in some white men's minds in Northern Nigeria.

What has been stated can be read in connection with my own situation. That situation was this. I had settled to leave Naraguta on November 4 for the southward trek to Jemma. Everything had been arranged to the utmost detail. It was to be the last chapter, though not the last stage, of this portion of the journey and, bearing in thought former delays, I was firmly determined nothing should detain me a day. So much for human calculations.

The start was to be on a Monday. On the previous Friday morning I found myself without house-boys. Two of the three had gone for causes which need not be intruded here, and Oje was manfully going through the daily task single-handed pending the arrival of assistance. Friday morning Oje announced his wish to leave " for 10 days." It was not the labour he had to do which prompted the step; in fact, he had asked to continue alone. The story he gave—I am convinced the true one—was that a man who owed him £4, 16s. was at Zaria—at least 3 days' journey for him, though he used the railway—and he desired to go and claim the money. No persuasion or sternness could induce him to stay. I offered to give him the £4, 16s. He was worth that and more. No use. Go he would. He knew the serious trouble he would give me and said he was sorry, but nothing could alter his attitude. It was one of those strange aberrations of the native from down country which defy reading by the white man, however experienced; for between the lad and myself there was a strong attachment. Evidence of it had occurred unmistakably a few days earlier.

He wanted to leave next day, by which time, he explained, he would find me a cook. When I saw it was hopeless to make him remain, in order to show independence I told him he could go at once. He did, notwithstanding he thought he might be forfeiting several sovereigns I was keeping for him. Although I knew it was not easy to obtain houseboys at short notice at Naraguta, I hoped to, and whether I did or not, I was set on starting Monday morning. It was a serious position to go without at least one, but I would be deterred by no inconvenience—to use a moderate expression—taking my chance of picking some up en route. So much for human calculations.

Next day occurred a much more severe blow to the plans. One pony which had not been very well became seriously ill and the other suddenly went quite lame. It was clear to even my limited veterinary knowledge that neither could be taken out for more than a week. To obtain fresh ones in the required time at Naraguta was out of the question. I was for walking. A man to whom I mentioned this spoke of it as "downright madness under the conditions." He said I would be meeting disaster and that I ought to regard myself as fortunate if I were as much as carried back.

Moreover, the servant difficulty was not easily adjusted. The first applicants were obviously to be shunned at any cost. Their presence would prove a great deal more trouble than their absence. For three days I was completely without house-help of any kind. For those three days, with the anxiety on my hands of a horse becoming weaker and weaker, in spite of all done for the poor animal, I had nothing to eat beyond hard, thick, dry cabin biscuits and a cup of tea morning and another in the evening. This was the only time I could spare from writing to make up a fire. There was a single deviation from the diet. It was a morning when I had been invited to breakfast. I had to walk nearly two miles in the heat and glare of 9 a.m. without the preliminary morning tea. My host, Mr F. Beckles Gall, the Resident at Naraguta, one of the kindest of men, will on seeing these lines in print learn to his surprise in what a plight was his guest of that morning.

It may be asked whether I could not avoid so much discomfort and prevent such risks in a country where food is a prime consideration for health. The answer is that I had gone up under the impression that anything could be bought near, whereas transport of supplies was not then in the more advanced state to which it has since been brought, and although fresh meat and poultry are for sale in the public market, there are some things a white cannot do; one is to go to market. You might as lief see a Duchess on knees cleaning her doorstep in Belgrave Square.

There were, possibly, several men within a radius of five miles—which here corresponds to the distance of a short street in England—who would have had me at their table had they known. But one does not care to run about with all one's small worries. There is so much done by some people for a stranger that he does not wish to put their goodness at undue strain.

Yes, in Naraguta, which away from a town is regarded as rather a large centre, I have endured— I will not say suffered, for I do not make a suffering or a trouble of it—I have undergone more hardships in the matter of food than anywhere in the whole course of this journey. My inconveniences are given in detail as a signal to others, though probably they will not be subject to the same limitations. Expansion of purchasable supplies is likely to be full.

Oje returned Sunday afternoon, very tired, downcast and contrite. He had been overcome by a kind of home-sickness and at Rahama turned from his purpose. He begged hard to be taken back. I subsequently learnt, not from him, that although money was in his pocket, he had had no food for two days. Water had been his only sustenance.

Still without house-boys, I rejoiced at seeing him, though sorry for the hard time he had evidently experienced. My liking for Oje was too strong to be destroyed even by the way he had acted. I was convinced he had been led to it by somebody who hoped to victimise him.

But it would not do to let him see forgiveness could be had on request, so I sternly told him I would not have him again.

He stayed near for the remainder of the day, sometimes sitting on the ground at the side of the bungalow, always looking wistfully when I went outside. Once, as I sat writing, he came into the room and commenced to make the bed ready for the night, as he had done for so many months, but I ordered him out and declared he was never to think of doing anything for me again, though I almost broke down before the sentence was finished. He went out with tears trickling. That night he slept in one of the outhouses and directly I opened my door at 5.30 next morning he was waiting and commenced " I beg, sir-r."

I told him to come back at 10 o'clock. He elected to remain on the spot. Another boy was engaged as steward and then poor little Oje was reinstalled a step lower, as cook.

The horse difficulty remained. On Tuesday the one that had been growing weaker died. I must not overlook the attention it received all through from doki boy Kolo, not the one originally in my service but a Beri-Beri. Kolo is not handsome to gaze upon—he has one eye, a phenomenally long mouth and wears a short pig-tail falling from the crown to the side of his head—but I liked him from the first meeting.

It was clear I must obtain horses if my stay was not to be prolonged to a length driving me to lunacy. But no Glendower can conjure them up at Naraguta within a fortnight of the great Hausa festival known as the Salah. However, if I did not try I certainly would not succeed, and, making efforts and my wants known in all directions, at last a Hausa dealer brought a strong-looking pony he had purchased from Pagans. It stood about 12 hands and, all being well, was just the kind of beast for trekking. The dealer rode him a short distance, and, although not taking kindly to bit or saddle, he seemed all right. I then walked, trotted and cantered him, and a friend having done likewise and pronounced him passable except for a defect in the shape of his legs, I bought the animal for £5.

The same evening the pony broke his tether and wildly tore about the compound seeking who of his kind he might fight and bite. For 20 minutes he was pursued by half-a-dozen doki boys, whom he repeatedly evaded by sharp turns and wheels to the left or right. Eventually wary tactics were adopted. The pony was quietly allowed to approach another horse and, as the Pagan beast stood for a moment, one of the doki boys threw his arms over the neck and the others closing in, the runaway was held captive, in spite of frantic plunging, backing and kicking.

Kolo held him whilst ropes were being sought, and maintained the charge when the pony recommenced the contest by biting a gash in Kolo's leg, from which the blood came freely. At last the beast was put in a doki house, both fore and hind legs hobbled, a stout rope round his neck and tied to the roof, but of sufficient length to allow lying down.

The entrance was crossed with heavy beams and the barricade made complete by a large iron wheelbarrow against it. A peace-offering, in the form of a heap of cut grass, was placed on the ground to keep the rioter quiet during the night. He rejected all these overtures and frequently signified his protest at the restraint imposed by attempting to break away, but that had been too carefully provided against.

I had thought during the performance that I would give him as much galloping as he wished for, and more, next morning.

At 10 a.m. the little brute was led to the bungalow. He was in anything but an angelic mood. Ears set back, a spiteful look in his eyes, seemingly spoiling for a fight, he seemed generally typical of the wild people who had bred him. I calculated that all this vicious energy would be fully expended in the couple of miles' gallop to and up the hill on which the post office stands. The pony had other plans.

It was a long business getting him to take the bit, which was only done after the beast had been tied to a post by a halter round his neck. The two doki boys had all they could do before the bridle was in position. The saddle was then put on and the halter taken off.

But the pony by no means entered into the spirit of what was intended. He jumped about and swung round, never giving chance of a foot being placed in the stirrup. At last the doki boys had to hold his head firmly, and a moment afterwards I was up and they let go to give a clear course. Instead of starting off like a flash, as I expected, he not merely reared but threw himself backward, his full length on the ground.

Taken unawares, I was not in time to check the movement and fell sideways, as fortunately only the extreme end of the boots were in the stirrups. To add injury to insult he attempted to roll on me—I had by chance fallen a little too widely—and then he jumped up and made off madly.

This part of the programme I heard of afterwards, as the fall stunned me. A thick, pith helmet—the gift of a friend in London—had been providentially strapped under the chin, and therefore remaining in position had thus prevented my cranium coming into direct contact with the stony ground. Had it, the more or less valuable contents thereof would probably have been deranged by concussion of the brain or some similar pleasantry.

When after a minute or so of unconsciousness I came to, the delinquent was being held near by. He did not appear to be the least ashamed of his handiwork. At first I could not get up and assumed some bone had been broken, especially as assistance to rise gave such pain that I asked to be left. Presently I was able unhelped to change from the horizontal to the perpendicular position and at once proceeded to take stock by feeling the ribs and shoulder-blade for fracture. All were intact.

Then about the mail, for I was taking to the post things written for the *African World Annual* and this was the latest day for forwarding them. The sport of a further try with the Pagan pony involved too great a risk of missing the mail, so I had another horse, which I had on hire, brought out, saddled

TROUBLES OF THE TREK

and reached the post office just before the bags were closed.

Next day it was clear I had been hurt more than I thought. The pain in the side had increased and any movement such as sneezing caused the agony as of internal knives cutting. The following day the signs having intensified, with added pain when in the prone position, I made an appointment to see Dr Costello, the Government medical officer. He promptly diagnosed the symptoms as contusion of the muscles. I was not able to ride and he, with the usual care given to each individual case, offered the use of his own hammock for the trek.

That is a mode of progression few use if they can avoid. With a squad of bearers not trained to work together, the discomfort on a journey of length has to be experienced to be realised. Moreover, lying down was bad enough in bed; in a jolting hammock it would be impossible.

However, I still determined to leave on the appointed day of the following Wednesday, though I had to walk. Annoyance at the continual delays was felt to be more risk to health than trekking in the tropics on foot over a bad path.

But a difficulty much harder to remove than absence of horses presented itself. The great, national festival of the Salah—the Hausa Christmas, as it is termed locally—was approaching and carriers would not move from their homes and miss the two days' jollification. No reasonable remuneration would entice them. Though I were prepared to go without the necessary couple of horses, the indispensable carriers would not be forthcoming. There was, therefore, absolutely no alternative to possessing my soul in patience as best I might until the human and equine elements shaped into propitious form.

The Salah over, the Pagan pony having been disposed of—thereby hangs another story, which cannot be told now—having been promised hire of a second horse, and the carriers been engaged, I am leaving to-morrow morning southwards.

CHAPTER XXVI

INCIDENTS ON TREK

The changed seasons—End of the rainy season—Bush fires—Rolling downs and kopjes—A 25-miles march without food or drink—Return journey commenced—Ascent of the escarpment, 2,200 feet—A Hausa and Pagan affray—An ugly situation.

LEAVING Naraguta and making direct south, about four miles along an excellent broad road, Jos is reached, past which one takes either a branch, still wide, road or a path which can scarcely be termed a bush one, for the character of the country is changing. There are granite boulders of moderate size. The merely undulating plains with small hills correspond to the impressions one has gained from the descriptions of Transvaal scenery, with its expansive veldt and kopjes around.

Travelling is no longer amidst torrential downpour and flooding tornadoes. The rains have ceased. No more will fall for at least three months, probably four. The rains ended with the advent of the October new moon. They stopped almost as automatically as the municipal turncock checks the supply from the main to the household pipes in English towns. A storm came and, continuing during the evening preceding the new moon, a bet was made at 8 o'clock that the fall of water would last over the astronomical change, which was to occur between 1 and 3 a.m. The man who backed the affirmative lost. The shower ceased at 11 p.m.

The roads just here are new, smooth and hard. Bridges of earth and wood, easily swept away by the swollen, rushing streams of the wet season, have been rebuilt, and therefore there is no wading across rivers of doubtful depth with deep holes in the bed or large rocks under water.

No need to watch for the sign of a storm. The sky is generally clear, blue flecked by a little white. The surrounding land is altering its appearance. The universal green, hitherto freshened by the rains, has largely become russet, with fields of light yellow grass. This dry, long grass has already provided the running ground for bush fires, too frequently started by a lighted object thrown thoughtlessly among quick-burning material. You can see these bush fires at night, sharp and distinct against the blackness around. They may be small and easily beaten out by the natives using sticks. Sometimes the fire will extend to a half-mile front. Then it must proceed until a large river or other barren space gives it no passage and it dies away. At the end of the rains, the European will clear the space round his house for hundreds of feet. So will the careful native. Should he have neglected, his dwelling may be smouldering in a flash; and whether from the bush or by internal cause, when a fire lays hold of a village scores of families are homeless in a few minutes.

These bush fires of Northern Nigeria are not, however, of that wild, devouring character seen in Canada and Australia, where the fierce roar can be heard a mile away and where everything staying within the line of advance must be destroyed entirely. Though here there is the sharp unpleasant crackle and uncomfortable heat as the flames roll onwards, the grass is not very high and being comparatively sparse does not give the fire that firm grasp which makes it invincible to subdue.

Over the blackened ground where it has run, within a few hours you will notice new blades of grass sprouting, so wonderfully ready to respond to nature is this soil, poor though it is judged by the soil more to the north, the west and the east.

There are other signs of the changed season. The harmattan haze hangs on the hills, and presently will come those dust storms which in no slight degree make themselves felt however you may try to protect yourself in a dwelling of any kind.

There is little cultivation along the route we are passing. Dwarf guinea-corn, about four feet in height, and similar millets nearly constitute the whole. There are a few flowers bearing rich yellow petals which easily transport one's fancy to English counties. The impression is emphasised by rolling downs, which remind you of Sussex scenery.

I have a wholesome fear of tiring readers with overmuch detail of travel and therefore pass over with a few words the several days' trek to Jemma, with one march of 25 miles in a severely hot temperature, mostly on foot, lasting from morning to evening, with not so much as a drink of water or a biscuit to eat, and entailing a descent of more than 2,200 feet from the Bauchi Plateau to Nassarawa Province. I take up the story where my little caravan, emerging from a long lane through high grass, dipped into a plain backed by high hills.

A pleasant little episode marked the entry to the plain. Passing a circular mud house a white man came out of it and seeing me in doubt as to the direction to be taken spontaneously asked, "Can I be of assistance to you?" and then probably noticing the betravelled condition I presented, offered refreshment. As the day's journey was practically ended the invitation was declined, but it was a kindly spirit that prompted it, a spirit general among the best type of Northern Nigeria Government Officers. The individual in this case was Captain F. P. Soper, Assistant Commissioner of Police in charge of the Jemma district.

My stay at Jemma was not long enough to go to the head-hunters' village four miles across the valley, though I should have greatly liked to have made their acquaintance. There was, however, a great deal of ground still to be covered, so after two clear days at Jemma, the return journey was commenced. (The various Pagan tribes visited in the course of the several treks are dealt with together in Chapters XXIX to XXXII, instead of referring to them here and there, piecemeal.)

Though for several reasons I should have preferred to have gone by the old caravan route westward to Loko and thence along the Benue River, or by the lower road northwards, considerations led to the decision to go back on the line by which I had come.

That, of course, entailed ascending the escarpment, some 2,200 feet. Plans were arranged

INCIDENTS ON TREK

accordingly. It was done on the second day's trek, and instead of a march of 25 miles, as when I came down it, one of 18 was fixed. The weather was very hot, which was also taken into consideration. The decision was made to leave Karshi rest-house at 4 a.m., and though the sun does not rise until a little past 5 o'clock, a broad pathway clearly showed the way to the carriers.

Getting up at 3 o'clock, by 4 o'clock breakfast had been finished, the table, chairs and the beds made into their usual loads, and we were off a few minutes earlier than the appointed time.

The idea governing the programme was to reach the mountain path to the Plateau at daybreak and then cover it in the cool hours of the morning, instead of doing so under a fierce glare, the heat intensified by reflection from the high rocks that seemed on touch to be burning, which was the experience on the outward journey.

The ascent to the Plateau proved much less trying than the descent had been. True, in the latter case the hardest part was done under the most severe heat of the day and an extra seven miles had been put on the span, whilst on the return tramp the worst section was left behind before the sun had put forth full power, and cold tea, kept so in a special flask, gave relief to a parched throat and produced a general refreshed feeling. Still, not until 12.30 was the rest-house at Hos reached and the loads put down for another day.

Temperature on the Plateau was in marked contrast to that felt in the lower ground of Nassarawa Province. On the higher altitude cool air and strong breezes temper the heat rays. Instead of being charged with moisture, the atmosphere is dry, rarefied.

At one part of the march I was walking, to ease the horse and for a change of movement to myself, when an incident occurred which might have produced an unpleasant result to each side in the quarrel.

The carriers were ahead, out of sight, for, notwithstanding their 60 lbs. load on the head, they will swing along on an even path at $3\frac{1}{2}$ miles an hour in dry weather and 3 miles an hour over wet ground, soon outdistancing a horse that is not trotting. With me there was only one of the doki boys. We were passing along a winding path flanked with a long hill on the left and high grass on the right. The noise of shouting in front reached us, which at first I thought came from some ju-ju celebration or other jollification at one of the Pagan centres. A bend of the path showed a crowd of men struggling and the angry voices conveyed unmistakably that passions were roused.

Running forward I saw a Hausa man on the ground being dragged by half-a-dozen Pagans towards their compound and houses at the side of the path, whilst eight or ten Hausa men were trying to prevent it. At the moment more Pagans, who had evidently been summoned to the scene, were hurrying up, spears in hand, though not poised ready for thrusting. I pushed my way into the middle of the struggling mass and motioned the Pagans to release their hold on the Hausa, which they did immediately. He then attempted to rise, but I promptly and none too gently pushed him down, so that adjudication could be done without giving either side the impression of favouring the other. It was better the relative positions remain.

The Hausa was one of a party, under a Headman, taking loads across country. I demanded from the Headman the reason for the disturbance. He attempted to represent the Pagans as the aggressors, but his story was easily sifted and the truth ascertained. As I expected, the Hausa was in the wrong. Some of the labourer class frequently adopt towards Pagans insolence and a sneering manner they would not dare unless for the knowledge that the British have forbidden violence and the use of weapons to vent a grievance, under any conditions. In the present case, the Pagans, noticing the Hausas approaching, had gone out with ground-nuts to sell. The man on the ground had taken a handful, eaten nearly half, and then given the remainder back, refusing to pay the penny due, on the plea that the nuts were not good. He had further exasperated these simple people by grinning at them as he proceeded to go away with his fellows. They thereupon seized, and were dragging, him into their village.

I said the Hausa man must pay the penny. He asserted he did not have one. I asked the Headman if any of the party would pay for him, and the answer given was that none had money—a palpable falsehood. Then, I announced, the blanket—a highly-valued article for use at night—belonging to the one who had eaten the nuts would be torn up. I put it on the ground, placed a foot determinedly on the edge and gripped the thing as though to rend it. I had mentally decided that, if the penny was not forthcoming at the last second, sooner than destroy the rug I would give the penny; but obviously it was infinitely better that the fellow or another of the gang paid. Just as a tug was made at the blanket the man on the ground cried " Baboo " (" Do not do it "), and asked the Headman to hand over a penny for him. The coin was offered to me, but I directed it be given to the Pagan.

I told the man to get up and ordered the Headman to lead the gang away at once, warning him against any additional provocation at villages on the way. I stayed 15 minutes to see that the Hausas got well on the road without trouble; then mounted, waved a farewell to the Pagans, who were mightily pleased at the settlement, and rode off.

The question may occur: What plan would have been followed had either party to the dispute resisted the intervention? To tell the truth, I did not have a thought on that aspect until an hour or so later. Only then, whilst jogging along on horseback, the humour of the situation presented itself. What I should have done in the event of the Hausas or Pagans showing hostility I really do not know.

As a matter of fact, the advent of the white man was welcomed by both sides: the Hausas at once realised that their brother would not be speared and the Pagans instinctively appreciated that justice was to be done. What would have befallen the man they were dragging into the compound is uncertain. Probably killed, and so would those of his gang who participated in the scuffle. A few years ago no Hausa dare venture within many days' journey of this Hos-Karshi bush-path. The British authorities have made the Pagans understand that

INCIDENTS ON TREK

any attack on people passing along the main track will be severely punished, at the same time promising that their villages shall not be entered by any strangers unless they are messengers from a Resident. Warnings and cautions to that effect are issued to all who go through the area.

A few days' later I saw the Resident at Bukuru and told him what had taken place. He approved.

A further 16 miles on the following day took me to Bukuru, whence, after the night's rest, I struck at right-angles off the main path for South Bukuru.

CHAPTER XXVII

INCIDENTS ON TREK—(*continued*)

Information and advice in West Africa—Different men, different manners—Ritz by comparison—A Samaritan by the way—Dried streams—Primitive transport—A visitor from Rhodesia—Omitting anti-fever precautions.

THE last stage of these months of trekking presented one of those questions of distances which different persons solve in various ways. The start was from Jos and the destination Rahama, 48 miles. The journey could not be divided into three stretches of about 15 miles each, if for no other reason than that I was not to leave Jos until 4 p.m., in order that I might transmit from mind to paper the impressions and reflections collected, get them in the post, and thus be clear to gather more as I went along. It was plain, therefore, that, to cover the ground within three days, on one day a long march must be made, as the position of rest-houses did not allow more equal averaging.

Which day did not matter much. It was largely a case of personal preference, and I mention the subject to show how men's advice differ as to what you should do in West Africa. There is seldom lack of advice and information, on ship or ashore. The only element doubtful is whether the advice is reliable.

INCIDENTS ON TREK—*continued*

In Northern Nigeria—these parts, at least—that does not apply. Opinions, however, vary. One man counselled an entire rearrangement of the programme in the sense of leaving Jos very early in the morning, doing 23 miles that day, 15 the next, and winding up with an easy 10. Another urged me not to overdo things, and rather to make a four days' time-table than to court being knocked up by too much exertion in the hot season. It is well to respect experience; nevertheless, some things must be decided by the individual affected. It may be he should avoid risks, and it may be that risks which ought not to be invited at an earlier period, when a breakdown in health would be a serious derangement of plans, should not have the same influence as a deterrent towards the end, when the main portion of the work has been done.

I elected to act on my own devices, to put the longest march to the last, and I determined to get through by Sunday. The governing motive in not being later was the desire not to delay at Rahama. Only one train a week was scheduled, and as I did not know which day it left, or the hour, by reaching railhead on Sunday the chagrin would be avoided of arriving a few hours after the train had gone.

It was seven o'clock and dark by the time we had done the nine miles from Jos to Gurum. The carriers had been told that the stay for the night would be at the rest-house there, but, instead, they made for the Anglo-Continental Mines Camp, which is about ten minutes' walk from the rest-house. On seeing the mistake which had been made, I hung back out of sight and sent the steward boy, who could speak a little English, to the camp to enquire the way to the rest-house. I did not wish to intrude, which I thought would seem to be if I appeared uninvited and unexpectedly when the evening meal was due.

The steward boy returned with a message that "The white man want you." I knew who the white man would be, so the steward boy was sent back, as though I had not understood, with the reiterated request to know what path led to the rest-house. After a few minutes there came from the lighted bungalow and through the darkness "the white man." It was Mr T. H. Driver, one of the most lovable characters on the tin fields. He had been ill and could not walk without trouble, though he had the aid of a stick; yet he must undergo the effort to invite almost a stranger to food and better shelter for the night than the rest-house afforded.

He then had swept out an unused shed, with cement floor, brick walls, and iron roof. It seemed a Ritz Hotel in luxury by comparison with another place of recent memory. In the shed my camp-bed was put up and to it I retired with thankfulness after dinner with Mr Driver and his staff.

You may assume that there was nothing more in this than ordinary politeness, and that anybody would act similarly. I should like to be able to say so. You may think I make too much of common courtesies and small hospitalities. Travel across a country such as this and you will appreciate them, the more by contrast. I suppose a great deal depends on character and temperament, otherwise there is no understanding the difference which marks men.

INCIDENTS ON TREK—*continued*

Not long ago I was located in a mud hut which was clean and roomy and in which I was quite happy. The second night I was informed it was wanted for someone else—a junior member of the staff of the concern—and although there was plenty of accommodation for either him or me in other buildings on the ground, the quarter given me to sleep in was of a kind that, in preference, I went to the hovel where two of my native servants—the horse boys—were passing the night, and had the bed brought there.

Of course I could have had the place to myself, but the boys were there first and had made a fire to keep themselves warm during the cold hours. Had I turned them out, they could not then have secured further fuel, and to have gone into a cold hut from a warm one, with their single blanket apiece, would be dangerous to health.

You may not regard highly the Englishman who puts another into the position stated, though it be merely a passing traveller. I make no grievance of the incident, unpleasant as the situation undoubtedly was. When, therefore, a T. H. Driver appears in the path, with his considerate heart, too much can scarcely be said for him.

My own case is not the only one I have witnessed. When passing through Gurum on a previous occasion I saw a man being carried in an invalid's hammock towards Rahama. His health had broken. He had been sent home and was too ill to ride a horse. The bearers stopped a little way from Mr Driver's bungalow, and the sick man sat under the shadow of some trees as a temporary rest from the tiring hammock. I looked on as

Mr Driver went over. He exchanged a few words with the man, who was a stranger, and then led him across.

The miner had been a burly, strong fellow. Now he was in a shattered state and could not stand alone. With arm round the poor fellow's waist and as tender and gentle as if he had been a girl, Driver helped him along with slow steps to his own bedroom and bade him lie and rest there until the midday intensity of the tropical sun had abated. And when the invalid resumed his journey Driver had given him a proper utensil for boiling water and thus added to the stranger's chance of retaining life whilst in the bush. "Good luck! Drop me a line to say how you are on reaching the Coast," were Driver's parting words. They constitute a tactful paraphrase of a request to know whether a man has lived to get to the sea.

I was away from Gurum in the early morning, and we easily arrived at Raffan Governor, 14 miles, about the time people in England would be finishing breakfast. There was thus a clear day for writing, and the carriers would have a good rest, away from the nocturnal attractions of a large village, for the long march on the morrow.

The carriers were aware that on the last day they had to do the longest—though, as regards the ground, not the hardest—march since they had been with me, and there was no trouble in parading them early and getting away.

Since I previously came over this ground the aspect has altered considerably. The rain-torn roads, making them into ditches and ridges, have been repaired and are now smooth enough to have wheeled along them frail bassinettes. The surface is as level as an ideal sand road. No one who had not seen would think that it will be washed away to a condition impassable for wheeled vehicles in a few weeks of the rainy season.

The streams, some impassable after a short storm, are in many cases now completely dried up. There are a number which would not be recognised as watercourses. Even rivers as broad as the Thames at Windsor are sufficiently shallow to be crossed on stepping-stones.

Other signs are to be noted. One sees that one has returned to a caravan route. Instead of two or three persons met during the day, the 20 feet wide road has carriers—a file of 30 or small detachments of a larger party—about every 100 yards.

But carriers, donkeys, and bullock wagons, they all seem so primitive, the method so ancient. It recalls the Biblical period. One thinks of mechanical transport; if not the railway, which, with a single train at its slowest, would whirl along in half-a-day the load which thousands of carriers need six times as long to transport, then of motor lorries, a couple capable of doing in a day work that requires 150 men with head-loads three days. Such lorries are due up a fortnight hence and will be the first distinct step in utilising the latest product of mechanical science to supersede the old, human manner.

A pleasant companion for several miles was Mr Speed, a grey-bearded veteran who had come to Northern Nigeria to judge its value for ranching. He has seen much of the world. Born in Australia, and a few years ago associated with mines in

Rhodesia, he knows the whole gamut of colonial life.

He is as enthusiastic over this country as man can possibly be. He considers it admirable for cattle-raising and for wheat production. Any question of hazards to health he waves aside. He thinks there is no reason why Englishmen should not settle permanently on the land, as they have done elsewhere. He argues that, by reasonable precautions, danger from the sun's rays can be avoided. He says they are bad, if not so strong, in Rhodesia and that there white women and children live and thrive, though a few years ago it was declared to be fever-ridden and impossible to any but the hard, inured campaigner.

Why, he asks, should not the present health conditions in the Chartered Company's territory be brought about in Northern Nigeria? He affirms that, as far as he can tell from intense observation, no cause exists to deter that consummation.

Mr Speed is one of those exceptional cases where an individual ignores some of the prime safeguards of two kinds against fever. In spite of the fact that he is much older than is regarded as safe for men to spend more than a fleeting visit to West Africa, he tells me that he never has a net to protect him from mosquitoes at night, as such an adjunct on his bed would prevent him sleeping by impeding free passage of air; and also that he does not use a filter, merely taking care that drinking water is simply boiled. That line of conduct with many men would be tantamount to signing their death warrant.

CHAPTER XXVIII

CLOSE OF THE TREK

Character of carriers—The only blow given—Native grooms' monetary transactions—Material for a *cause célèbre*—Dispensing justice on the road—Headman Dan Sokoto—Dan's sharp practices—A long march.

I LEFT Mr Speed at the Gidden Gombo rest-house in order that I might push on to railhead the same day. The distance was only 10 miles and the carriers quite fresh and fit at this stage. It is surprising what difference a few miles additional to an ordinary march will effect. Though my men would, of course, have preferred to have stayed at Gidden Gombo with Mr Speed's carriers, they offered not the slightest demur to going forward; and after stretching themselves on the ground for about 20 minutes they rose willingly and headed their loads with smiles.

There are shirkers and wasters and defaulters among the Hausa carriers, as there are among bodies of men of lighter colour skin; human nature does not become perfect, whatever the externals; but treated properly—by which is meant, with tact, firmness when necessary, and consideration—my testimony is that the Hausas are as good-tempered a class as can be found anywhere, and always ready to respond to whatever call is made upon their endurance.

Do not conclude they are free from frailties and failings found elsewhere. Justice is, however, the talisman for ruling them, justice with self-control, never allowing your temper to master you, be the cause what it may.

This particular gang had been with me nearly four weeks, and it is scarcely probable that in that period there would not be among themselves cases of quarrels brought to the white master for settlement or an occasional act which needed some disciplinary step.

Both were surprisingly few. Only on one occasion was the strong measure taken of striking a blow. The steward boy, Oje, during a temporary halt on the road objected to a carrier sitting on a box containing food, and as the man would not move Oje attempted to draw the box from under him, whereupon he slapped the boy's face with such force as to make him stagger. Oje responded by hitting with a light cane, and then the carrier—a rather tall fellow—advanced menacingly towards the lad. As he did, I, who unknowing to them happened to be standing by, stepped forward and with a single sharp cut from a short riding whip recalled the carrier to his senses.

A few words of admonition on the cowardice of a big man striking a little one brought approving cries from the gathered circle, and the man expressed his regret on the spot. Later he spontaneously apologised to Oje.

The two horse boys—Kolo and Mama—usually the friends of a common fraternity, sometimes had mutual monetary dealings. The outcome of a transaction of that kind—the loan of 3d.—was a dispute.

CLOSE OF THE TREK

The alleged debtor, Kolo, asserted he had paid. Persisting in the declaration, Mama flew into such a rage that, in his exasperation, he tore the other's robe. This was clearly wrong, so, to maintain good order, I awarded Kolo 6d. from Mama's wages, subsequently, in order that Mama might not feel embittered at the loss, taking care he should do a special service with a reward of 9d.

After the reconciliation which followed the judgment, and notwithstanding my reiteration of Polonius' advice to Laertes, rendered colloquially, a week later a feud broke out between the same two over the loan of a penny. The matter was brought for my decision. To have gone into the question would have incurred very much longer time than could be spared, so, warning each disputant against a resort to violence—threatening to have both punished if they fought and to have the one who hit first thoroughly flogged—I told them that, as the trek would end in a couple of days, they must take what would possibly be regarded as a local *cause célèbre* to the court of the Alkali, the native judge.

The Headman of the carriers, Dan Sokoto, was quite a character, as most Headmen are. He was a strong contrast to Headman Hanza, with whom I first set out on trek. Still, I got to like Dan. Rather under the height of most Hausamen and an age that would be looked upon by them as old, he was wiry and as alert as the youngest. He did not wear a turban, like the stately Hanza, but affected a white embroidered linen cap, conical shape, cocked rakishly to incline to the right eye. His goatee beard he would stroke whilst he smiled benignly when the steward or the cook asked for the money which Dan made a point of getting either as a temporary personal accommodation or to buy for them some extraordinary bargain of clothing or a sleeping mat from any market we happened to be passing. Dan was always ready with a reason why the purchase was deferred and why he should in the meantime retain the money.

His industry was to be admired. Whenever we stopped, whether it be for a few minutes or as a rest in the course of a long day's march, out would come his needle. He plied it incessantly either in making himself nether garments or in fancy woolwork. At both he acquitted himself well.

Dan started his service badly. I had engaged 20 carriers. Dan turned up with 22. Asked why the requisite number was exceeded, he answered that the loads were too heavy to be apportioned to the lesser figure. As he had not seen them, it was unmistakably an attempt to have more men under him than I considered necessary. He would no doubt have drawn an illicit commission from the wages of the couple unwarrantably enrolled.

The superfluous couple were dismissed. Really, made up into about 60-lb. loads, only 18 men would have been wanted, but going away for a month from the chance of refilling any vacancy, it was desirable to have two spare men in case any of the others fell ill. In order that all might do their share as long as possible, the loads were arranged into 20 divisions.

At the close of the first day's trek I called Dan Sokoto and told him I did not at all relish the trick he had tried and that if anything of the kind occurred again I would send him back and appoint another Headman.

The answer was characteristic. He did not attempt to justify his conduct. He said he was sorry for what he had done; that he hoped to remain with me; that if I forgave him I would have no further cause for complaint. Put in a more blunt way, he meant, "I tried to get the better of you; I failed. There is no necessity to make a fuss about the thing; let it pass and allow me to serve you." So I regarded the matter.

Perhaps I should apologise for making this digression from the narrative, but progression on trek depends so much on one's carriers that I thought these glimpses into their personality and manners might be of interest.

I have mentioned that a few miles added to a normal march will occasionally mean much more than the distance appears. Though the men went on from Gidden Gombo buoyantly and light-heartedly, after a couple of hours, with the sun's rays increasing in power, the pace fell off considerably. The men held on bravely and were as good-tempered as ever, but were unable to maintain the rate, and by the time we had entered the last five miles there were signs of distress among some. I encouraged and stimulated them, referred to this being the end of their present efforts; joked of the " dash "—i.e., present—to be given when we reached Rahama and of their having light work, or none to do, the next day.

The heat and dust had become very trying, and although the carriers could march easily in the early mornings bearing their loads for 10 or 12 miles without a stop over fairly rough roads, they were now so done up on this last stretch that in the final 5 miles they had to rest three times.

It would have been easier for me to have cantered on, but I felt it due to the excellent fellows with whom I had been across and back over the Plateau for so many days to stay with them; and so together we at last reached Rahama; again saw a railway, and found Mr Garrard, the local senior representative of the Niger Company, as cheery as ever. The men, each carrying at least 60 lbs. weight on his head, had covered 26 miles in a typically torrid temperature.

It was well the march had been maintained, as the weekly train was to leave at 8 a.m. the following morning.

CHAPTER XXIX

TOWARDS THE PAGAN COUNTRY

Hausa and Pagan—Distinction of dress—Deeper divisions—The price of peace in former days—Public highway—Revenge and brotherhood—Scope of an Assistant Resident.

THE inhabitants of Northern Nigeria may be broadly classed as Hausa and Pagan. Each comprises many tribes. The Hausa is generally regarded as a Mohamedan, though no more so than that everybody in England who does not attend chapel, synagogue or meeting-house is to be counted as Church of England.

The distinction between Hausa and Pagan is easily seen in dress. Any Hausa worth the name sports a flowing robe and wide linen trousers. A well-to-do man's garments of that kind will make those of a British Jack-tar appear puny and of spider proportions. Costume affected by the Pagan sexes will be referred to presently.

A less visible but far deeper division between the two is that formerly the Hausa people raided Pagan tribes wherever it could be done, dragging prisoners to slavery, killing the villagers unfit for it, burning the houses, destroying the crops and food stored for the lean months, and leaving any persons who had escaped the raiding bands to death by exposure and starvation. The price of peace to a Pagan tribe was tribute, which usually took the form of an annual quota of slaves. They were mostly obtained by raiding other Pagan tribes, and, as an area that was secure from raiding found a vent for its energies and war-like skill by inter-fighting, the whole countryside for hundreds of square miles was in a continual ferment of bloodshed.

The advent of the British made a radical alteration. When a Protectorate was proclaimed it was announced that whilst the Pagan would be preserved from being raided he was to allow free passage through to the Hausa, for a few years ago no Hausa dare enter these regions where the Pagans were strong enough to resist attack. Caravans which came near enough to the danger zone were assailed or harassed by the wild men from the hills.

With the inception of the new conditions, a public path, corresponding to a highway in England, was marked out, wherever possible away from the Pagan villages, and it was proclaimed that any peaceable stranger passing along who was murdered would be avenged by the British. Although that is enforced to some extent in the neighbourhood of large centres of administration, it cannot be the uniform rule over a vast territory where means of locomotion are almost entirely confined to bush and mountain tracks. Held in check by the supreme authority, the fierce hatred and enmity of Hausa and Pagan remain. You cannot eradicate in less than a decade the memory of wrongs for generations, nor at once replace with a spirit of sweet and loving brotherhood the intense desire for revenge. The feeling manifests itself around out-

TOWARDS THE PAGAN COUNTRY

lying posts in minor ways. Murder is, however, seldom resorted to.

Seven days' marching has brought us to the middle of the Bauchi Plateau, 4,000 feet above sea-level, although the spot could have been reached in four days by a more direct line from Rahama.

I speak of "The Pagans of the Plateau," but the term should be understood to comprise a number off it. There are two reasons for the extension. First, some tribes are spread from the Plateau to the lower land, and, secondly, it is better that certain of the customs and practices should not be precisely located, for, notwithstanding they are known to the higher British authorities, no Resident or other official would wish them placed to his discredit by people unaware how limited were his resources. It is not realised at home that large tracts of the country are no more than nominally occupied, and it would be unreasonable to expect that close supervision and control of social habits are to be effected by an Assistant Resident responsible for a district extending to anything between 5,000 square miles and 10,000 square miles, where he is expected to maintain peace between sections mutually yearning to fight; where he exercises magisterial functions and enforces sentence; where he has to collect taxes from quarters none too willing to pay; and where, to carry out these duties with force and pressure additional to his own personality, he has a garrison of 10 native policemen. If he failed to do all these things he would be sharply called to account by the Governor of Northern Nigeria; and if in his zeal to do any of them he caused a rising that needed troops to repress, then he would be asked why he could not, like others, accomplish his task without requiring the use of the military.

There are dozens to whom the description applies. I shall presently show part of an Assistant Resident's functions in operation and an estimate can then be formed of what these men do in Britain's name for the people placed in their charge. Every one with whom I came in contact was imbued with the desire to administer the principles of humanity and justice between man and man, or man and woman, and to do so in a common-sense spirit.

This preamble is given so that readers may not be unduly shocked at the introduction of cannibalism, especially at the fact that the diet is indulged in merrily in a British colony. Other customs are given precedence.

CHAPTER XXX

IN A PAGAN TOWN

Bukuru Residency—Bukuru town—Its ingenious defences—Traps for an attacking force—The blacksmith—Musical instruments—Pagan orchestras—A royal male Pavlova—The Court band—A King's reward—Pagan homesteads—The sleeping apartment—Farming—Incentives to obtain money—Enhancing nature's charms—Male and female decorations—Bareback and bitless horsemanship—Races—Care of horses—The hunt—Sign language.

AT Bukuru is the post of an Assistant Resident, typical of several. Formerly no Hausa would dare to penetrate so far into the Pagan country or within a week's march of this part. Now there is a Hausa market established within sight of the highway, for the convenience of caravans passing through.

About half-a-mile away is the Residency, a ramshackle mud dwelling not nearly as good as a farmer's stable in England. Living in such places, out of sight and out of mind of the public at home, badly housed, these Residents are paid immeasurably less than the value of the service they render the nation. A few feet from the entrance, at the top of a thin flagstaff planted in the ground, a Union Jack flutters. It is the symbol of a power—accepted by faith rather than by sight—strong enough to enforce peace and to hold the scales evenly in disputes brought to its representative.

Two miles from the Residency is the nearest Pagan town, that of Bukuru. It is not situated, as some are, in the mountains or on a high hill. It spreads, roughly, six miles by two, on ground slightly above the level of the surrounding country. But the approach is impossible to traverse without a guide. Nearly a mile before the first batch of houses is reached you enter a narrow avenue of cactus. Not the form of plant seen in English public parks but strong trees clustered from the ground to the crown with thick, hard leaves each edged with a dozen or more prongs sharp enough to tear a man's clothes and his flesh to ribbons. These cactus trees are planted so closely that, the branches interweaving, you cannot see between them. The top ones cross and intertwine, forming a tunnel 15 feet high.

It was a scheme of defence in the days when a swarm of Hausa horsemen might swoop on a Pagan town and overwhelm it. The cactus avenue is planned on the principle of a maze. It winds, twists, turns, has branching courses leading to blind alleys where the sides are too close to allow a horse to be turned: a perfect ambush. Other narrow ways take you back to places you have passed in coming inwards, the design having been to bring the front sections of a hostile column of mounted men, hurrying on, face-to-face with the middle or the rear sections of the force, who would also be impetuously pushing forward, anxious to be clear of the trap in as short a time as possible.

The confusion produced is easily imagined. From the side walls of cactus through which the Hausas could not break, even with the weight of their

APPROACH TO A PAGAN TOWN.
A maze of impenetrable cactus. (See page 248.)

A PAGAN HOMESTEAD.
Built against a rock to prevent rear attacks. (See page 251.)

IN A PAGAN TOWN

horses, the Pagans sent showers of poisoned arrows, galloping on ponies from point to point as the situation required.

Nearer to the town the cactus sides compress to almost touch your elbows as you sit in the saddle; and, making it still more difficult for hostile horsemen who had managed to get so far to either go on quickly or to retreat, the pathway slopes into trench-form, sufficiently deep to reach to a horse's knees and with so little width that the animal cannot stand with the forelegs side-by-side and therefore must keep moving. An enemy forced to fight in such quarters would be helpless.

No wonder those Pagans of the Plateau maintained their towns inviolate against the raiding Moslem tribes.

Having passed through the cactus maze we are entering the town. The first house differs from the others further on, not only in size, but in use. It is about 15 feet in diameter and is the only place of business in the town. It belongs to the blacksmith. The spade-hoe, spear points, broad swords and knives, the jointed bar which is placed on the nose and under the chin of a horse, a small bell that hangs from the pony's neck, these are the manufactures. All are of iron. The metal is obtained by smelting ironstone, but customers must bring their own charcoal, so scarce is fuel. Payment is by accha, the native grain.

Everything else each Pagan produces for himself, though there are exchanges, such as a man who has aptitude for making musical instruments swopping one to a neighbour good at, say, shaping pipes.

Musical appurtenances range from a harp, 20 inches by 8 inches, made entirely of reeds, and drums, to wind instruments of a score variety: flutes, piccoloes and an article resembling an orange which is hollowed, hardened and three holes bored on top thus: °o°. The bottom one is whistled through, fingers placed on the smaller holes regulating the sound.

Every village has its band and no orchestra is without a drum. Tunes are beyond the comprehension of white men, but undoubtedly the Pagan learns on some distinct principle. Usually the music is of a low, sing-song tune. A common practice is for the performers to form a circle and walk behind one another whilst playing, which increases the monotony of the music.

I have, however, heard spirited, enlivening airs, as at Fedderi, where the Chief, or King, of the Jarawa tribe performed a skirt dance in honour of my visit. Gathered round was "a large and appreciative audience" of his own folks. The old Chief's everyday dress does not err in the direction of excess, but, to constitute himself a royal male Pavlova, he donned a Hausa robe, which was kept at his hut exclusively for the purpose. The musical accompaniment was "by special request" rendered by the Court band, who wore their State uniform. What that was can be seen from the photograph facing this page. The dance proved really entertaining, and, like the music, developed on settled lines; it was not a mere inconsequent throwing about of the limbs.

I gave each of the instrumentalists a threepenny-bit and the King a shilling. His Majesty was so

PAGAN FARMER USING HIS ONLY IMPLEMENT, A SPADE-HOE.
(See page 253.)

THE KING OF THE JARAWA PAGANS DANCING IN HONOUR
OF THE AUTHOR'S VISIT.
The accompaniment is by his Court band, in State uniform. (See page 250.)

IN A PAGAN TOWN

overjoyed at this munificence that I believe I could have made a treaty of alliance, with any clauses I liked, straightway. I mean a treaty in the domain of diplomacy, not of matrimony. That has been offered to me times out of number in West Africa.

A few hundred feet beyond the blacksmith's establishment we are abreast of the first cluster of houses. The scattered Pagan settlements are called towns for want of a better title. They could as well be spoken of as big villages. Bukuru is one of the largest.

A single family, perhaps two, will have its own plot of about a quarter-of-an-acre. This is enclosed by a fence of cactus, not nearly so formidable as the outer defences of the town; merely to prevent marauding sheep, goats and dogs of neighbours from enjoying themselves on the cultivated part of the compound.

The ring-fence used to be stronger in days when the lust of combat induced disputes between a couple of men to result in an assault on the domicile of one of them, though, if blood did not boil too rapidly, the disputants usually agreed to fight out their differences at a suitable spot away from the dwellings, so that the friends of each party could have a hand in the fun.

A Pagan homestead comprises a cluster of huts. Whereas the Hausa house may consist of one room screened by hanging mats into two or more compartments—though, among the well-to-do in cities such as Kano and Zaria the buildings have interior walls making distinct rooms—the Pagan has a separate hut for each part of his daily life. They are small, circular, very neat, about six or eight feet in diameter, of mud with a roof of the same material lightly covered with thatch. One or more will be the grain store, where the gathered crops are kept and drawn upon for food whilst others are growing. The supply is reached from the top, by tilting the roof, which makes thieving less easy than if there were a door. The solid wall also prevents insects getting through. To safeguard the contents against ants the grain huts are built on big stones and are placed high enough for the fowls to take shelter from storms and to go to roost at night.

Various members of a family have different huts for sleeping; the younger children in one, grown-ups in another, and possibly an aged parent of wife or husband in a third. His spouses will be accommodated either singly or in couples and the requisite number of huts built.

In the centre of the cluster of huts meals are prepared and the evening one eaten round a fire. At many parts of the Pagan country wood is scarce. Fuel consists of dried cattle-dung and sapless cactus. A leaf or grass without moisture takes the place of the English kitchenmaid's paper for lighting the fire. Flame is obtained by striking flint on a bit of iron or focussing the sun's rays by means of a piece of glass, probably part of a broken bottle dropped by some Hausa miles away and picked up in the fields. Where a Hausa village, which always means a market as well, is near, matches are being introduced.

As the keen, evening air strikes chilly, the family huddle round the fire, and, shortly after eating, retirement to rest takes place. A 86° or higher temperature when the sun is up falls in the dark hours to 44° or less.

No lights are used in the houses. Lamps are unknown. How, then, is warmth gained during the cold night? People who wear no clothes by day are not likely to don pyjamas or fancy bedgowns. Civilisation has not touched them to the use of a blanket, like the Hausas.

When sleeping huts are built a broad shelf of mud is made to the wall. This is the couch of repose. Under it a fire is lit, and, every crevice of the doorway being closely covered, temperature soon rises. There is no ventilation whatever, so the smoke disposes of any mosquitoes and other insects, though I should say that the carbonic thickness of the atmosphere would alone effect the purpose. The marvel is for any soul to emerge alive. Asphyxiation seems certain. Yet I gathered from the Pagans that they enjoy the hours in comfort and tranquillity.

In the plot of ground in front of the huts small vegetables are grown: a kind of kitchen-garden and kept scrupulously clean. I have looked over dozens of plots without finding a single weed in any.

The farm land is not in the towns. It may be four to eight miles away. A man, riding a pony, goes to his farm in the morning when the sun has made its warmth felt and remains at work until about 4 o'clock in the afternoon. The pony is not tethered. A hobble-rope is put on two legs and the animal allowed to wander. A bell attached to the neck indicates its whereabouts to the owner, who occasionally has to penetrate through grass higher than himself to bring back the steed. The heavier work of the field, such as hoeing, is done by the farmer and his sons, whilst the ladies of the household assist at sowing and reaping and alone do the weeding. That arrangement applies both in the farm land and the compound adjoining the dwelling. But the feminine units are expected to walk to their tasks. The wife on domestic duty goes out with the food for her husband and for those of his other wives and sons and daughters who are with him on the farm.

The main crop is accha. There are also an inferior kind of guinea-corn known as magaragara, which grows about 4 feet high, douro, gwaza, doiya, tamba, risga and tobacco, which is smoked in long pipes by both men and women. In some parts the ladies do not smoke; they chew tobacco. Bees are kept in hives of mud, and though there are few flowers, honey is obtained plentifully.

A pony is not possessed by every farmer, and at first it is a strange sight that of a farmer walking to or from his ground with a string of four or five wives, the party in single file and absolutely no clothing on any of them.

The Hausa is a skilled agriculturist, who has nothing to learn in that respect from any white race. He, however, is distanced considerably by the Pagan, who tends his land cleaner. The soil is much poorer than that of the Hausa country and needs greater skill and effort for cultivation. At present the Pagan raises only sufficient for his own requirements, which besides the matter of food remain small. When he and his womenkind yearn for the gee-gaws of what is termed civilisation, and he wants money to purchase them, then he will make

IN A PAGAN TOWN

more use of the nearest Hausa market to transform his corn or other produce into cash. So far, the principal luxuries which attract most Pagans are matches and cigarettes. In some places the people are developing a taste for meat, for which, of course, money must be earned. Though sheep, goats and, in instances, cattle are bred, seldom are any killed for food. They represent a man's wealth and in the owner's view it would be rank heresy against political economy to consume them.

There is a large open space—three or four acres—in Bukuru town. Nobody farms the ground, nor is it used for individual purpose. There the people foregather for public celebrations, which take place at least twice a year. Events that prompt these assemblies are gleaning of the farm crops and other agricultural periods in the calendar. Then it is that the fashions of Bukuru can be seen in all their glory.

Clothing does not enter into the pageantry. Paint is the agent employed to enhance nature's charms. Earth and tree-bark are ground into a red paste and with it the fair young dames cover between the ankle to below the knee, where a narrow white colouring marks fhe limit of the decoration. Only this; nothing more.

Men dab the red paint on chest and nose and also use it on their ponies. More attention is bestowed on the animals than the owners give themselves. The hindquarters are painted red on which, at equal distances, white circles the size of a five-shilling piece are superimposed. The breast of the horse may likewise be embellished with red pigment, and on its face brass ornaments or a band of the same metal across the forehead are fixed for festive parades.

No stirrup or saddle is used, though on show days a piece of goatskin is put on the horse's back as a decoration, not for utility or comfort. Nor is a bit utilised. A light iron, jointed, across the nose and another under the jaw are connected by a ring on the left-hand side of the head. To that ring a single grass rope is joined, passing under the animal's neck and held in the hand of the rider. By that means a horse is pulled up and partly guided. Its movements left and right are regulated by the rider's feet in the inner side of the forelegs.

The equestrian will perhaps have a plait of straw encircling his head or possibly wear a hat of the same material. Besides half-a-dozen spears in his hand, he will likely carry a long knife or sword in a brass sheath hanging from his waist. A grass bag in the left side, suspended from the right shoulder, provides a receptacle for trophies of the chase or any other article, such as a pipe.

At the public assemblies at the open spaces everybody who has a horse brings it. The men ride in line and in file, throwing themselves into various attitudes to amuse the crowd.

Short races take place across the 1,000 yards or so of ground. There is no settled plan for the contest. One of a group challenges another, and at once off they dash, most likely accompanied by a third or fourth who heard the summons. On pulling up the chances are there will be pushing, either as a joke or in the course of a dispute as to which has won. Then spears are flourished and a thrust is almost a certainty, though seldom is there

A NAKED PAGAN RIDING HIS PONY BAREBACKED.
(See page 255.)

PAGAN HORSEMEN.
(See page 255.)

more damage than a slight flesh wound. The day winds up with a general carouse, in which the local-made beer has a leading rôle.

Bukuru men are excellent horsemasters. The appearance and condition of the animals are better than those belonging to Hausas elsewhere and are equal to any except the very best kept by Englishmen. Horses belonging to others which were lame or would not thrive have been taken by the Bukuru people, who returned the animals in first-class health and fettle. They will not disclose the details of their methods. One includes hot water drunk by the horse and another is that of salt and other ingredients made into a ball which the animal is forced to swallow.

The Pagan hunt is a mild performance. It takes place in the dry season. The high grass is burnt and the flames beaten out when sufficient space has been cleared. Some distance from the clearance the grass is again fired, whilst the huntsmen, waiting on their ponies for the rats and lizards which dart out, spear the vermin. A few small, bush deer are obtained in the same way. A free fight is not an uncommon wind-up to the hunt.

The folks of Bukuru are people of few words, signs being largely used instead of speaking, though, estimating from the number of wives acquired in some quarters, I should say that the language of love must be an extremely easy dialect.

To express "No" in the sense of there being none, the right forefinger is brought past, touching, the lips, at which the slightest semblance to a whistling sound is made.

"I do not know," such as the answer to where a person is for whom the questioned individual has regard, is replied to by raising the shoulders.

"I do not know and I do not care" is conveyed by the open hands and the forearm at right-angle to the upper limb.

Answer respecting the age of anyone not the person questioned is made by the fist held vertically at a distance from the ground, indicating the height of the individual, from which illustration the age has to be gauged. The people have no sense of calculation beyond four or five years.

A gift or anything given in payment is usually received without word or sign. Should it be sufficiently liberal to impel stronger feeling the equivalent of "Thank you" will probably be uttered. Should the recipient be stimulated to add emphasis he will say "Mr feng"—the first word pronounced Mer—translated, "I rejoice," and with the elbows of bent arms strike the ribs repeatedly.

The figures in the photographs which exemplify the sign language were placed at my disposal by the kindness of Mr E. Evans, one of the two men of the Sudan United Mission station in Bukuru. The natives were in his service, which accounts for wearing so much clothing and also, possibly, for their rather fleshy appearance. The Pagan working in the fields is lean, wiry, active, yet strong and healthy.

What is to be said of this mission station planted in the heart of the country of wild tribes? Medical attendance is given, and it was pathetic to see the look of appeal by women, children and men who

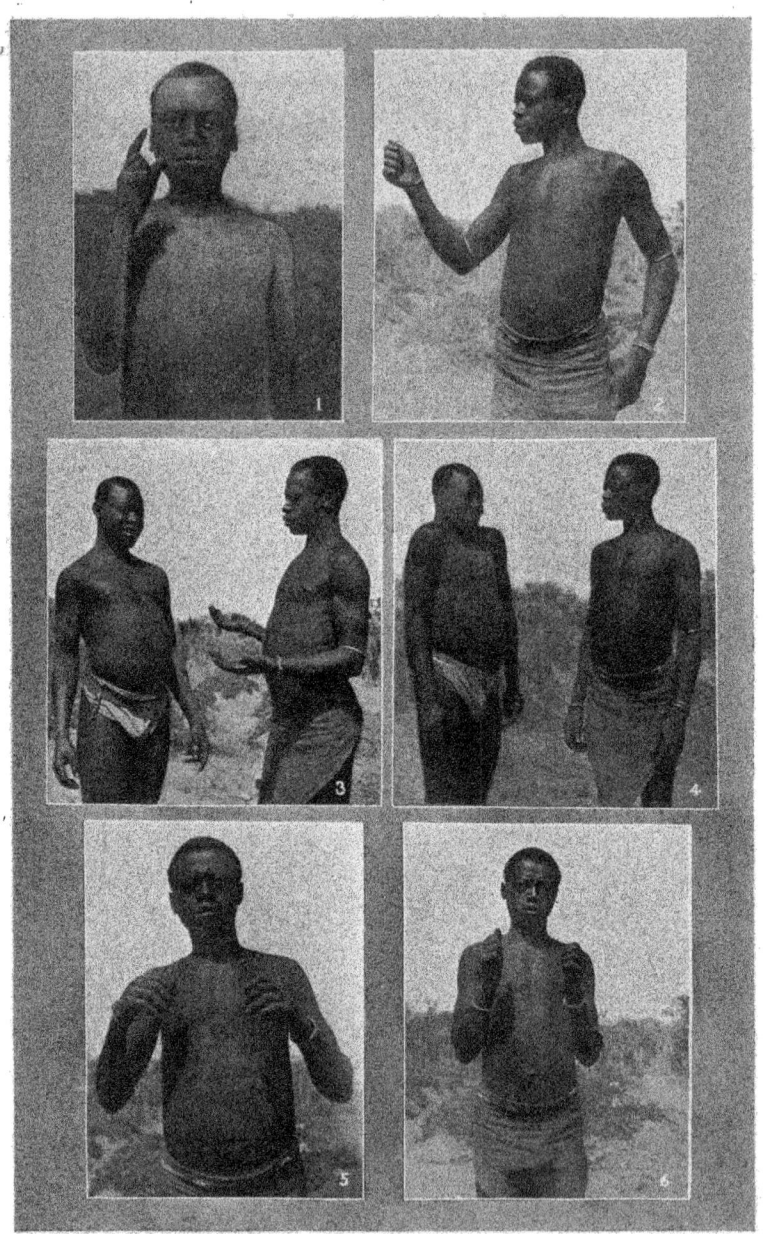

BUKURU PAGAN SIGN LANGUAGE.

(1) "No." (2) Indicating a person's age. (3) "Don't know and don't care." (4) "Don't know." (5) Gratitude. (6) Large numbers expressed by beating the fists together. (See page 257.)

came for wounds and ulcerous parts to be washed. Several young natives had been trained to the use of the antiseptic syringe and dressing and they carried out that part of the treatment after a case had been looked at by one of the white men. In this humanitarian course the mission is doing angel's work, though I cannot refrain from wondering if it was necessary to go so far afield for needful patients. As to the religious aspect, I cannot understand why this out-of-the-way part of the world was sought to spiritualise the heathen whilst so many of that description abound in Great Britain.

CHAPTER XXXI

ADMINISTERING JUSTICE AND TAXATION

Direct rule—Cases in a Resident's Court—Wife and "another man"—Trial by ordeal—Modification of that method—Kidnapping for slaves—"The liberty of the subject"—Extenuating circumstances and even-handed justice—Benefits that are not welcomed—The joy of fighting—Graduated taxation—How to express numerals to people who have no such terms—Two tax collectors—First lessons in administration.

POSSESSING no corporate existence or regular system of government the Pagans must therefore be ruled in a direct way by the British. The authority and influence of their Kings and Chiefs vary and is seldom strong and capable of being exercised in accordance with equity and humanitarian principles. Where in touch, the Residents are endeavouring to stimulate them to accept responsibility, but it must necessarily be a slow process, as the men shirk incurring unpopularity and dislike among their own people by discharging unpleasant tasks. At present the main thing is to prevent fighting, which until recently was the usual manner of settling a dispute, either between individuals or 'twixt tribe and tribe. Tribal warfare had become a recognised part of existence. Quarrels had engendered aloofness to such an extent that to-day there are villages 15 miles apart which do not understand each other's dialect.

JUSTICE AND TAXATION

The British have endeavoured to impress on the Pagan that any quarrel which cannot be composed amicably must be brought to the nearest Resident, who acts the part not merely of Judge but also that of friendly adviser.

Whilst at Bukuru I spent two mornings in the Court held by the Resident, Mr S. E. M. Stobart—he has the rank of Assistant Resident—and what was seen will perhaps give an idea of one portion of the excellent work performed by the British political officers in these all but unknown areas of Northern Nigeria.

The first case was that of an elderly Pagan who complained that a young wife of his had gone to the house of " another man," who struck him when he went to interview and claim the lady. Mr Stobart sent one of his native staff to make enquiries. The report put a fresh complexion on the story. True the girl was living in the house of " another man " and he had assaulted the veteran Benedick; but the girl was his daughter and she had sought refuge from the ill-usage of her husband. Mr Stobart told the complainant that when he was satisfied the young woman would be properly treated she would be ordered to return; not until.

The next suit dealt with a plot of farming land near Bukuru. Each of the two men claimed it. As tribal convention tinged with a dozen local considerations would be a determining factor guiding a conclusion, the Resident had referred the question to the sub-chiefs of the respective wards in which the men lived. Previous to the advent of the British, if a fight had not been desired the issue would be tried by ordeal. At the direction of a

Chief, poison would be prepared by a medicine man for both parties, which they would swallow, and the one who survived or better resisted the effect of the draught would be adjudged the award.

Trial by ordeal is now strictly prohibited, but until the Pagan people have developed more intelligent methods a substitute remains unbanned. This consists of each party to a dispute providing a fowl, which is given poison. The owner of the surviving bird secures the verdict. It is a process not encouraged by the British Residents, who strive to make the leading men decide matters on their merits.

The two sub-chiefs had come to say they could not agree—no doubt because neither was willing to give decree against a person in his own section of the village—and they thought trial by fowls would be the best way of reaching a satisfactory conclusion. Mr Stobart pointed out that when he had to solve a difficult case he did not call for two fowls and that sub-chiefs of such intelligence should be able to rely on their own brains. He would not sanction the use of fowls. They must themselves judge and bring adjudication to him within three days. They promised to have another try.

A young Pagan presented himself to the Resident and stated he had been twice sold into slavery. His story was that whilst working on his farm he was seized by a Hausa, taken several days' journey and disposed of for two horses. The vendor explained to his victim that he had to do it owing to severe need and told the sufferer that if he escaped —giving a scheme by which he might—and came to the captor he would see that the captive got home safely with at least part recompense for

JUSTICE AND TAXATION

what he would have endured. The unsophisticated Pagan did escape and came back, whereupon he was again made prisoner and sold for three horses. A second time he escaped, and having learnt wisdom he went to the Resident of his district, who sent for the accused Hausa and committed him for trial by a higher Court. If found guilty he would forfeit the five horses to the injured party and be liable to five years' imprisonment.

Although slave-raiding on the scale practised a few years ago is now impossible, kidnapping and slave-dealing is by no means stamped out. One plan is by various pretexts to induce individuals or a family to journey to some place near the French or the German frontier and sell them over either border, where apparently the crime is not regarded nearly so seriously as by the British authorities.

There had been a party of Hausas who caught young fellows, sent them by go-betweens along routes off the main track to confederates north of Sokoto, by whom the captives were sold over the French boundary. When the English authorities first learnt part of the scheme they kept quite quiet until the whole plan and those engaged in it were known. Then, suddenly, descents were made simultaneously at both ends and all the principals and their subordinates arrested. Evidence was overwhelming. The main offenders are serving five years' hard labour.

A slave case of a different character came before Mr Stobart whilst I was at Bukuru. In this instance it was a Pagan who was charged with having in his house, prisoner, a boy, son of a Fulani. The lad had been in charge of a herd of travelling cattle which instead of keeping together and on the move whilst going through cultivated ground had been allowed to stray among the Pagan's accha crops. To his remonstrances the youngster answered defiantly. The farmer marched the boy off and informed his father that the child would not be given up until compensation for the damage was forthcoming. The Fulani went to Mr Stobart, who sent his police for all the parties and, having heard what they had to say, delivered judgment, in effect, as follows: The Pagan had done serious wrong by interfering with the "liberty of the subject." Technically he had made the boy a slave and therefore was liable to severe punishment, especially as he should have known that redress was always exacted for damaged crops. However, taking into consideration the provocation, for every day he had held the lad prisoner he must go to prison for 4, making 16 in all. On the other hand, the Fulani was responsible for not taking care that his cattle were controlled in a way that would prevent them damaging the crops of the Pagan and therefore the order was for him to pay all the compensation claimed.

A case which arose from a similar cause was that of a Pagan having speared a Fulani in the leg. Only a flesh wound had been inflicted. The Fulani's bullocks, passing the farm of the Pagan, had eaten his growing guinea-corn. The sentence of the Resident was that although the Pagan suffered a grievance he had no right to take the remedy into his own hands and would accordingly be fined eight spears—all he possessed—whilst the Fulani, who should have precluded his animals straying off the path, must requite the complete damage specified.

I gathered that Mr Stobart uniformly exacts full compensation for damage by cattle to Pagans' crops, as, being only agriculturists, their crops are their all-in-all. The award is made even when a Pagan is punished for retaliating. Further, now that the Fulani, the Hausa and similar tribes have right of passage through Pagan country, not infrequently going with herds of cattle, they must understand that the property of the inhabitants has to be scrupulously respected.

Another Pagan was charged with slightly spearing in three places a Hausa living in the public market recently opened near the highway path a few miles from Bukuru. The Pagan, evidently excited from indulgence in the native beer, had attempted to pass through the Hausa's house, and, the occupier barring the way, declared he would go where he pleased. On the Hausa advancing, the trespasser struck him as stated. A hue and cry was raised and the Pagan made off across the fields, throwing away his spears to facilitate progress. I saw the fugitive running, with a large, gladiator-like sword unsheathed. As the pursuing crowd was rounding him up he cast off the sword, was arrested and at once taken before the Resident.

The case was heard patiently, the situation illustrated by rough diagrams drawn on the earth floor, as the Pagan asserted it was a " near cut " through the house to his village. Mr Stobart asked what he would say if a Hausa endeavoured to go into his house without permission. The Pagan answered that that was different. He was convicted without extenuating circumstances of any provocation and received the light sentence of 14 days' imprisonment, which merely meant being kept under restraint, not sent a long journey to a prison. He would be set to gardening work in the Residency compound. But the four spears and the sword thrown away were confiscated, as it was against orders for men to be in the public market carrying such weapons; for obvious reasons, though no notice is taken if the people pass along the centre path and do not stop.

A Resident's duties are by no means confined to exercising judicial functions. He has to collect taxes, which are no more popular among the wild Pagans of Northern Nigeria than is the rule in English cities. Most of the tribes never experienced a requisition until recent days. Still, it is desirable that, either as tribes or individuals, they should pay. It is the most convincing lesson of the power of the ruler. They have value for the impost. Peace and security for life and property are maintained. The Fulani and others are prohibited from swooping down with armies of cavalry to raid the country for slaves, and inter-tribal warfare among the Pagans themselves is sternly forbidden. But, sooth to say, these benefits are not welcomed. The people do not thank us for them. They would infinitely prefer to be without taxation and to take their chance. They say that over very large tracts of country, particularly on and around the Bauchi Plateau, they were well able to take care of themselves against Fulani, Hausa and the kind, who would not venture in the area; whilst as to fighting among themselves, why, it was that which made life worth living.

JUSTICE AND TAXATION

Efforts of the Residents have been to persuade unwilling tribes to accept the principle of taxation; to get in the thin edge of the wedge, as it were. Reasonable increase can be made as the British control becomes firmer. Taxation of the Pagans therefore ranges from a goat paid yearly by a village of between 700 and 800 inhabitants to 2s. 6d. annually per male adult of other villages.

A taxation census is taken where that can be done without using troops. Only an approximate result is obtained. The Resident goes to a village and notes the compounds, asking how many men live in each. The people cannot count nor express themselves in numerals. They have names for figures up to 10 but do not give them with confidence after 5. They may be able to speak of 6, 7, 8 or 9, though not at all sure. At the figure of 10 they are, as that simply means two 5's. The fingers of one hand keep the mind fresh up to the lower number. As Mr Stobart goes through the villages of the Bukuru division he collects at each village a small bag of stones and uses them as denomination for questions relating to figures. I saw an answer given in that form as to the number of wives a man had. Fortunately the bag of pebbles was ample for the expression.

The same method is employed in conveying details of taxation. One day I was in the circular mud hut which Mr Stobart has as his Court and office and some taxes were brought in from Bukuru village. Village Chiefs are appointed for the collection, so that by degrees they may learn simple administration. They are given 10 per cent. of the amount gathered. Recalcitrant individuals are reported to the Resident, who takes measures to make them do as their neighbours. The usual method is to send a couple of native police early in the morning to bring in the defaulters. They are told that if payment be not forthcoming in a reasonable period certain of their goods, such as a goat or a horse, will be confiscated.

Bukuru village is taxed at 1s. per adult annually. On the occasion referred to, the sections whose payments the two Chiefs had brought should have yielded £5. The amount counted on the ground, in shillings, was £1, 10s. short. The couple of worthy gatherers, who probably wondered why in their mature years they should be afflicted with the mental worries of revenue and finance, were made to understand by means of 30 small stones that there was that quantity of backsliders who must be made to toe the monetary line or the names given to the Resident. They went home, I believe animated by the honest desire to do their best. But this tax-gathering must be a sore trouble to the Pagan village Chiefs, who formerly never knew the need of money and who regarded wealth only as represented by horses, sheep, goats or oxen.

In no instance is taxation oppressive, harsh or even hard to pay. Corn is easily grown by the Pagans, and the sale of a single sackful produces a year's tax on the highest scale. The establishment of Hausa markets on the main caravan paths provide places where the corn is sold easily. The markets have been made possible by the British declaration that neither Hausa nor Pagan shall attack the other.

MR. S. E. M. STOBART,
THE RESIDENT AT BUKURU, AND HIS STAFF.
(See page 261.)

BUKURU RESIDENCY.
(See page 247.)

CHAPTER XXXII

MARRIAGE AND DEATH CUSTOMS

Fashions—A wedding-ring warning—The former way with undesirables—Succession to a Chiefship—Marriage—Dowries—A perpetual leap-year—Widows—Burial usages—Cannibalism—Eating those who die from natural causes—Etiquette of the practice—A credit and debit account:

IN referring to social customs of the Pagans on and just off the Bauchi Plateau it is desirable to survey the subject comprehensively in order to avoid repetition and overmuch detail. First, fashions. Little can be said on that topic. Men in the outer districts, who for some time have been more-or-less in contact with the Hausa people, rejoice in a loin-cloth, and, in a few instances, a short, loose shirt which once was white, whilst the women wear a large bunch of leaves in front and another at the back. Towards and in the inner areas of the Pagan country transition of male attire is abrupt to nothingness.

As one travels through the country one sees that the ladies of the various tribes exercise more gradation. Change is not so sudden. The two fronds of leaves give place to one, which is worn either fore or aft, according to individual fancy. Further on, a bunch of grass stalks, six inches long, secured by a string round the body, hanging behind and looking like a table crumb-brush, constitutes the sole extraneous adornment to the female form divine.

Then, presently, even so much is not used. In some of these last areas, during the first few months of married life the matron dons a thin plait of skin or grass round the waist, as a kind of wedding-ring, probably to warn all and sundry gallants that henceforth they may not pay their court to her. In one large village I saw some unmarried girls each with a walking-out costume consisting of a small bell, made by the native blacksmith, tied by a string round the loins and suspended in front tinkling.

The absence of any corporate government, civil or military, among the Pagans makes getting into touch with the people a slow and tedious process. They never, like the Fulani and Hausa tribes, had police, prisons and other adjuncts for ruling. Questions that affected the community were decided by public opinion. If there were persons who were a danger or a nuisance, the villagers assembled and settled what was to be done to the delinquents. They might deny an indictment and be tried " by ordeal "; or, waiving that test, the verdict would be death or being despatched to the Hausa country and sold for slaves. Pagan villages and hamlets which paid annual tribute of slaves to the Fulani Emirites disposed of their own desirables in that way, filling up the quota by raiding other villages.

There are Pagan " Kings " and Chiefs, but their

MARRIAGE AND DEATH CUSTOMS 271

authority in many instances is slight and always confined to a limited area. The Burrum tribe—one of the largest—comprises 26 large villages, called towns, each with a separate and independent Chief. The regulations for succession to a chiefship are not uniform in all tribes. At Burrum towns the eldest brother of a deceased Chief takes his place; in the absence of eligible brothers, the son of the defunct occupies the post. With the Jarawas, the Headmen of a town elect a Chief from the family of the last one. It is usually the eldest brother. The Rukuba Chiefs, whose authority is stronger than in most Pagan tribes, nominate their successors, which is either a son or a brother, according to preference.

Marriage is of extreme simplicity in most quarters. The Teria folks, although so isolated in their lives that no other village speaks their language, are not alone in the manner of mating up. With them merely a nominal dowry passes for a wife. But no woman of theirs has more than two children, and as infantile mortality runs its course the town is rapidly becoming depopulated.

The word dowry is used, though among all the tribes of Nigeria where the usage prevails it is payment by the husband to the girl's father or guardian.

The Jarawas have no regular dowry system. "Free love" is carried to the most extreme line and no claim by a man to a woman is allowed. When, however, a swain from another tribe comes wooing his affinity in this one he has to pay a dowry of a horse and five goats and then, in the event of infidelity of his wife, he is held to have a claim against his father-in-law.

The Rukubas do not understand chastity on the part of unmarried girls. This tribe also has no regular practice of dowry, which is quite formal: perhaps either some beans, a hoe, two goats, pots, or 10 calabashes. If a wife leaves her husband he seeks out a discontented couple and pairs off with the lady.

The Burrum population honour a rigid dowry scheme, which consists of payment of a horse and five goats. Marriage is not recognised until the dowry has been paid. If a couple elect to go in double domestic harness without that preliminary, all children born to them can be claimed by the woman's father. Should a wife desert her husband for another, he must pay the original consort the counterpart of the dowry. Failure to do so, or husband number 1 declining to accept the solatium, children born to the couple are forfeit to the grass widower. Their value is apparent. The girls would be a source of potential wealth to whoever gave them in marriage, whilst the boys could be set to work on the farm from an early age.

With the Angass tribe courting is a perpetual leap-year, for the girl selects the husband and tells her mother whom she has chosen. Of course, Barkis must be willing, as the dowry is from 20 to 30 sheep. Provided the prospective bridegroom is agreeable, he liquidates the dowry by instalments, leaving about seven sheep to be paid when the girl is to go to him. That is decided by her mother, upon which the balance is handed over. There is no special wedding ceremony. The marriage tie is

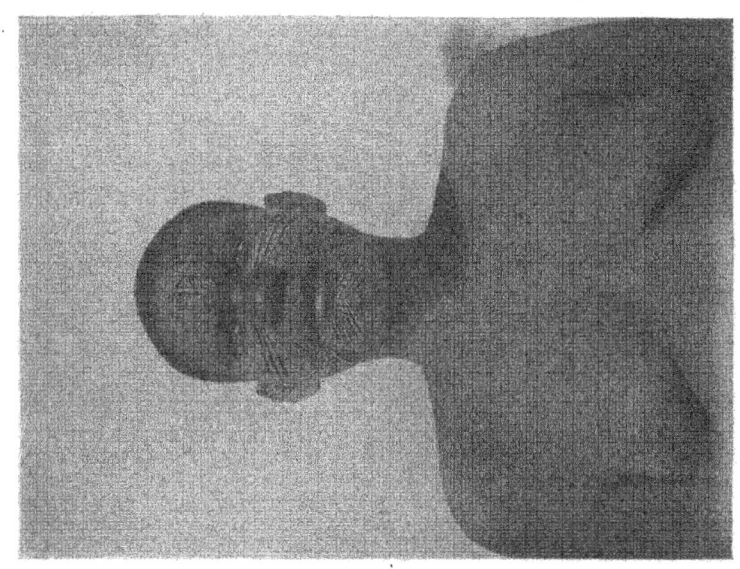

A PAGAN BEAUTY OF THE DASS TRIBE.
The incisions on the face are tribal marks.

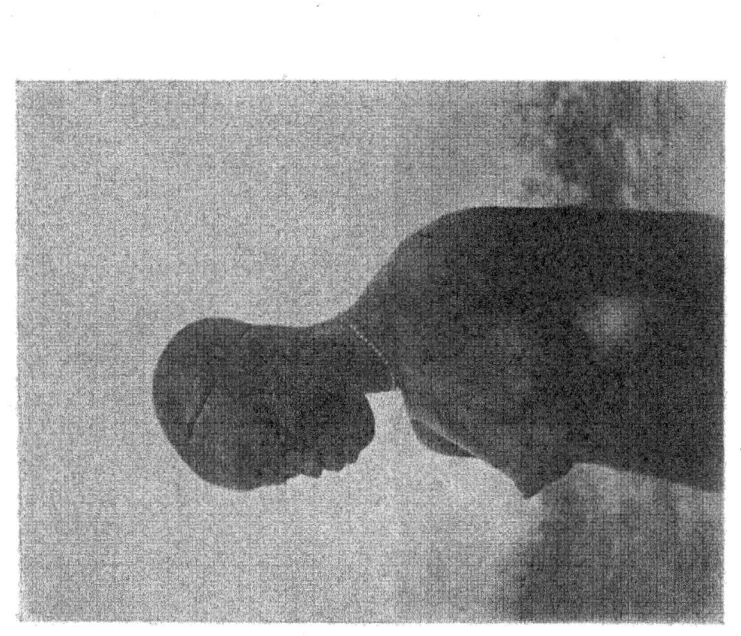

GIRL OF THE JARAWA TRIBE.
The cuts on the face are made when she reaches the age of puberty.

MARRIAGE AND DEATH CUSTOMS

a loose one. If the girl does not find her husband congenial she is free to leave him, but her parents or the next husband refund the dowry. Until she marries again she is at liberty to distribute her qualities as a wife to whom she likes and to as many as she pleases.

In this tribe no marriages are permitted among blood relatives or even with those connected by family.

On the demise of a father who has grown-up sons, in most tribes his possessions pass to them. A widow becomes the property of the eldest of any sons the deceased husband may have had by another wife. At times this works out that the widows are divided up among the sons. It may be assumed that the practice is a hardship on the head of the household which takes in the widow. By no means. The man who wishes to marry her has to pay dowry to her guardian, and, in the meantime, or if she is on his hands altogether, a woman is always welcomed to help in the field or to relieve another from cooking for that purpose. As a matter of fact, unless quite aged, widows go off splendidly. They are usually a thorough success. As was explained to me on a previous journey by a Chief in another country who offered a rather ancient matrimonial gift from his own ample store, it is not always the youngest who are the most tractable or industrious.

On the death of a widow having a young family her property, i.e., the children, go to her husband's brother.

Burial usuages are marked by great diversity,

according to tribal tradition. The Teria tribe, in this as in many observances, is distinct. Mourning is notified by a rope round the loins. The dead are sewn in grass mats. Cooked beans and mai—fat— are buried with him. Ten days later gia—native beer—is poured in the grave. Members of the same family are buried in one grave. When an interment takes place the remains of the preceding occupants are taken out, the latest tenant put in and the disinterred corpses—or what is left of them— placed last. This must be quite an exhilarating and healthful exercise. The top man cannot improve by the repeated handling.

The Jarawa bury anywhere in the bush, a few inches deep, the face of the dead covered with a cloth. There is no regular cemetery.

A Burrum man of position is sewn in the skin of his horse and buried behind his house. Individuals of lesser rank are enclosed in goats' skins and put under ground at a place in the bush kept for that use. The flesh of the animals whose integument has formed the shroud, whether horse or goats, are eaten at the feast which immediately follows the funeral. If a man expresses a wish that his other horses be killed at his death, that is done and the hides buried with him.

The Narubunu tribe consists of four towns, or villages: Buji, Gurrum, Gussum and Jengre. At the last two there is a ceremonious washing of the corpse by the subordinate members of the household of the Madaiki. (It is a Hausa word meaning the second man of the town.) Burial takes place in a large hole in front of the entrance to the Chief's house, resembling a catacomb, which must make it

MARRIAGE AND DEATH CUSTOMS 275

quite a cheerful residence. The corpse is laid on a mat and carefully covered.

But a number of the tribes, more than are assumed, eat their dead who die from natural causes. Possibly you shudder at the thought of a corpse which came to that stage by disease being consumed for food. I admit it does not seem nice, according to our tastes and ideas, but if I am ever to be the dainty served up at a meal I greatly prefer the cannibal company having the feast through my having shuffled off this mortal coil more or less of my own volition, so to speak—by fever or other illness—rather than the diners should hasten the consummation by means of spear or poisoned arrow. If they enjoy the tit-bit, I am sure I shall not mind. The trouble, in the event of any of my friends wishing to make a pilgrimage to the sepulchre, would be locating it.

None of these cannibal gentry ever hunted or specifically killed human beings for food; certainly not in recent times.

The causes which operated to make mortal remains find their way to the cook-pot were that of the vital spark having been quenched in fight; the frame which held it put to death for an offence against the community; or that it gave up life in the ordinary way.

With tribal and inter-tribal wars forbidden and exaction of the death penalty in the hands of the supreme authority, menus in which human flesh figures are now necessarily fewer.

In this eating of the dead there is a certain etiquette. You will appreciate that the pleasure of the palate must be tinged with some sadness, or at least regret, in the knowledge that—assuming you to be a cannibal—your meal is made from the man who lived across the way or further up the path and with whom you had been on visiting terms; whilst obviously there must be some sentiment against consuming one's near relations.

Count is taken of these human traits, and a village which indulges in cannibal luxury will exchange bodies with another village. It occurred to me that mortality would not invariably be equal between the contracting villages and I asked whether a debit and credit account was kept. The question was put jokingly, as I expected the thing would be allowed to work itself level, but I found a rough-and-ready record was kept of the village exports. An epidemic, such as smallpox, may yield quite a harvest of material to the larder—whatever the disease makes no difference to those who sit down to the feast; they are not at all fanciful or capricious—and so pile up the debt beyond chance of quittance within a reasonable period. Therefore a settlement is made at regular periods and the balance defrayed by cows or goats.

The number of bodies is not alone computed. You need not be an epicure in the business to understand that a fully-developed individual who becomes *non est* is, in a table sense, worth several ancient, withered carcases. All this is calculated in the settlement.

There is also a kind of payment in advance, to facilitate the process of exchange. If a village sends a corpse or two, the receiving parties hand over any persons who are very old or extremely ill. That saves the visitors, who have perhaps come

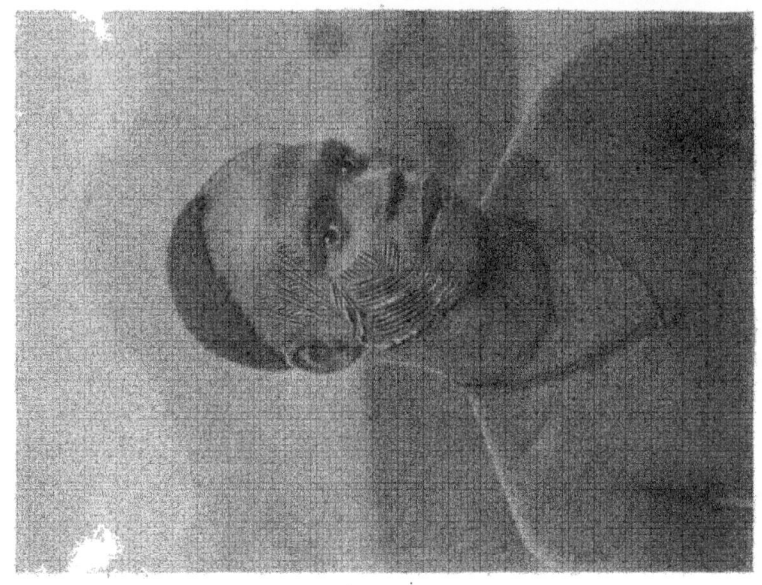

JARAWA PAGANS.
The marks are produced by the flesh being cut and charcoal placed in the incision.

MARRIAGE AND DEATH CUSTOMS 277

5 or 10 miles, a double journey. It is considerate and courteous. Whether the tramp to their new abode improves the health of the departing ones is another question.

Some tribes are gallant enough not to eat women.

CHAPTER XXXIII

SOLDIERS AND THEIR SPORTS

British-trained troops—Little-known Mr Atkins—Swearing-in recruits—Hausa and Pagan oaths—Native priests on active service—Number of wives allowed—Artillery on men's heads—Gun drill—Dipping for toroes—Mounted infantry—Signalling tuition—Teaching the band—Inculcating self-reliance—The military classification of white civilians.

NORTHERN NIGERIA is 255,700 square miles in extent, more than twice the size of the United Kingdom and Ireland. A few years ago nearly the whole of Northern Nigeria, with its 10,000,000 inhabitants, was more or less hostile: at the best, that portion in British occupation no more than sullenly acquiescent to the condition and quite " good enough " to eject the white intruders at a suitable chance. That stage has been passed, and, although a considerable territory remains merely nominally occupied, most of the country has been brought within thorough control. Warlike tribes, spending much of their lives in systematic exercise of arms and periodically engaged in severe battles, have been overthrown. They are now entirely engaged in agriculture or trading. The land is pacified.

The position has been attained without employing as much as a Corporal's guard of white troops as a separate unit. The wonder has been attained by

SOLDIERS AND THEIR SPORTS 279

using natives, not as auxiliaries and in loosely-formed bodies for merely scouting or outpost purposes, but in properly disciplined and strictly supervised regiments prepared to withstand the shock of an onslaught from hordes of formidable warriors. Not least remarkable has been the breaking up in combat of large armies by comparatively small numbers of Nigerian soldiers. The secret of this superiority has been firmness, steadiness in defence, daring in attack; qualities due to British schooling and leading in the field.

The regular military force of Northern Nigeria consists of the 1st and 2nd Battalions Northern Nigeria Regiment, a battery of 6 guns and a company of Mounted Infantry. The corps are entirely unknown by sight in England. They have taken no part in royal processions and a detachment has never figured at the Military Tournament. There are less than 1,000 whites in the whole of Northern Nigeria, and only comparatively few have seen the troops with which we have won the country.

A widely-prevalent practice at home is to speak of West Africa comprehensively, as one would of Europe. There are greater differences between peoples in the former regions, though of the same race, than there are between the Scot and the Turk or the Celt and the Circassian. Neither the West India Regiment—one battalion of which is usually quartered at Sierra Leone—nor the Gold Coast Regiment are Northern Nigeria men, notwithstanding that representatives of the first two sometimes figure in London picture-shop windows as "Our Army in West Africa."

As stated in other chapters, the term Hausa is no more distinctive as a class than is "English" when it embraces the town-bred wastrel of the south and the hefty, pure Highlander of the north. Moreover, Mohamedanism as a faith sits as lightly on large sections of Hausas as the tenets of the Church of England do on many recruits in the United Kingdom. But every regard is paid to whatever scruple a Nigerian may have in the way of sentimental denominationalism. Whether he has any or none he is expected to be true to his oath as a soldier.

On enrolment, therefore, the Mohamedan—orthodox or nominal—is sworn on the Koran; the Pagan on the bayonet. Holding the blade and having expressed in his own tongue the declaration of fealty to the King, he touches the bayonet with his tongue and declares that, should he be false, may it destroy him.

There is no separation in the regiment according to faith. Companies and squads are composite. That system has not given the slightest trouble or difficulty. A "palaver" among them over divinity matters has never occurred. A lay Mohamedan does not seek to proselytise his fellow, and the Pagan is not interested in the devotion of the other. The best of comradeship prevails. If a fairly large number of soldiers go on an expedition, Mallams—priests and religious teachers—are detailed with them for the Mohamedans, as Army Chaplains do on active service with European troops; and if the Mallam, who is under military law, does not attend at the proper times to conduct prayers he must answer for it in the orderly room.

This perspicacious measure was initiated by Sir George Taubman Goldie, the founder of Nigeria, in his advance against Kabba, in 1897, which was the first time Hausas had been called upon to fight people of their own religion. The presence of Mallams counters any attempt to stir up a jehad or to represent a campaign as due to endeavour of the white man forcibly to convert the Mohamedan. It also prevents that argument being used to undermine allegiance of the troops.

Social usages are likewise interfered with as little as possible. The main consideration is that the men shall be made into thoroughly efficient soldiers. That is what they are paid for, and nothing is allowed to interfere. Beyond it their own customs, approved by law, are permitted. Otherwise there would be very poor material in the ranks, for service is quite voluntary.

Marriage prevails practically without exception among adults in West Africa. The Tommy Atkins of Northern Nigeria, like his white comrade here, must obtain permission to take unto himself a wife. Should he do so without that preliminary she is not "on the establishment," in which case he must provide for her living outside the barracks. If the young fellow is well-behaved the Commanding Officer gives permission for matrimony.

Of course there must be a limitation in number. A Private is therefore allowed one wife; a Sergeant, two, and a Sergeant-Major, three; with an additional spouse to individuals in each rank on completion of three years' exemplary service. When I heard of the regulation my early aspiration for a military career recurred strongly. Forgetting the question of race, I reflected that I might rise to be a Sergeant-Major in the Northern Nigeria Regiment.

The regiment has English officers, who are attached for five years. They are assisted by non-commissioned officers from home, locally styled Colour-Sergeants, with a Sergeant-Major as senior. They supervise the barrack-square drill and instruction, which is given by the native non-commissioned officers, who, as has been indicated, can attain the rank of Sergeant-Major.

The guns are carried on the men's heads. As a faithful attendant at many Military Tournaments in London I declare I never saw a smarter bit of work of its kind, either by the best Royal Horse Artillery battery or by picked men of the navy, than was witnessed on the drill ground at Zungeru.

At a whistle signal from the battery commander, Captain Maclaverty, the men advanced about 50 yards, with the guns, in pieces, on their heads. On the signals, "Halt," "Action Front," the several parts were put together and brought into action, firing four rounds. The guns were then broken up, the sections hoisted on the men's heads and retired to the original position. All this was done with the rapidity and precision of bluejackets, without the slightest flurry or confusion, and, from beginning to end, carried out in well under a-minute-and-a-half.

I had taken a kinematograph apparatus from England and secured moving pictures of the operations, so there was the double test of time by watch and the amount of film used.

The battery can, however, from the halt, walk a

SOLDIERS AND THEIR SPORTS

distance, put the guns together and fire a round in less than 30 seconds; in fact, anything longer is considered bad. The movement specified is that of firing case-shot to repel cavalry attack.

The projectiles used are: shrapnell shell, $12\frac{1}{2}$ lbs., effective at 3,400 yards; double common shell, 18 lbs., effective at 2,000 yards; case, 15 lbs.

The white personnel of the four guns I saw at Zungeru—the remaining two were at Sokoto—was made up of a Captain in command assisted by a Subaltern, and a Sergeant-Major, whose chief work was that of Quartermaster-Sergeant. Further, there were the native Sergeant-Major and other black N.C.O.

Gun-carriers are enlisted for two years, and actual gunners for six years. Re-enlistment is allowed. The native Sergeant-Major has 15 years' service. Though recruiting can be direct into the battery, the artillerymen are drawn mainly from the gun carriers.

All gun orders are given in English. Although very few of the men understand the tongue, they learn to recognise the meaning of the words of command. Every officer must, however, pass a colloquial test in Hausa. Recruits are put through their early stages by the native non-commissioned officers, who take most of the parade drilling. All these native Sergeants and Corporals, and most of the Bombardiers, are capable of commanding the battery and of taking a series.

Do I labour detail too much in stating the items of transportation? The process is as follows:

The gun itself, weighing about 240 lbs., is borne

on slings, the poles of which rest on the heads of four men.

The cradle, into which the gun fits and to which are attached hydraulic buffers to take the recoil of firing, weighing about 240 lbs., is carried in the same way as the gun.

The trail, or carriage, which has a spade to assist in checking the recoil, weighing about 240 lbs., is transported as those stated above.

The two wheels are each carried by a man, who has a 70 lb. load.

The axle, about 70 lbs., is a one-man load.

A box of spare parts and cleaning traps, about 70 lbs., is carried by one man.

There is also a Headman to superintend and assist.

Similar guns were used in the capture of Kano, in 1903, the great Hausa city with mud walls 40 feet thick and 50 feet high. Against these walls, which it was thought would be knocked to pieces by the artillery, all ammunition was impotent. An entry was at last effected by smashing one of the heavy gates with a shell.

The sports in which the men of the regiment are encouraged to indulge are mostly of British origin. They are very keen on wrestling and tug-of-war and greatly enjoy dipping for toroes. A toro is a threepenny-bit. A large basin of flour, in which a number of toroes have been buried, is placed on a table. At the side of the table is a pail of water. Competitors, stripped to the waist and with hands behind back, one by one dip their faces into the water and then plunge them in the flour, attempting to pick out a coin with the teeth. The crowd of sightseers at the public display I saw at Zungeru shouted with delighted amusement at the ludicrous appearance of each contestant as his features emerged from the flour.

The favourite sport of the mounted infantry is wrestling on horseback. That itself is pretty exhilarating. A spice of added excitement is provided by the mounts, which enter into the spirit of the situation with zest, by darting at and attempting to viciously bite one another.

I may explain that in their ordinary training the men of the mounted infantry do not pass back into the unmounted branch. The uniform somewhat resembles that of the Sikh, and, though their arms includes a lance, they are taught to fight as foot soldiers as well.

Not least interesting is the moulding of the signallers. Obviously it is of vital importance on an expedition that detached parties, perhaps unexpectedly surrounded by overwhelmingly superior numbers whom they may be able to keep off temporarily, shall be equipped with means for making their position and plight known to the main body.

Whether the men selected for signalling tuition are Hausa or Pagan matters not. Scarcely any can read, much less write, their mother tongue. That, to say nothing of English, would be as Greek is to the average recruit in Great Britain.

You will gather what pains and patience the British N.C.O. exercises with his charges when it is said that these Nigerians—some, wild men from the hills and mountains; others, simple labourers or farming hands previous to the equivalent of " taking the King's shilling "—can not alone signal by flag, lamp and heliograph a message handed to them in English but—it seems almost marvellous—receive from any of the three instruments mentioned, and write, such a message, not knowing in the least what it means.

The explanation is simple. They learn that a figure—for example, B—is sent by a particular form of flag-waving, lamp-flashes or helio-rays. Conversely, certain movements of flag or the other instruments mean that the man receiving them has to draw the character—i.e., letter—associated with the sign; space between words, of course, being recognised as well.

Imagine what it must be to teach that to simple creatures who know no writing and can read none and who never fingered a pencil until they entered the signalling squad, for, as has been said, they have not the least idea what meaning is conveyed by the messages they despatch or receive.

The value of signalling was utilised for civil purposes two years ago, when early in the tornado season the telegraph connecting Zungeru with the important centre of Minna, 38 miles distant, was destroyed by storms. For 10 days, until the line could be restored, communication between the two places was uninterruptedly maintained by the signalling section of the First battalion.

A message was flagged under my observation by the Second battalion, at Lokoja. Beyond handing the paper to the native Corporal, no white man gave instructions or interfered in the slightest. On page 290, photograph 1 shows the original communication; photograph 2 is as the receiving signaller wrote it. I asked Major Baker, tempor-

SOLDIERS AND THEIR SPORTS

arily in command of the battalion, to use the words employed, as I wished to have a kinematograph illustration of the operation.

Then there are the bands, and excellent they are. Both the Hausa tribes and the Pagan tribes have a multiplicity of musical instruments on their native heath, wind and even string. A detailed catalogue would occupy space of an article as long as this. But the military band of each battalion is quite in the lines of English regiments.

Instruction? Well, the men are as innocent of eye-understanding music as they are of caligraphy. You might as well show them the signs of the zodiac or the combination of any other astronomical constellation. The English bandmaster teaches his pupils through their ear. Heaven only knows how he obtains the result from such raw material. Listening to the band playing alternately popular tunes and classical airs outside the officers' mess in the evenings, you would indeed wonder.

The titles of the pieces might naturally puzzle, or at least confuse, the performers. They could scarcely be expected to differentiate on an order for Cavalleria Rusticana or one for Rule Britannia. Therefore, the simple expedient is adopted of giving the compositions numbers, which obviously are much easier borne in mind. Thus, on the bandmaster ordering, for instance, "One," God Save the King would be rendered; "Two," Rule Britannia; "Three," A Life on the Ocean Wave; "Four," Hearts of Oak; and so on.

It is not found specially difficult to replace a fresh tune to an old number. On one occasion you might hear, in response to the order "Five," selections from The Bohemian Girl; a few months later the same word of command would produce The Policeman's Holiday.

You should see the Drum-Major, who is a native. He bears himself as though leading the Grenadiers, the Coldstreams, the Scots or the Irish Guards. His imposing staff is swung and twisted and twirled in the air, and presently balanced horizontally as he guides the front rank of the band wheeling, or he holds it aloft as a sign for the files to counter-march. He is quite conscious of his importance as regards his own men, I assure you; yet he knows his work so well that when Sergeant-Major Slaney, who had been detailed from the Coldstream Guards for Special Service instruction, told him how to take the band round the ground for kinematograph purposes, it was necessary to tell him only once.

That induces me to mention the admirable method followed in handling the men. All words of command by the whites, whether officers or non-commissioned officers, are given in quiet, cool tones. There is never any undue bustling in a manner to make the men frightened or nervous. Nor are they treated as automatons. Every opportunity is taken to develop the intelligence of those capable of exercising any. I noticed both at Zungeru and Lokoja that whenever an officer wanted a section to go through a movement he invariably gave the order to the senior native non-commissioned officer and allowed him to move the squad accordingly. In this way these non-coms. become self-reliant and of immeasurably greater value in an emergency on active service, where they may be thrown on their own resources.

SOLDIERS AND THEIR SPORTS

I witnessed a march of the Second battalion through Lokoja, traversing the native quarter. It was done for recruiting. How the drums and fifes and bugles brought the young women to line up on the route and gaze on the troops as they proudly swept by! And there were the small boys, as yet entirely minus clothing, trotting along to the martial sounds.

For days some of the bigger lads hung about the encampment of huts where the troops live, desirous of enlisting as buglers but not venturing to enter the trimly-kept compounds. At first they shrunk back with awe as a white officer or non-commissioned officer passed in or out. But as one of either class smiled at the youngsters or patted them on the head they gained courage and eventually several asked a native soldier how they could enlist. The majority of the youthful buglers are, however, sons of soldiers or of ex-soldiers.

The military spirit has a large influence among the civilian Hausa population. They classify all Europeans in the country into practically two classes: " Colour-Sergeant *bature* "—*bature* is Hausa for white man—and " *Bombature*." The latter is equivalent to big white men—not in stature but status—and the former is the mark of subordinate rank. The " Colour-Sergeant *bature* " will be men of the class of overseers on the mines or second-class officials on the railway and others of corresponding rating in commercial concerns, as distinguished from their seniors. Occasionally there is an individual between the two classifications. He is provided for by the designation " Sergeant-Major *bature*."

T

In the estimate of the Hausas, there are no whites to be ranked as Privates. All are regarded as in some degree above themselves. It behoves Englishmen who go to Nigeria to remember this and to bear themselves accordingly. That does not warrant arrogance but entails self-control.

PHOTOGRAPH I.

No. of Message

Prefix ... Code ... m. | Words | Sent | Recd at ... m.

Office of Origin and Service Instructions. | At ... m. | Date | To | From | By | By

WRITE DISTINCTLY. CURTAIL ADDRESSES. TO BAND

SENDER'S NUMBER. | DAY OF MONTH. | IN REPLY TO NUMBER. | AAA

GOD SAVE THE KING

FROM O · C

PLACE

TIME

PHOTOGRAPH II.

No. of Message

Prefix ... Code ... m. | Words | Sent | Recd at ... m.

Office of Origin and Service Instructions. | At ... m. | Date | To | From | By | By

RMOMA A COY

WAUWDU BAUCHI F COY

WRITE DISTINCTLY. CURTAIL ADDRESSES. TO BAND

SENDER'S NUMBER. | DAY OF MONTH. | IN REPLY TO NUMBER. | AAA

GOD SAVE THE KING

FROM O · C

PLACE

TIME

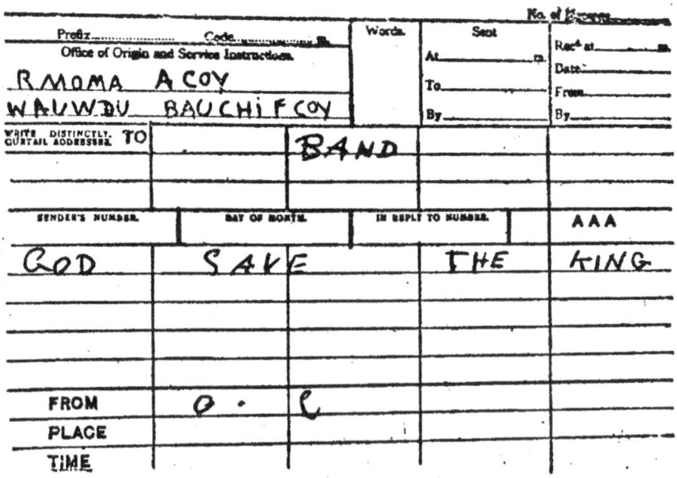

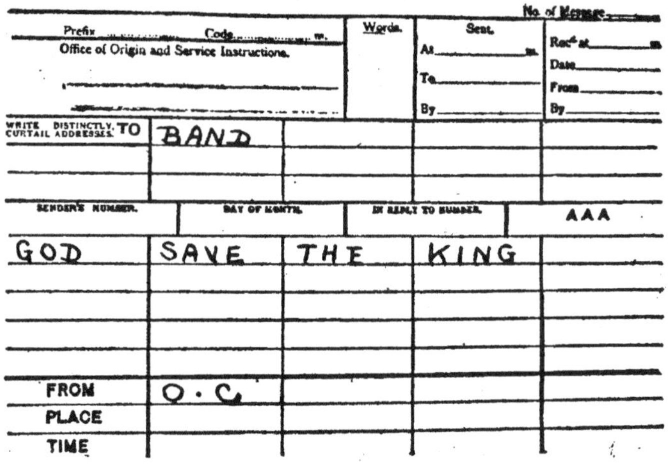

BERI-BERI WOMAN WITH ARTISTIC HEADDRESS.

SWEARING IN A PAGAN AND A MOHAMEDAN FOR THE
NORTHERN NIGERIAN REGIMENT.
(See page 280.)

CHAPTER XXXIV

ZARIA CITY AND PROVINCE

Prominence of Zaria—As a produce and trading centre—The gold discoveries—Opposite deductions—Model, native town-planning—Various taxes.

On the railway route from Lagos to Kano the largest European trading centre produced by the opening of the line is Zaria. Several factors have contributed to making the place prominent and important. Until Kano was subdued, in 1903, Zaria was the foremost Hausa city which had submitted to the British. Secondly, the idea of making Zaria, instead of Zungeru, the administrative headquarters of Northern Nigeria, and the steps taken towards that object, which included building a suitable house for the Governor and others for the principal officials, mark Zaria as a Government station of distinctiveness, for though the commodious bungalows are not occupied by the class originally intended the men there are a senior grade.

Thirdly, the junction of the Lagos-Kano trunk line with the branch, Bauchi Light Railway, and the fact that passengers from either to the other must stay at Zaria at least one night necessitate the provision of several rest-houses and has encouraged the increase of European stores to cater for items supplementary to the outfit and the "chop boxes" which people take from England.

Fourthly, Zaria possesses several districts in which produce is raised of the kind readily bought by exporting firms, and the railway has enabled natives who cultivate such material to bring it with ease to a comparatively large purchasing centre. The chief descriptions are shea-nuts, ground-nuts, benniseed, and a little beeswax. There are also hides and other skins.

Of the European Stores, the Niger Company, as usual, was first in the field, opening in the middle of 1911. It was followed shortly afterwards by Lagos Stores and the Tin Areas of Nigeria. These were joined in time by John Walkden and Co., and Paterson and Zochonis. Sites are now being built upon by Ollivant and Co. and John Holt, whilst plots are in the hands of the London and Kano Trading Co., Pagenstecher and Co., Geiser and Co., and the French Company. Most of the establishments buy produce as well as retail European goods.

No doubt in time Zaria will outgrow its present condition beyond recognition, but I am by no means sure that already the supply of stores is not well in excess of the demand for several years, both for selling to Europeans and for the purchase of native produce. Even as matters stand, there is not nearly enough to go round remuneratively, and, though the amount is sure to increase, a long time will pass before it is of sufficient quantity to warrant the number of establishments which have been and are being run up.

Moreover, Zaria is more likely to diminish, rather than increase, in importance as a stage on the railway when the gauge of the trunk and the branch lines have been altered to uniform gauge—the work will have started weeks previous to this being published—which will avoid breaking bulk for transhipment and will enable travellers to continue the journey without change of carriage; the acceleration providing a through service thus making unnecessary the present enforced wait at Zaria.

The Niger Company is gathering the fruits of having been the pioneer firm at Zaria. The mud houses and sheds are being replaced by more permanent structures. The retail store is of brick and is 80 feet by 35 feet. There are also two iron buildings with cement floors, one for warehousing the trading goods and the other for keeping the produce purchased. In addition an 80 feet long, open shed is used for weighing produce bought and to give shelter to the sellers whilst they wait their turn. The large compound in which the buildings stand is itself a public market on a small scale. Natives foregather there, sit down as at a meeting-place, and small traders assemble to sell food to the people who dispose of their produce, which may have been brought several days' journey.

Although it is generally assumed that the gold discoveries made are in Zaria Province, the only one of which the finder says he is satisfied lies just over the border, in the Niger Province. That belongs to Mr L. H. L. Huddart, who has shown me specimens from the ground which look enchanting. Whether the mineral is to be won in payable quantity is a question I am not prepared to answer. There is Mr Huddart, who was first in that field and who declares he is content with that on which he has lighted; whilst, on the other hand, some of the smartest mining men in the country have prospected around the centre and have reported adversely. Of course, both may be right.

Apart from this matter of gold, Mr Huddart evidently believes in the country's minerals, for a couple of miles from the European cantonment at Zaria he is putting up permanent buildings to be used as offices and a laboratory at which he proposes to carry on his profession as a consulting mining engineer.

Zaria, the administrative headquarters of the province of the same name, consists of three parts: the native city—a large, walled town resembling Kano—four miles from the railway, so that the native life, under the Emir, may be as free as practicable from disturbing influences; the Government offices and officials' bungalows; and the European merchants' stores.

The group of stores and the group of bungalows are quite near each other and within a stone's-throw of the station.

A quarter-of-a-mile from these centres there is the small sabon gari—i.e., native town—established for the requirements of natives who draw supplies there which they retail to the resident Europeans, in the way of daily household requirements. The sabon gari is also a great convenience to the large number of natives who bring in produce to sell to the exporting firms. Compared with Zaria City, this sabon gari is of limited dimensions. It differs markedly from Zaria City in having been laid out on Sir Hesketh Bell's plan for model native towns.

It is divided into rectangular blocks, or plots, 50

feet by 100 feet. The rent for a plot is 12s. or 16s. a year. The main avenue is 100 feet wide, and other roads have a breadth of 50 feet, whilst streets parallel with the houses—which, of course, are of mud—are 15 feet across; 183 plots are occupied.

Rentals from plots are divided evenly between the British administration and the Beit-el-Mal, but dues from the market stalls go entirely to the Beit-el-Mal. This institution—which is the Treasury for native administration—is described in Chapter VII.

General taxation in Northern Nigeria in every province is adjusted to local custom and usage. Therein lies one of the secrets of our success in governing the country, that the ways of the people are interfered with as little as possible.

But the population must pay taxes. They have always done so in one form or another. Whereas formerly they had to render service, or its substitute, for war or for slave-raiding and were squeezed in actual taxation according to the requirements of the Emir's Chiefs and, in addition, any man who prospered became an object of cupidity for the taxing Chief, now everybody is rated on a general plan and the amounts levied are decided upon in consultation between the British and the native authorities. Perhaps it will not be considered unduly out of place if, as an example, the system in Zaria Province is stated.

There is, first, the kurdin gidda, or house tax. Every owner—lessee, as we should term him—pays 1s. 6d. annually for occupancy. The kurdin kassa, or farm tax, is levied on every adult male farmer, whether working on his own account or for somebody else. The amount depends on the wealth of the town and the facilities of the inhabitants for earning money, such as proximity to trade routes and a railway. The tax ranges from 3s. to 6s. annually.

The kurdin gari—tax of the town—is paid by adult males who do not farm, whatever their work or occupation, or if they have none. The actual sum paid is fixed on the capacity of the payee to earn. The average is about 3s. a year.

A special tax which has been in existence for centuries is the kurdin karra, or tax on sugar, charged on sugar-cane plots, at 4s. yearly, independently of the size of the individual plot and of the number of men working on it.

Native non-Moslems are levied for a hoe tax, which is imposed only on adult male farmers, who pay from 3d. to 3s. a year on the same principle as that applied to the kurdin kassa.

As in every Hausa Province, all these taxes are collected by the district Chief and paid into the Beit-el-Mal. Fifty per cent. is taken by the British administration and goes towards the cost of the supreme Government. It is the price for protection from aggressive wars by neighbouring peoples and for the control of their own rulers against the extortions and oppressive demands which past rulers exercised. No part of the present taxation is taken out of the country.

The 50 per cent. balance is divided roughly into two. One of the two parts is for the Emir of Zaria Province, who has a fixed civil list for his personal expenditure and the expenses of his Court and for the payment of native Judges and police and the upkeep of a central prison; the other part is apportioned among the town Chiefs of the Province, who pay their subordinate officials a salary previously decided on the proportion it shall bear from the collected taxes. The salaries must not, however, exceed the figure decided when each appointment is made.

Of course, any attempt, detected, on the part of the Chiefs or village Headmen who collect the taxes to act in an irregular manner is dealt with severely. The natives know they can appeal against injustice to the British Resident. But the Residents do not interfere between the native Chiefs and the population unless some great principle is violated. By utilising the machinery of social organisation, which has existed for hundreds of years, for the purpose of native government, a Civil Service has been obtained of men who understand their own people in a way no white could be expected to, and is obtained at a fraction of the cost incurred in having the work done by Englishmen, who could not carry it out with a tithe of the efficiency.

The Government officials' bungalows at Zaria are the best in Northern Nigeria. Nearly all are of brick. The roads are excellent. They were laid out by the Public Works Department, with the exception of the main trading road to Zaria native city, which was made by the Emir with his own people, directed by those of them who had been on railway construction. The highway is 60 feet wide and is planted both sides with trees, which give a comforting shade.

Two groups of rest-houses are at Zaria. One is within a few feet of the station, in charge of the railway staff, and is very convenient for persons who arrive by a main line train and leave the following day by a branch line train, or *vice-versâ*; the other group is used by the Resident for travellers who may be staying a little longer.

It was to the latter group I went on my first stay; and it would ill-befit me to omit mentioning the courtesy shown at each visit. When here previously the Resident, Captain Fremantle, was occupied with preparations for moving into the native city for one of the usual periodical visits, lasting a few days; but the morning following my arrival he sent his next-in-command, Mr M. P. Porch, to enquire if I was comfortably quartered, and Mr Porch so thoroughly carried out his mission as to spontaneously ask whether I was short of any supplies, as, if so, he would willingly send me some of his. Dr Johnson, the medical officer, did not wait for the formality of an application for condensed water—that or the filtered variety is indispensable—but offered the necessary authority to draw a daily supply from the man in charge of the condenser. Dr Johnson had sufficient thought and human feeling to reflect that a new-comer might lack the appliances to convert liquid poison into drinkable stuff. He did not put across a polite note a pencil scrawl, "Apply to the railway people," whose place is a mile away.

On reaching Zaria this time I find Captain Fremantle, whom I had looked forward to meeting, temporarily invalided to England, his place filled for the time being by Mr A. C. Francis, who had been described as one of the most delightful men in the Northern Nigeria Government service. That is just what I should say of him.

FIDDLE

A HAUSA BOY

CHAPTER XXXV

THE BARO-KANO RAILWAY

Emirs' assent—Compensation for palm trees—A locomotive's food—Engine whistling preferred to Caruso—Official opening—Natives' curiosity—A Mallam's impressions—Horse *v.* train.

PREVIOUS to taking my last railway journey in the course of the present stay in Nigeria, it will not be out of place to give a sketch of the building of the Baro-Kano line. It starts, southwards, from Baro, on the River Niger, to Kano, joining at Minna the system running from Lagos. The portion of that system in Northern Nigeria was constructed with funds advanced from rich Southern Nigeria, whereas the Baro to Minna portion was built from the Northern Nigeria exchequer exclusively.

Although the line was imperative both for strategic and commercial purposes, care was taken not to ride roughshod over the susceptibilities of the people nor to run full-tilt against any prejudices of theirs. The Emirs through whose territory the track passed were formally asked to signify assent, which they readily gave. They are highly intelligent men who, long ago having realised that British ascendency was inevitable and permanent, saw clearly that their own positions would be strengthened by increased facilities of the paramount and protecting Power to move troops should that be necessary.

Every palm-kernel or other trade-value tree cut down was paid for at five years' purchase, assessed at the rate of 10s. annually, the money handed to the Chief of the area. This policy earned the hearty goodwill of the population directly affected.

The line passed through the county of three Emirs: those of Bida, Zaria, and Kano. All displayed the utmost cordiality and co-operation in the construction. They directed and encouraged their subjects to work in building the railway, though labourers were paid personally and individually.

The Emir of Zaria evinced so much interest in construction that he was in the habit of sitting on the embankment, with his officers of State around, watching the rails laid. He would repeatedly enquire how much the locomotive ate, in the matter of fuel—wood—and what quantity of water it drank. He regarded it quite as a living creature. Above everything, he loved to hear its voice, to listen to its whistle and shriek. For his greater enjoyment, the whistle would be kept going at its loudest for several minutes at a stretch. That appealed to him more than the finest tones of a Caruso or the sweetest notes of a Melba or a Tetrazzini.

The Emirs were each invited to perform the ceremony of opening the railway in his own Province. In 1909 the Emir of Bida opened the 43 miles' section from Baro to Badegi, Sir Percy Girouard, then Governor of Northern Nigeria, being present with his staff; early in 1911 the Emir of Zaria opened the extension to 267 miles' point, Mr C. C. Temple, Acting Governor, attending;

and the lengthening to Kano was opened by the Emir of that name. The Emirs were presented with bronze spanners—a material more highly valued than silver—with which they screwed up the last fish-plate bolt.

For the first few months or so that weekly trains were running to Kano, natives from the city and the surrounding villages displayed curiosity concerning the locomotive to the degree of assembling in crowds on the track at the railhead—there is no station yet—to gaze again and again at the engine. Quite polite and giving no trouble to the officials, they would examine it from every point of view, some lying on the ground to look underneath the phenomenal thing.

Last January, shortly after the railway started, a treat was given to the pupils of the Government schools at Nassarawa. The establishment is used for instruction to the sons of Emirs and Chiefs and to men for public duties, of whatever age, to equip them better mentally for their tasks. The treat consisted of an outing by train. One of the pupils, a Mallam from Bornu, 70 years old, was with difficulty persuaded to go into the truck. Covered carriages had not arrived. Eventually he did and was soon at his ease. He watched intently all that took place during the trip and on returning was asked cheerily by one of the young engineers what he thought of it all. The old man thanked the railway officials for so much education given in so short a period, but in reply to the question he said he could tell them only by writing a big book. One pointed out that some of them might not live until he had finished, in which event they would die in ignorance of the knowledge sought from him. Therefore he should speak at once.

After thinking, the Mallam replied that he might tell them a few of his impressions in a long speech, and was preparing to gird up his loins for the operation. That prospect was not at all alluring to the audience, so he was urged to give voice to the one thing which impressed him most. He at once answered, "The fact that the engine drank more water than a thousand elephants!"

Some Chiefs from outlying districts were brought in for a joy ride in trucks. When the initial uneasiness at the novel form of movement had passed off, they seemed to enjoy the thrill of being whirled along at 20 miles an hour by no effort of theirs. Asked whether the sensation was not better than travelling in the saddle they replied, "Certainly not, as the horse did not spit hot sparks at a man on his back or behind him."

A little after 6 a.m. the train by which I travelled left Zaria for Baro, which is a two days' journey. The first night was spent at Minna, 155 miles from Zaria. The line from Lagos and that from Baro roughly form the apex of a triangle at Minna, with the Niger, between Baro and Jebba, as the base.

Two years ago railhead from Baro was at Minna, then a small, temporary station, really merely a stopping-place. Now there are platforms 300 yards long, and the station offices are of red brick, made on the spot, with cement facings. The station is lit by incandescent oil lamps, the oil forced up 30-feet standards. It is the only station which has semaphore signals, three in each direction. There

THE BARO-KANO RAILWAY

are six tracks of the standard West African gauge —3 feet 6 inches—and a turn-table capable of taking the largest vehicle on the railway, 50 feet.

One sees as many as 50 trucks, brought up or down the line, waiting to be made up for their several destinations. They contain cotton goods from England, cement and machinery for the tin mines, kola nuts from the Gold Coast Colony for the great Mohamedan centres of Zaria and Kano. Formerly the nuts were taken by head carriage.

After the first few stations from Minna towards Baro permanent buildings are in existence: square, brick buildings, with an annexe consisting of a roof on pillars, used as a waiting-room for native passengers, where they can go for protection from the rain. I noticed, too, that the open trucks, which were all that could be obtained for the unexpected dimensions of the native traffic in the earlier months of the opening of the line, are being converted into covered carriages.

It is good to see on this Baro-Kano Railway, so much used by native passengers, the provision made for their reasonable comfort. They are regarded as human beings, not merely freight. Their fares contribute considerably to the revenue of the railway. There were people in England, and plenty in Nigeria who had not been through the district, who saw in the scheme of the line from Baro to Minna, running as it does parallel with the section from Jebba to Minna, only an unnecessary competing span with the latter stretch, just built, so they said, to satisfy Sir Percy Girouard's idea, he being "out" to propound a scheme of construction in accordance with his reputation as a railway builder.

Persons who formed so ungenerous a judgment thought of merchandise alone; they took no note of the inhabitants of the land. Such persons should see the immense convenience the line is to the native; to what an extent it has lightened his life, in more ways than one, and then they would recognise both its utility and necessity. This is stated independently of considering the Baro-Minna section in the general, broad policy of railway development.

A gladsome sight at some of the stations south of Minna was bananas brought by women for sale. A bunch of 12 for a penny was the price, which my boy, who made the purchases, told me was double the charge he would pay if marketing for himself. Still, I was eager enough to buy at the higher rate, for I had had no fresh fruit, and, with the exception of onions and potatoes, very few vegetables of the same character for about six months.

The appearance of the fruit showed I was passing into country where the cultivation and climate differed from that lately seen. There were other signs. Flat, open, grassy land, fairly wooded, but not to the extent of marring the landscape view, the general effect in several respects is to make it indistinguishable in appearance from English country. This effect is rather added to than otherwise by an occasional sheet of water. But a characteristic of the tropics is distinguishable in the aristocratic-like palms, standing separately and much higher than the other trees.

Near some villages along the railway are a few small patches of tobacco growing, the long and broad leaf drawing attention to the plant from the

THE BARO-KANO RAILWAY

surrounding greenery. There is a freshness of verdure in these low-lying lands of more marked kind than the higher, cooler, and drier reaches yield. It is here and still further below in the valleys of the Benue that cotton will be produced if the plant is to be cultivated in any quantity in Northern Nigeria.

The train was due at Baro on Saturday evening, and my plan was to go straight on board a launch, if one was available, leave in the early morning for Lokoja, there to join the first mail stern-wheeler for the sea. During Saturday afternoon a telegram was handed me at a station, sent by Mr E. N. Coleman, Transport Agent of the Niger Company at Baro, who had been a fellow-traveller on the voyage from England, containing an invitation to the hospitality of the bungalow there for the night, and stating that the launch was ready for continuing the journey next day. It was quite dark when the train drew into Baro.

CHAPTER XXXVI

BARO ON THE NIGER

Baro port—A Selfridge-Whiteley 400 miles up the Niger—London frock-coats in West Central Africa—Fretwork and ladies' garments—An untutored eye and its guide—The rat a table delicacy—Oje's local patriotism—Baro and Jebba; hygienic problems—A superfluous hospital.

UP early the following morning, to make most of the time before starting down the Niger, a quick look round at once gave a view more like the general pictures of West African towns seen along the Coast than the plains and highlands recently left. Small, square, and oblong houses, painted white and with red roofs, surrounded by a horseshoe-shaped hill 400 feet high, covered with green, bring to mind some resemblance to Sierra Leone and Monrovia, as seen from the sea at a distance.

Baro is 130 miles below Jebba, and was selected by Sir Percy Girouard for the terminus of the railway. The Niger is 1,000 feet across, divided into two channels by an island about two miles long, on which the native town is located. The south channel—the one nearest the railway—is only 100 feet wide, and you can walk over it, on sand, at lowest water.

Formerly Baro was an important produce-buying

BARO ON THE NIGER

station of the Niger Company, principally for shea-nuts and ground-nuts. Since the opening of the railway the place has become important as a transport point for transference from the river stern-wheelers—run in connection with the ocean liners—to the train, for passengers and material bound for the tin mines. Now an average of 5,000 packages are handled weekly, ranging from personal baggage to heavy parts of machinery.

There are a number of people, particularly those going to the tin fields, who have little time to make purchases in England and who cannot supply the deficiencies when at the mouth of the Forcados River, as there is direct transhipment from the ocean ship to the stern-wheeler. Practically any requirement can, however, be satisfied at Baro, where there is always some interval between the arrival of the stern-wheeler and the departure of the train. The stay is long enough to make any outlays. The store of the Niger Company was stocked as I had not seen an establishment stocked for a long time, not since I had been in Zungeru more than six months earlier. There was everything actually on sale needed for a man going to the mines or prospecting. I walked up and down the building, as big as a large drill hall, and noted light tools for joiners and carpenters; oil stoves, useful for doing cooking on the train when a carriage has no facilities of that character; table and wall lamps; medicines, including quinine; tinned and bottled fruits; table necessaries and delicacies; liquids, from lemon squash, lime juice and Wincarnis to champagne; clocks and wristlet watches. I counted 6 brands of cigars and 20 kinds of cigarettes, camp-beds, deck chairs, men's clothing, from soft felt and tweed hats to boots of various sorts, even to sock suspenders.

Then, to my surprise, I saw black frock-coats, just as the doctor or other professional man would wear in England. Although second-hand, I was staggered on learning that they are sold at 3s. 9d.! Fancy being rigged out in a respectable frock-coat 400 miles up from the Coast in West Africa at a cost of three shillings and ninepence! And, presumably, this figure leaves a profit after payment of transit from home.

And who wants to wear a black cloth frock-coat in these sultry regions, where white linen is more appropriate? I ask.

The answer is that there are two destinations for the articles. Natives in the district who are well off—such as a petty trader—buy and use them as rain-coats. They enquire at the store for " a water, black gown."

The second destination to which a frock-coat goes, which may have graced the figure of a company director, or even a member of the House of Lords, is as a present to some native Chief in Southern Nigeria, who will don it on State occasions, as the Lord Mayor of London comes out resplendent in his robes of office when an imposing ceremony is afoot.

In this store there was an array of another garment which my untutored eye took to be men's undervests having intricate fretwork at the neck and on the short sleeves and under the fretwork what I thought to be blue and pink blotting-paper. On enquiring the correctness of my surmise, young Mr Coleman, who was showing me round, said in a rather loud tone, half-scornful at ignorance and half-pitiful, "What! Men's undervests! Why, they are ladies' chemises, with insertion. What you call fretwork, as though it were wood carved, is embroidery. Did anyone ever hear of embroidered men's undervests!" And he laughed. After a pause he added, "Aren't you married?" "No." His rejoinder was merely "Oh!" I learnt he was.

Naturally I wondered what female form was decorated with such trappings and was told that the belles from villages miles around were particularly partial to this adornment, worn without anything over it; whereas in more civilised lands—so Mr Coleman informed me in a confidential, fatherly way—a dress covered the artistic production.

I always try to understand a subject in all its bearings, but you who may regard me as woefully deficient in knowledge on this topic please bear in mind that I have just come down from country where fashions and styles and manners of dress are much simpler and approximate—in fact, in many cases have not even attained—to the Garden of Eden stage.

The large number of rat-traps for sale led me to enquire whether there was a plague of the rodents. I was told No, but that the folks of the neighbourhood esteemed the vermin as an article of diet, properly cooked. The traps were used to secure the delicacy. My boy Oje informs me his people —the non-Moslem Yorubas of Ibadan—also enjoy the dish of rat, but he made clear that they would not demean themselves to eat the house variety, as the Hausas at Baro do, instead catching the field rat, "because he chop (feeds) on corn and be big and good past the other." Oje never misses an opportunity to give reasons why his tribesmen and tribeswomen are superior to all the coloured race. He has a bump of local patriotism fully developed.

After looking over the excellent Railway Institute—a great boon to the employees—closer examination than had been practicable the previous evening was given to the Niger Company bungalow for staff quarters. It is built of cement blocks, with an overhanging verandah of wood and a roof of tiles, which has the immense advantage over iron or tin in that rest is not disturbed at night during the wet season, as, at the most, the rain merely purrs on the tiles. Under them is a wooden ceiling, giving coolness, and corresponding effect is obtained on the hottest day by use of cement blocks for the walls. The cement came out in barrels and the blocks were made by a Cyclops hand machine on the spot. When the railway authorities saw the bungalow a similar block-making machine was immediately ordered for their own purpose.

The whole bungalow is large and airy. It contains eight bedrooms—the verandah is suitable for sleeping during the highest temperature—and downstairs there are a lounge for smoking and reading, a dining-room, and a domestic store. All the rooms have been made mosquito-proof.

Baro presents a peculiar hygienic problem. The mortality formerly associated with Jebba baffled doctors as to its cause. Baro, on the other hand, used to be regarded as possessing peculiarly unhealthy conditions in the marshy land along the river shore. Yet, with the exception of the first year of railway construction, cases of illness have

HAUSA HOUSEBUILDING WITH GRASS.
The Foundation.

THE FINISHED MANSION.
It is put up by two men in a couple of hours, including cutting the grass.

averaged few and are now lower than ever. So much so that the hospital has been closed some time as there were too few cases to keep the staff employed. There are not many of that kind in West Africa. This qualified immunity could probably be traced to personal precautions. The lesson should not be lost by new-comers to the country, not necessarily new-comers to this part, as the same principles apply all through West Africa.

There were other spots at Baro I should have been glad to visit, but, being due at Lokoja—70 miles—the same night, at 11 a.m. I went aboard the small steam-launch the *Rattler* and commenced the 406 miles' journey down the Niger.

CHAPTER XXXVII

LOKOJA

First stage down the Niger—Lokoja's past—The discovery of the brothers Lander—Previous theories—McGregor Laird's enterprise—Eighty per cent. mortality—The 1841 expedition—Richardson, Barth and Overweg—Laird's second endeavour—The House of Commons scuttle policy—Its reversal—First Fulani battle—Imperial control—Commerce of Lokoja—Vessels at the beach—Loading boats—Freedom of contract.

"STEAM at 10 o'clock, Cappy." That was the order given by Mr Coleman at Baro in the evening to the skipper of the *Rattler* launch for the following morning. "Cappy," of course, was an abbreviation of Captain. This commander was of the Nupé tribe, and the craft in his charge was used by Mr W. H. Hibbert, Divisional Agent of the Company, for inspection tours of the stations in his division. He had kindly sent it up from Lokoja to save me waiting three or four days for a large sternwheeler coming down the Niger.

The wish, however, of several people that I should see the places in which they were specially concerned made the hour 11 a.m. when the *Rattler* steamed away on the 70 miles' run to Lokoja.

The launch, propelled by a screw, was 75 feet

long, with a beam of 8½ feet, and 4½ feet deep, drawing 2 feet 9 inches. The boat is used as a habitation by Mr Hibbert for weeks together as he travels up and down the main streams and tributary creeks to visit the many stations of the Company where produce is purchased by the men in charge and European goods sold to the natives.

Just below Baro the Niger is 1,200 feet across, as smooth as the Serpentine lake in Hyde Park. The banks of the river are low, in some cases edged with narrow strips of sand and in others completely grass covered. As one steams down, the crowded trees make a wall to within a quarter of a mile of the bank, whilst in spots this thick wooding comes to the edge of the water and continues along it. Occasionally, in the background, are ranges of hills, giving a higher and less regular sky line. Clear and distinct on the sand beaches crocodiles can be seen at intervals snoozing in the sun.

This broad river is not so easy for navigation as it looks, for there are plenty of shallows and submerged islands where our little craft might easily run aground. "Cappy," therefore, does not take a direct line, but frequently has the boat in a diagonal course, as though he were tacking against the wind, giving directions by a slight move of the hand to the sailor at the wheel.

Although no stop was made on the journey down, it was quite dark half-an-hour before arriving at Lokoja, where Mr A. Coombe, also a fellow-passenger on the voyage from England and District Agent of the Niger Company, was waiting on the beach with a lamp to guide "Cappy" to his moorings alongside the bank.

Lokoja has a past. Not in the sense applied to Mrs Ebbsmith, but in the place it has occupied in the record of West African exploration. The story, even given briefly, may convey some notion of the climatic deterrents on the one hand and, on the other, how the British outlook on colonial expansion has changed—completely reversed—and how that policy was, it may be said, almost involuntarily effected.

I do not propose, at least here, to take a literary jaunt along the 2,500 years since the Niger River was first mentioned by a writer, the worthy Herodotus. I merely venture to sail lightly over the 82 years that have elapsed since the course of the waterway was discovered by the brothers Lander. That is done by reason of the very important trading position Lokoja occupies and the dominating influence it has had in the political advancement of the country.

The connection of Lokoja to the Niger is as strong as London is to the Thames or Liverpool to the Mersey, though the famous African town does not correspond topographically to either, for it is 337 miles from the sea.

That part of the Niger was unknown to whites until the brothers Lander came down the stream in a canoe from Boussa and, continuing, traced the river to its outlet. Europeans had traded in the delta for hundreds of years but did not suspect it was the same stream Mungo Park and other travellers had struck in the hinterland.

Two men had, however, formed theories concerning the course of the Niger from Boussa. One, Herr Reichard, argued in print, in 1808, that the river took the line which was to a large extent eventually proved, but he did not indicate accurately how it was disposed at the mouth. The other, James McQueen, issued in 1816 a small publication in which he traced the direction of the Niger to the sea; five years later he elaborated his views in a volume, illustrating them by maps. As McQueen —a merchant of the West Indies—had never been in Africa, his conclusion was scorned. Nine years afterwards he heard its accuracy verified, when Richard and John Lander came out at the southernmost arm of the mighty stream.

The news acquired by the Landers in 1830 that the river was navigable from the delta, in 1832 induced two vessels propelled by steam to be fitted out at Liverpool for trading up the river. The expedition was financed and organised by the pioneer of British commerce in this part of Nigeria, McGregor Laird. The vessels together carried a crew of 45, of whom, in a couple of years, the climate killed 36. This heavy mortality shocked people at home, and for some time the country was looked upon as impossible for Europeans.

However, in 1841 another attempt was made, though for a different purpose. Three steamers went out from England, carrying 145 persons. Their object was towards the abolition of slavery solely by peaceful measures. The officers were all drawn from the Royal Navy. The expedition, like the former one, were absent two years, and although the deaths were not so overwhelming in this case, they were appalling: practically 33 per cent., for 49 succumbed. In the main design of the journey nothing was effected. A piece of land was purchased adjoining the river. The intention was to work it as a model farm, using free labour. When the ships turned homewards the plot of ground was abandoned. It was, however, subsequently to be one of the most-talked-of spots in Northern Nigeria. Lokoja stands there.

In 1850 the British Government sent a small expedition, consisting of Richardson, a German named Barth, and another of the same nationality, Overweg, to march from Tripoli southwards across the desert and explore the eastern territory of what is now Northern Nigeria. The trio broke up. Mr Richardson died in Nigeria, and whilst Dr Overweg went to report on the country in Lake Chad district, Dr Barth reached Yola, on the Benue River, 467 miles from where it forms a junction with the Niger facing Lokoja. Barth advised the Government that the Benue be utilised for trading with the interior, Lander having demonstrated that the double waterway communicated with the sea.

On the strength of Barth's reports, and notwithstanding the deplorable experience of the previous parties, McGregor Laird in 1854 applied to the Government for permission to explore and trade on the Niger. His request was granted and he built a steamer, the *Pleiad*, for the purpose. It carried quite a mixed consignment, consisting of trading goods; a zoologist, who was to pursue his own branch of study; and several native missionaries in the service of the Church Missionary Society. Every health precaution was adopted, including quinine daily; and, in striking contrast to former results, after about five months every one of the Europeans was brought back.

LOKOJA

Laird's expedition had proved so promising that in January 1857 he offered, for a subsidy by the Government, to place a steamer on the Niger and maintain communication between the sea and about 400 miles up country. The proposal was adopted, and a few trading centres were soon established along the route. These, however, resulted in friction with the natives, and, after a period of three years, Laird's death and other causes were followed by abandonment of the centres and almost the complete relinquishment of direct British interest in that part of the territory.

Dr Baikie, R.N., who had been in charge of Laird's first expedition, on the second being arranged was sent out as British Consul and took up quarters on the river shore which had been acquired for the 1841 model farm and which in Baikie's consulate was named Lokoja.

In 1868, in furtherance of the policy of the period to reduce, not to extend, British influence, Baikie was withdrawn, and the Niger territory, beyond a few miles from the mouth of the river, cut from our control. The ideas of the day had been expressed by the House of Commons Resolution of 1865, which directed that: ". . . the object of our policy should be to encourage in the natives the exercise of those qualities which may render it possible for us more and more to transfer to them the administration of all the Governments with a view to our ultimate withdrawal from all [West Africa] except, probably, Sierra Leone."

Well, where pusillanimous Cabinets feared to go unofficial enterprise boldly stepped, and, whether the Home Government wished it or not, circumstances so willed that the Union Jack came to be eagerly planted on the Niger territories and subsequently carried far into the interior, or the British would have been hemmed in on the coast by other Continental nations. The former attitude of general withdrawal had in the course of a single generation become utterly discredited. In 1886 the Niger Company received its Charter, and from that time the peace and prosperity of Northern Nigeria has proceeded apace.

Lokoja was the administrative headquarters of the Company. Here, in 1897, Sir George Taubman Goldie—the Mr Goldie Taubman of those days—organised the force to proceed to Kabba City, which was the initial occasion Hausas were put to fight against their co-religionists. The care and thought these pioneers gave to the study of local feeling and tendencies is shown by the appointment for the first time of Mallams to accompany the troops, and, like army chaplains, minister to their spiritual requirements. That step prevented the enemy from undermining the soldiers' staunchness on the subject most likely to touch their sentiment, and it also counteracted the risk of a jehad being preached on the ground that the white man sought forcibly to convert the Mohamedans to his own faith.

It was from Lokoja that Sir George Taubman Goldie set out the same year, and, with native regiments which numbered all ranks between 500 and 600, defeated, in a two days' battle, the Emir of Bida's army, estimated at from 10,000 to 15,000 first-class fighting men, including the famous Fulani horsemen, who until that encounter had been looked upon as invincible in war.

LOKOJA

The Company's Charter was taken over by the Imperial authorities at the opening of 1900, and Jebba, 200 miles higher up the river, shortly afterwards made Government headquarters.

If Lokoja does not possess the former political predominance, its business importance is more than ever. The town may be said to occupy a strategic commercial position. It stands, as has been stated, at the confluence of the Benue and Niger rivers, which here are together about two miles across.

The Benue flows into the Niger at an angle of 45 degrees and is navigable to Yola, 467 miles distant. It runs through the Bassa country, remarkably rich in agricultural and sylvan produce, of which not a tithe has yet been tapped.

There are eight European firms in Lokoja, namely, the Tin Areas of Nigeria, the British Cotton Growing Association, the Niger Company, Messrs Pagenstecher, John Holt, G. W. Christian, J. D. Fairley, and the Bank of British West Africa. The first five are buyers of produce as well as storekeepers, whilst the remainder only engage in the latter form of business. The exception to both descriptions of business is, of course, the bank, which does not go beyond its own sphere.

Kabba Province, in which Lokoja stands, is noted for the rubber, palm-kernels, and shea-nuts cultivated by the native farmers, with comparatively little beeswax and a few hides. The Niger Company is the largest buyer. Away from the headquarters, at Burutu, it is the largest station of the Company. In the sheds I saw tons and tons of palm-kernels, shea-nuts, rubber, and other forest products brought from the interior and exchanged for British goods and for the small amount of Continental articles which British manufacturers cannot make; and there are also large cash transactions—in fact, most of the purchases are paid for in cash—of which only a small proportion is expended on the spot.

This is not done at once, nor is it necessarily carried out with the firm to whom the native farmer or trader has sold the produce. He is not the man quickly to launch into outlay. He is cool, careful, calculating, and, having disposed of what he has to sell, will sit down for two or three days to cogitate on what he shall buy in the way of presents to take to his folks at home. Having brought himself to the mood of expenditure, he probably inspects all the stores before deciding where he is to bestow his patronage, which may be no more than 5s.

A somewhat similar procedure is followed when he is a seller. Each European firm will be tried and the amount it will give for the produce ascertained previous to one being selected. Time is no object. If anybody fresh from England and not conversant with native methods sought to inculcate new ideas and method by refusing to pay the price offered and declined a few days earlier for the native produce, then that merchant would simply take it away and probably never bring more to the same place.

Lokoja has this difference from its Lancashire prototype, Liverpool, that whereas the Mersey and the Manchester ends of the Ship Canal are the water termini of sea-borne merchandise,

Lokoja is a kind of clearing-house for general distribution. To its beach are moored screw and stern-wheelers, from 10 tons' freight to the larger ones of the "Naraguta" class, for freight of 600 tons; barges drawing 12 to 15 inches, for passing up the broad though very shallow creeks of the Niger and the Benue, carrying goods of English make to the inhabitants of districts which can give our home manufacturers those essential oils and other products of the soil necessary for their industries, and which they scour the world to discover.

To other parts of the beach come and go native canoes of infinite variety in shape and size, some as long as vessels seen on European canals, and decreasing by degrees until there is the plain dug-out made from the trunk of a tree, in which the perambulating trader, with wife and child, makes his peregrinations perhaps 500 miles up the Benue, buying and selling and exchanging at the stopping-places, and at night sloping his mat on a pole fixed horizontally, thus providing a house and shelter for sleep. Lokoja is the great centre of them all.

It is also the Northern Divisional Headquarters of the Niger Company, the division supervised by Mr W. H. Hibbert, and comprising 6 districts, with 30 trading stations and stores, reaching as far as Ilorin in one direction and Jemaa and Loko in the other.

Loading or unloading the larger river boats is worth describing. Word goes round the native town when the operation is to take place and a great crowd of all sorts and conditions foregather to take a hand. There is no elaborate and intricate supervision to

X

ensure that each labourer shall prove himself worthy of his wage. He is paid piecework in the most direct, precise, and simple manner. The honorarium is rendered at every load.

Suppose it is a case of loading fuel—wood—for a stern-wheeler. The corps of workers assemble where the material is stacked, are given baskets, which, being filled, they hoist on their heads, and half-run, half-walk, close on one another's heels, in a long, winding line to the boat.

As they pass along a plank from the shore to the craft there stands on it a native clerk who hands to every person payment. Wages are high at Lokoja, compared with what they were when I was up at Jebba three years ago. At Lokoja, as in some parts of England, there is the cry of rise in the cost of living. Consequently a few cowries no longer suffice as an inducement for beach work. A journey with a load to or from the boat is rewarded by a tenth of a penny. Nickel coins of that denomination are sent from England for currency in Nigeria. The native name is nini, pronounced neenee. Tenth of a penny is the minimum payment. Do not conclude that these very casual labourers would be content with whatever you cared to offer. Nothing of the kind. The tenth is for a generally-agreed distance between the points of taking a load and discharging it. Should the points be wider apart, two, three, or even four tenths must be disbursed as each worker performs his, or her, task.

An amusing crowd it is that scampers along at this work: men, women, and children of all ages and sizes. The most complete freedom of contract obtains. Everybody is free to enter and head a basket, and anybody can give up when they please. In hurrying over the narrow plank to the boat, occasionally bearer and load will overbalance and topple into the river, at which the noise of shouting with which the work is carried on will be heightened by loud laughter, whilst the fallen warrior collects basket and contents from the running stream and completes the task of depositing his charge at its proper destination.

CHAPTER XXXVIII

LOKOJA—(*continued*)

A cosmopolitan town—A Baron Haussman—The Cantonment Magistrate—Some of his duties—Expenditure and economy—King Abigah—A plea for generosity—The hospitals—A black Bishop's legacy—The missionary question—Critics and the converse.

THE commercial aspect of Lokoja has occupied the main portion of the preceding chapter, but, of course, a large business centre necessarily attracts other adjuncts of life. The coloured population is 13,484, of whom 11,680 are natives of Nigeria and 1,804 come from Coast towns. The 72 Europeans are composed of 38 Government officials and 34 engaged in the stores and missionary work.

Lokoja is a cosmopolitan town, in an African sense. It is Lagos on a small scale. In it you can see the West African of every kind to be met along the Coast belt, from the educated type of the Coast and portly mammies of Sierra Leone to the Mohamedans of other countries.

There is thorough segregation. Lokoja proper may be described not even as oblong but in the form of a narrow strip—nail-like—parallel with the Niger. At one end of the strip is the native quarter, forming a kind of oval head to the nail-shaped town. A wide thoroughfare—Camp Road—stretches about a mile. At each side and sometimes a little way back are the European stores, and at the further end—the point—the Government offices and residential bungalows, the barracks, and the hospital.

On the excellent principle of keeping European commercial development separate from the purely native administration of the country—so that the former does not disorganise the latter—that is fixed at Kabba. At Lokoja the political officer has the rank only of Cantonment Magistrate, but the heavy duties he performs, the hours I have seen him at his tasks, their multifarious nature, and the way he has of "getting on" with all kinds of people, all mark Mr Bertram Byfield as among the best type of official to be found in British colonies.

He is the Baron Haussman of Lokoja. He takes as much pride in it as did the famous improver of Paris in his own city or as a man might in the garden to his house. Mr Byfield walks along Camp Road and into the native quarter always alert to detect in the course of his peregrinations what may be necessary for public health or convenience. He seems to regard himself as always on duty. In the course of each of my walks with him he noted half-a-dozen things to be done.

He has completely rearranged the market on the plan of Sir Hesketh Bell's model town-planning. The streets are in straight lines and run sideways and at right-angles to one another. To an eminence high enough to be approached by a zigzag path he has removed the Court house of the Alkali, in order that cases may be heard clear of the turmoil of the market-place. Cheaply-made bridges he has placed across dykes, and so given a short and direct cut between parts of the native quarter formerly connected only by a long detour. Another phase of his daily life is holding his Court for the trial of offences which do not go on the " list" of the Alkali.

The first occasion I called on Mr Byfield he was doing none of these more or less dignified acts, but (also in pursuance of his duties), of all things in the world, haggling over the price of old, disused kerosene cans from the military people! Such is the variety to which the qualities of capable officials in Northern Nigeria have to be turned.

What has the Cantonment Magistrate—he really should be a Resident—to do with cast-off kerosene cans? you ask. This. Although there is a sort of native Mayor and municipality—all appointed by the C.M.—for the native quarter of the town, the C.M. must see that they carry out his directions, for he would be held answerable if a serious outbreak of illness occurred. They needed the tins for hygienic use. But, again, why haggle over 3d. more or 3d. less per can? Because the strictest economy is the order of the day in Nigeria, and if when the accounts came to be overlooked the Governor saw that the C.M. of Lokoja had paid more than somebody elsewhere, His Excellency would demand the reason why.

You may remark that the procedure is straining a principle to pedantry, as the expenditure merely transfers money from one public department to another. Your assumption would be incorrect—at all events, incomplete. The outlay on military needs comes out of the general funds, raised by Customs, and by further revenue on all classes of the population, European as well as other; whereas

LOKOJA—*continued*

such local requirements as the cans are discharged by direct native taxation. British administration says that whilst it is fair and proper that indigenous dwellers should pay taxes for increased advantages to themselves, every care must be exercised that the money of these people is laid out with scrupulous economy.

A historic figure is Abigah, King of Lokoja, with whose son I had the illuminating conversation on domestic felicity detailed in Chapter XIV. Mr Byfield kindly sent for the old man to meet me in the market. I had, of course, known that the King had been brought by Dr Barth to Europe and that he had visited England and seen Woolwich Arsenal. He told me that Dr Barth also took him to Berlin, and introduced him to the Emperor William I. (then simply King of Prussia), who, noticing Abigah's strong and healthy appearance, tapped him on the chest and declared he was "a piece of black mahogany." Although more than 50 years have passed, Abigah is still as active in walking as a young fellow. He speaks English quite well, not in the pidgeon manner.

I omitted to ask what the King's means are. As he must be over 70 years of age and has been useful to England since Barth visited Lokoja, I hope the Government of Nigeria will take care that the old man's latter days are not embittered by poverty. This remark is made as I had heard up-country he was badly off. I am sorry the matter slipped my memory when speaking to Mr Byfield. In maintaining our rule in Northern Nigeria we depend so much on the cordial co-operation of the native, natural leaders of the people that it would be a great pity to jeopardise our good name for fair-dealing towards those whose supreme functions we have taken over by failing to be not only strictly just but somewhat generous in a case where that would be no more than discharging an obligation of honour, for Abigah has always been a staunch friend of the British.

At the other end of the town is the hospital, which fills an exceptional place in a mental survey of Nigeria. There are two routes from the Coast to the interior. One is by the railway from Lagos, the other the river route from Forcados. Along the former line, besides the large hospital at Lagos, there is a similar establishment at Zungeru, as well as a smaller one at Ibadan, and, all being on the railway, a patient living near the line is within easy reach of any of them.

On the river route, and then beyond it from Baro right up inland, there is no hospital approaching to that of Lokoja in size, technical resources, and with the unspeakable blessing of feminine nursing.

Do not, however, expect an institution the dimensions of those in English cities. The term Lokoja Hospital really means two hospitals—for Europeans and for natives. The first is of wood, bungalow shape, raised from the ground and resting on iron pillars with stone foundations. There is accommodation for 10 beds in wards made mosquito-proof, as is also the nurses' sitting-room.

Everything is done in a thorough, systematic way, for which purpose a laboratory and an operating room are provided. One of the patients came from Forcados. When there he was ill. Not sufficiently so to be invalided home but too low in health to remain. So he had been sent the 337 miles up the Niger to Lokoja Hospital to be nursed and was about to be returned " as good as new."

The staff consists of a senior medical officer, a medical officer, four nurses, and two Sergeants of the Royal Army Medical Corps, who are storekeeper and dispenser.

The hospital for natives is several hundred yards away. A brick building 90 feet long, it holds 35 beds, of which 2 (in a separate room) are for women, though there are seldom in-patients of that sex. The principal complaints which bring men towards the end of the year are sciatica, lumbago, and bronchitis. Malaria is always represented, but the most common case is tape-worm, due to dirty food. The operating-room and dispensary are in buildings apart from the wards.

The two white doctors have as assistants here— all natives—a wardmaster and three dressers, and also as dressers one Corporal and three orderlies of the Northern Nigeria Regiment.

In no part of Northern Nigeria is the native population, in health or in sickness, more solicitously watched than in Lokoja.

There are two further features of life in Lokoja which should not be ignored. One is the military, the other the missionary. The former is dealt with in Chapter XXXIII; as to the latter, I make no pretence about looking upon that aspect of European influence, as a rule, with disfavour. In one case I have criticised with perhaps extreme severity. All the same, I hope I have the spirit of fairness, and it is only bare fairness to say what is done by the Church Missionary Society in Lokoja.

The compound in which the house stands presents the gladsome sight of trees bearing oranges, guava, mangoes and sweet cassava. The only other orange tree in any part of the town is at the local headquarters of the Public Works Department. Apart from bananas, native cultivation of fruit in those parts of Nigeria through which I have passed is practically nil. But wherever there is a branch of the Church Missionary Society there you will see fruit trees. That is due to the late Bishop Crowther, in whose day all missionaries in Nigeria were, like himself, blacks. He insisted on every station showing at least one fruit tree flourishing.

It has been said, times out of number, in Nigeria and in many other lands, that the net result of even secular missionary education in most instances spoils the natives; that their innate reliable qualities are destroyed, and only the rote, not the practice, of ethics adopted instead. I merely express what is stated by opponents of the movement, without confirming or denying. But it is proper that the other side of the question should be given at a place where I had a better opportunity than anywhere else of learning what was being done there. The station at Lokoja is in charge of Archdeacon J. L. Macintyre.

The allegation of denationalising the native is warmly repudiated, as is that of spoiling him by unduly indulgent treatment and by overpaying those who may be employed and thus making them discontented for service with anybody else. I give a plain statement of the educational scheme carried out at Lokoja. No child is allowed to learn English till he or she can read their own language, i.e., Nupé, Yoruba, or Hausa. When passed in vernacular reading, children enter Standard I. and begin to learn English, though all the teaching is in the native tongue. On emerging satisfactorily from Standard IV., which is as far as is taught in the C.M.S. schools, a boy of good character may be engaged as a pupil teacher for three years. He is paid 7s. 6d. a month during the first year, increasing to 10s. and 12s. 6d. monthly in the second and third years respectively. A simple, native dress is provided. The pupil teachers teach five hours a day in school and receive two hours' instruction out of school hours. They are given quarters and shown how to play cricket and football. At the end of the three years' course the boys are free to leave. The majority go as clerks to Government offices or merchants' stores, but some stay as assistant schoolmasters at £1 a month, that amount rising annually 2s. 6d.

These details are set out for the reason stated above, and, I am informed, far from young natives being spoilt by the C.M.S., the grievance of the officers of that body is that their efforts to retain and conserve the simple habits of the country are frequently nullified by the action of those who disseminate the complaints.

Elsewhere I have been so severe a critic on the lay issues of missionary work that the least I can do, in the attempt not to be one-sided, is to pay a tribute of reverence to those who labour in what they regard as a sacred purpose. An example of their self-sacrifice is Archdeacon Macintyre. When with him he was in anything but robust health. Really, he should go to Europe to recuperate. The doctor urged that course, but Mr Macintyre was trying his utmost to avoid peremptory invaliding orders. A few days earlier he had got up from a sharp and trying attack of malarial fever, and was about to take a trip down the Niger, to be followed by a week on an Elder-Dempster liner at anchor off the mouth of the river, in the hope that the double change would patch him up for the remainder of his term. Twice he has had the dangerous blackwater fever. Disagree as one may from the outlay and the result of missionary efforts in West Africa, one must admire and honour the spirit shown by the noble men and women who give health and life for the cause, sacrificing these precious possessions in silent and obscure countries as freely as a soldier dies in a blaze of glory and renown.

I had several talks with Mr Macintyre, who, of course, had been made aware of my views on the subject of his work. We discussed it unreservedly. I said the position seemed to me that he was wearing himself out to small attainment, when there were so many heathens of our own colour, so much pain, poverty and misery in the great cities of Britain. Why, I asked, could not he and others look there instead of perceptibly putting themselves into the grave in malarious West Africa?

Mr Macintyre, whose age is probably about the thirties, replied that there were plenty of regenerating agencies in England if properly systemised and organised. He had been a curate, he related, in a poor district, and the various religious and philanthropic bodies tumbled over each other there in discharging their several tasks. There were more than enough persons to do all that was called for in England. There was no opportunity to break new ground. In West Africa, however, a man could feel he had fresh, untouched, unspoilt material to work upon and consequently facilities for tangible achievement; a man could be sure of doing something.

To do this something you see splendid fellows, of whom J. L. Macintyre is a type, sacrificing strong frames to a wasting condition, enfeebled and weak. He is paying still higher, for I gather that he has the happiness of a wife and a home in England. He is here on what he looks upon as his duty. I repeat, splendid. But, with much admiration and personal esteem, I remain unconvinced.

Four clear days were spent at Lokoja. In no corresponding period of the journey did I make more friends; at no place experienced a greater willingness to assist in obtaining information. Nowhere did I receive more individual kindness in the time; nowhere met better fellows. The four days were strenuous ones, spent amidst a torrid, damp atmosphere, but each hour was fully enjoyable and I said *au revoir* with regret at parting.

CHAPTER XXXIX

NAVIGATING THE NIGER

Rise and fall—A tideless stream—Comfort afloat—The uncertain river—Nasaru the Pilot—Altered channels—When aground—Breakdown of machinery and smart repair—Tropical scenery—The crocodiles' rest—Riverside villages—Where money is ignored—Estimation for old bottles and tins—Harmattan fog—An island trading station—Hazard and skill to maintain a time-table.

THE River Niger at Lokoja should not be likened to the fickleness of a woman but to the quick alternating of moods which distinguish that inexplicable and unfathomable sex. In a July the river has been less than 2 feet in depth, by an October it once rose to more than 35 feet. The respective averages in the two months are 3 feet 6 inches and 31 feet 3 inches.

Not an easy river to use for transport of heavy material, as the fall is as rapid as the rise, and by December it is generally below 8 feet, reduced in January to little more than 6 feet. Until the railway, which runs parallel to the river, starting at Lagos, 120 miles from the mouth of the Niger, was recently completed to the Bauchi Plateau, the river was the highway for goods eastward, i.e., in a line direct inland from the sea.

At Lokoja where, as previously explained, the

Niger is joined by the Benue, the former is three-quarters of a mile wide and the latter more than a mile. This two miles' expanse has a number of islands, most of which are submerged at the high-water months, but, whatever the depth of the river, their positions produce currents running side by side in opposite directions.

The Niger is tideless, in expression of ebb and flow; it is always running seawards. The rise and fall of the water are reflections of the rainy and dry seasons. But so long a distance have the floods to travel from the higher lands and so many tributaries empty themselves into the Niger and the Benue in the upper reaches that the wet season of one year does not make itself felt on the navigable parts of the rivers until 12 months later.

The strength of the current, which varies from three to seven miles an hour—always towards the same quarter—and the height of the river considerably modify the time-table of the larger vessels. Lokoja to Forcados, 347 miles, in the high-water season occupies two-and-a-half days. Forcados to Lokoja, at the same time of the year, is a day more.

At low water you may calculate anything beyond the periods given, but you should keep to calculating, not form any conclusion, for the precise, or even approximate, day and hour you reach your destination are largely on the knees of chance, in the matter of silted-in channels and quickly formed sandbanks; and though the skill and alertness of the native Pilot may evade these checks for a long time, he is sure to be caught by them sooner or later and the craft held up from an hour or so to a question of days.

I left Lokoja at 8 a.m. aboard the stern-wheeler *Mungo Park*, belonging to the Niger Company. She is the latest passenger-cargo boat on the service, carrying 220 tons on high water, drawing 5 feet, and 130 tons at low water, drawing about 4 feet. There is accommodation for eight saloon passengers, whose quarters are on the upper deck.

The vessel has electric light, electrically-operated air fans, and the bedrooms are mosquito-proof. I say bedrooms advisedly, not cabins, for the sleeping apartments are large, roomy apartments, with iron bedsteads which do not need the generally indispensable protection from winged insects of enclosing curtains. Every provision is here for comfort. Though we have no ladies this journey, the skipper, Captain W. H. Stephenson, has shown me, with pride, that their well-being has not been overlooked, for special accommodation has been furnished for them.

To me this form of locomotion is ideal of its kind. The barque is sufficiently large to give one the impression of being on an ocean-going ship, whilst the uniform smoothness of the stream sets the mind at rest. I am not oppressed by the uneasiness which ever haunts me on a liner and which prompts anxious looks to discern if there are signs of the wind freshening and enforcing a hasty retirement and abstinence from food. Whatever befalls on the Niger, there is no mal-de-mer. The most sensitive internal organism will not be disturbed.

We are propelled by two paddles at the back of the vessel and there are extra large balance rudders for sharp movement of the craft. They are frequently required at this season, as you shall learn. Our average speed is 12 miles an hour. Cargo is carried on the lower deck, where native passengers also settle.

There is only one European in the crew, the Captain. The other members are the Chief Engineer and his two assistants, the Pilot, Bos'n, four Quartermasters, and 22 deck hands. With the exception of the Engineers and the Pilot, all are river " boys " from the towns of Onitsha and Aboh and river villages.

The Niger Company does four-fifths of the cargo transport up and down the rivers—trading goods up, produce down—making no preference in selection between their own cargoes and those of firms who are side-by-side competitors in trading at dozens of places. The exception to this four-fifths division of carrying is Messrs John Holt, who have their own boats.

The first day the *Mungo Park* made 56 miles, measured by the direct course of the river, to Idah. It was not much to show for the full day's steaming, but the way had to be picked very warily. Though the broad river was certified as between 6 feet and 7 feet deep, that did not mean all the way across; it only specified the channel along which such a boat as ours could travel. Nor was the channel necessarily in the middle or the side of the river; it might twist from the former to the latter, or *vice versâ*; or it might take a zigzag course. As a matter of fact, it described all these gyrations, with variations made from parts of them. We tacked and turned from bank to bank; then, perhaps, for a few miles heading straight down stream, along the

Y

middle of it, presently to revert to forming angles and curves.

The guide to these evolutions is the Pilot. A Nupé, clad in the long flowing robe of the Mohamedans, capped by a white turban, Nasaru remains at his post on the bridge from dawn to dusk. He takes no rest or time off. He has his food where he stands. His eyes are unvaryingly directed on the surface of the stream, from which he reads the changing position of the narrow channel. That is the only line we can thread without being caught on a submerged sandbank.

How Nasaru remains awake all these hot, monotonous hours, scarcely moving, his gaze fixed on an inappreciably altering, dull scene, is remarkable. His principal movement is to raise his forearm at right-angle from the elbow and extending the fingers as signs to the man at the wheel which way to steer; and, without looking down at the instrument, he frequently uses the telegraph to the engine-room to alter speed. The only occasions during the 14 hours' run that Nasaru relinquishes duty is when he drops on his knees for the Moslem prayers. He does that on the bridge, at the spot where he stands throughout the day.

It is imperative the river be watched so closely and unremittingly, as during the low-water season the channel along which safe travel can be made changes continuously and the course up or back may be quite impracticable on the return. This is due to the sand washed down and the pressure of the current wearing a channel where there is least resistance from irregularity of the banks or any other cause, throwing the displaced sand into the

A NUPÉ PILOT ON THE NIGER.
(See page 338.)

MANICURE.
The fee is twenty cowries, *i.e.*, about one-fourteenth of a penny.

NAVIGATING THE NIGER

previously-travelled channel. How requisite it is to visually trace the course was proved on our approaching a double channel, one each side of a large sandbank, really big enough to be termed an island.

Nasaru did not like the look of the water. It did not now appear to have the same depth as when traversed on his previous journey. The vessel was stopped, and he went off in a small boat to explore the channel on the other side of the island. On coming back from his soundings he directed the *Mungo Park* through the new channel, which gave 5 feet and 6 feet of water, whereas we subsequently learnt that the one he had stopped at bore only 3 feet 6 inches.

During the journey from Lokoja to Burutu three times we have seen stern-wheelers fixed on a sandbank. Each occasion, after he had peered through his telescope, Captain Stephenson remarked, with a chuckle of satisfaction, " Not one of our Company's."

When a steamer of size goes aground there are three courses to be followed. Perhaps only one or two of them need be resorted to. The first is to try to get off by means of the propelling engines. If the vessel does not readily respond the engines are stopped, as to keep them going in such a position must cause the paddles to throw up sand, which, settling round, still further embeds the craft.

The first attempt yielding no satisfaction, the next step is to have the rowing-boat, slung at the side, brought to the bows and the anchor put in it and taken to deep water, dropped there, and a steel hawser attached. The other end of the hawser is led to a powerful windlass on the stern-wheeler, and on heaving away—in landlubbers' parlance, the windlass working—the vessel usually comes from her grounding. For this purpose a stern-wheeler of the *Mungo Park* type carries three Trotman anchors—respectively 10 cwts., 8 cwts., and 4 cwts.—besides the ordinary patent anchor for general use.

But should the vessel be so firmly fixed that she cannot be moved off by either of the means stated, then there is a third resource. At low water every stern-wheeler tows a barge alongside. On the most severe form of going aground the barge is piled with cargo from the stern-wheeler, and, when sufficiently lightened, that vessel is drawn into the navigable channel by again heaving on the anchors. But though the steamer has floated, the heavily laden barge, which was alongside it, is now itself obviously aground, so the cargo is once more transferred to the stern-wheeler, the operation being carried out by a roomy rowing boat, which may go backwards and forwards scores of times on the errand. Thus a couple of days are easily consumed. Less haste, greater speed is an axiom of navigation on the Niger for several months of the year.

Opposite the town of Onitsha, near where we stopped for native passengers, there was a large depression in the bed of the river, which a battleship would not cover, holding 40 feet of water, but no anchorage, as the bed was rock. Yet the other side of the deep water gave no more than 2 feet, except where the channel ran. It is easy enough to wreck a vessel in these parts.

At the close of the second day, which accounted

for 90 miles, we stopped overnight at a point 10 miles below Onitsha and 146 miles from Lokoja.

A fog on the morning of the third day prevented a start until 7.30, and later there was a breakdown of machinery, which brought us to a complete standstill. The mishap was not a slight one. A fracture had occurred to the shaft on the circulating pump, which forces water through the condenser to cool steam that has passed through the cylinder. The shaft was broken diagonally close to the flange. The nearest marine engineering shops were at Burutu, about 170 miles down the river. Had we been compelled to send there and wait for mechanics and new parts we should have had to remain helpless three or four days.

The Chief Engineer informed Captain Stephenson that he could repair and set the engines going with the material at hand. All the Company's large boats carry a forge, anvil and general outfit of tools. This Chief Engineer is a black, a Sierra Leonean, trained by the Niger Company at the Burutu workshops. He and his assistants were soon at work.

The flange was filed out, neatly fitted on the broken shaft by filing key-ways and securing the flange in position by steel keys, forged there and then, which held the shaft to the flange. I watched all this, which was done with celerity, yet in a cool, matter-of-fact way, as though it were all in the day's work.

At the commencement of the repair no statement could be made as to how long it would take. At the end of five hours' close application the skipper received the Chief Engineer's report that he was ready for the word to proceed, and the engines starting very gently at first, in a few minutes were once more full speed ahead.

All the way down there has been a full range of tropical landscape. At some places the forest comes to the edge of the water and presents a barrier to sight of what may be beyond. At other sections of the route trees are not so crowded and stand a few score feet back, whilst where they are more scattered there is opportunity to notice the aboricultural variety, in which the palm always stands out distinctively against the sky background.

Where a stretch of sand lines the shore or there is grass not shadowed or hidden by taller growths, crocodiles are frequently seen at rest. They sprawl on the sandbanks and seldom dive off unless the stern-wheeler passes quite near. There are plenty opportunities for a rifle-shot at the brutes, but he who fires does so at a risk of being fined £5, for that is the penalty the Government has fixed to deter shooting from a boat.

The usual scenery of the bank is occasionally broken by a trading station, usually consisting of two or three corrugated iron sheds placed adjacent to the beach but on rising ground which the flood-level does not reach.

Standing quite alone, many miles from trading stations, are the riverside villages, enveloped on three sides by the forest. The architecture tells that the Hausa country has been left. These lower-river tribes build their oblong houses of bamboo, placed vertically. On the approach of the stern-wheeler numbers of the male inhabitants paddle off in frail, dug-out canoes and plunge in the water

A EUROPEAN TRADING STATION ON THE NIGER.
(See page 342.)

ON A CREEK OF THE NIGER.

after anything pitched to them, as though there were no crocodiles on the prowl. Bottles are the articles most esteemed by the seekers of what they can get from the passing boat. If a bottle and money be thrown together, the swimmers will always ignore the coin for the bottle. Next in value are tin boxes of the kind which have held sardines or biscuits.

Apart from this crowd in the water to pick up unconsidered trifles, there is a turn out of villagers for the purpose of yelling a greeting to some neighbour who is among the crew. The exile will have made a hoard of all the discarded bottles and tins he could lay hands upon since the boat last passed, and over they go to delight his kinsmen and friends.

Captain Stephenson, in order to assist my having a photograph of the scramble in the water, told his personal steward boy to bring up some old bottles. The lad appeared with two, saying they were all he could find. He was sternly sent back and eventually produced six, declaring he knew of no more on board. Later the same afternoon, as we went by another village the skipper pointed to his steward boy perched on the deck where he imagined he could not be seen, flinging bottles with both hands, as quickly as he could pick them up from a pile of not less than two dozen. They were his collection on the voyage and now he was giving them to the folks of his home.

That night we stabled at a point two hours' steaming below Aboh, having done 64 miles since the morning. There was still a chance that, in the absence of any but small mishaps—and not many of them—we should complete the balance of 127 miles to our destination on the morrow.

We started at the usual hour, 5.30 a.m., but at 7 o'clock there was an ominous check. A thick, harmattan, dry fog compelled us to anchor. For what period we should remain no one could say. It must be until the air cleared. To go on would be madness, sure misfortune. That was plain enough, whatever remained obscured. Vision was very deceptive; the nearest bank appeared to be half-a-mile away, whereas it was less than 200 yards distant.

An-hour-and-a-half, and the mist lifted, and again we were under way. At places the depth of the narrow channel on which we glided became so reduced, nearly on the border line of safety, that great care had to be exercised and slow speed maintained for several stretches.

It is still broad, afternoon daylight as we pass Gana-Gana, 35 miles from Forcados, and therefore only 30 miles from Burutu, which is regarded as practically the same; so we may still reach the latter to-day.

Gana-Gana is the first trading station of the Niger Company from the headquarters at Burutu. The river is a-quarter-of-a-mile across. In mid-stream is a small island on which the station has been made. The manager's house is a medium-size sternwheeler hauled up on the island. The lower part of the boat is used as a store for bought produce; the upper part remains little altered from when the barque was afloat, the saloon merely modified to the conveniences of living on land.

A screw steamer has also been drawn up, roofed

with corrugated iron and is used as living quarters for the black staff. No one else remains on the islet during the night.

In addition there are three corrugated iron sheds for stores and another for trading goods. Produce is brought by natives in canoes from both banks of the river.

This placing of a trading station on an island was of considerable advantage in the old days when a general attack on a European store, firing the building and murdering the occupants was a periodical entertainment of inhabitants up the rivers. The station being surrounded by water which had to be crossed gave the defenders a chance, with the use of rifles, to beat off an assault.

All the trading stations are kept busy from morning to night, so there is little likelihood of anybody in one experiencing monotony; but in former days there was the additional exhilaration of always having in mind the probable need of a sudden run for firearms to keep at bay a howling mob of savages bent on killing and plunder. By comparison, things are quite tame nowadays.

Although the river, broad as it is, gives practically nothing to spare in depth, we spin along in the effort to reach Burutu to-night, but the channel occasionally becomes so shallow that, unless we are to be run aground after all, the engines have to be slowed; for, whilst it is urgent to reach Burutu without stop, as a mail liner leaves Forcados to-morrow morning for England and we have light cargo for her, if we go on a sandbank the whole scheme must be upset and a week's delay ensue. That means, instead of the goods being directly transhipped, the labour and extra expense of warehousing and handling them three times instead of once. Therefore, notwithstanding the brief twilight is passing and darkness coming on, the engines continue their regular sharp pulsation and the stern-wheels strike the water with their pat-pat-pat sound, and no halt is made as the night settles around, though we are still some 20 miles from Burutu. Fortunately, the moon is clear. Nasaru looks unflinchingly ahead. He has been doing so for 12 hours, yet he shows no sign of weariness and appears as visually alert as he was at the start.

Should anything untoward occur to delay us, it is the skipper who will be blamed. He is expected to be in time for whatever is to be transferred from his boat to the homeward-bound liner. If he does not maintain that time-table he must give a good reason why; it must be a very good reason. Still worse is it for his reputation if he runs aground. That may be no fault of his; still, he is judged from results. There is nothing like being careful; an excess of that quality, however, means that dovetailed arrangements and schedules are put out of gear. Whatever difficulties or obstacles come in the path of a skipper of a large stern-wheeler on the Niger—and many do—in thinking how to overcome any one of them he can always murmur truthfully, as did Desdemona, "I do perceive here a divided duty."

Steadily, yet with unrelaxed caution, paddling, the miles between us and our goal are reduced one by one, until, at nearly 10 o'clock, in the distance there is a cluster of white specks, too bright to be stars. As we move onwards it becomes plain they

NAVIGATING THE NIGER

are the electric lights on the wharf at Burutu. Half-an-hour more and we are up to them and at anchor.

It seems we have suddenly sailed into a new world, or, rather, into the old, strenuous, restless world again. The long rows of large sheds, the big arc lamps and the smaller ones together throwing a glare half-way across the river, and the wide-funnel ocean ships and others of lesser degree clustered, all tell you are at a large shipping port planted in West Africa.

Nearly everybody ashore has gone to bed, but Captain Stephenson promptly reports his arrival to Mr Price, the Burutu Agent of the Niger Company, and word is brought back from him that the *Mungo Park* is to leave at 6 a.m. for Forcados, so that anybody who desires to land at Burutu must do so before that hour next morning.

CHAPTER XL

BURUTU

A port in a swamp—Training native engineers—A composite village—Social grades—Medical provision—Mr John Burns on a Nigerian river—Back to the sea.

BURUTU, like Forcados, five miles lower down the Niger, was a mere mangrove swamp, a forlorn no-man's land. It has been reclaimed by the Niger Company for headquarters, and is now a bustling, thriving spot, large enough to be termed, by comparison, a small Glasgow in West Africa.

It has most of the characteristics of a port. On the 3,000 feet frontage two ocean liners can lie end-on—there is always one berthed—and seven of the eight hatches simultaneously discharging or loading; smaller craft—branch boats of 1,000 tons to stern-wheelers and launches for river traffic—are continuously bringing produce and passengers and taking up country small goods, among which bags of salt occupy an important place; whilst the coal wharf knows no rest. Awaiting shipment are 7,000 casks of palm-oil. Recently there were 10,000.

Besides, there are three hulks converted from two old sailing ships and a steamer. Two of the hulks are used to warehouse bulk produce of palm-kernels and shea-nuts; the third holds coal. But the

THE NIGER COMPANY'S WHARF AT BURUTU.

SHIPPING PALM-OIL
For direct transit to Liverpool. (See page 348.)

Company are building a new coal wharf of two tiers to enable the coal ships to discharge cargo direct into trucks.

Fifteen corrugated iron sheds, 90 feet by 30 feet, give accommodation on the wharf for goods which should not be left in the open, and also for the extensive engineering and carpenters' workshops, under a white Superintendent Engineer, who has with him three European fitters, a boiler-maker, two shipwrights and a large body of skilled natives from Coast towns. A couple of slipways take the river craft for repair, from launches to steamers up to 700 tons.

The coloured staff of fitters, blacksmiths, turners, moulders, and the rest of them are men from Sierra Leone, the Gold Coast, and Nigeria. They serve apprenticeship in the Company's engineering shops for five years. If their conduct has been satisfactory they will be graded as improvers. Next they may be drafted on a river boat as third engineers, rising to second or to chief engineer. Others may start on shore, either in the workshops or as house-boys. Should they wish it, and their behaviour be good, they go on the river steamers, commencing as stewards or deck hands and going through every stage, as quartermasters, boatswains, and mates, and rising to command the vessel, for, with the exception of three, all the stern-wheelers and small steamers are in the hands of black captains, and thoroughly capable they are. It was with such a "Cappy" I came from Baro to Lokoja.

Burutu does not consist of only a long line of reclaimed beach and workshops abutting. There is much more. Hundreds of labourers are employed

—400 on the commercial beach alone—and for them and others model villages have been laid out and the forest cleared for some distance back; for, previous to the Niger Company making Burutu its principal centre, the trees crowded down to the water edge, as they do at the opposite side of the river and at the ends of the nearly two miles of beach.

These villages have districts. You must not expect, say, the native clerk from Sierra Leone, the Gold Coast, or Lagos to have his residence cheek-by-jowl with the Yoruba labourer or the Ijaw river boys. Why should he not object? This is not said in an ironical tone. Do we not have a corresponding feeling? How shocked English suburbia would be, to be sure, if their neat promenades and well-laid-out boulevards were the resort of men who gained a living with pick and shovel! And who can say he enjoys huddling in train or tram against a navvy with the clay on his clothes, fresh from the exercise of his profession? The black man, too, has steps in his social ladder. He, too, has feelings, like all of us, whether he be the Coast person with elementary education and sometimes deservedly hated by the white; whether he be the Mohamedan of the hinterland; whether he be the Pagan of the uplands and the hills.

Therefore, the houses for colour men are in separate groups, according to the class occupying them. The labourers' dwellings of bamboo walls and palm leaves are being gradually replaced by buildings bricked to about three feet at the sides and continued with corrugated iron, the same material for roof, and with cement floors. The ten senior coloured clerks are given two large bungalows divided into two rooms for each married couple, a portion of the verandah walled off from the adjoining family. The newer houses being erected will include bathrooms and kitchens.

An isolation hospital for natives holds any case of a contagious nature. To the hospital for Europeans a dispensary is attached, and to it come daily between 50 and 60 of the black dwellers in Burutu, including mammies and piccaninnies. Most of the male patients' ailments are simple knocks or cuts received in the course of their work. The expenditure for all this is borne by the Niger Company, as well as the services of the Government doctor at Forcados, who is at Burutu every day except Sunday and attends to both Europeans and natives.

The European bungalows are made mosquito-proof. In each of the messrooms is a large overhead fan, electrically driven, and in the principal rooms portable table fans kept going from the same source. Even persons who live in a cold climate will realise what a boon these fans are in a quarter of the country where the heat is excessive and is always associated with a damp enervating atmosphere.

I suppose it is generally known that the Right Hon. John Burns, now a Cabinet Minister, in his younger years served a term, as an engineer, with the Niger Company. The statement is frequently made in West Africa that it took place at Burutu. That is incorrect. In Mr Burns's time Burutu was a desolate mangrove swamp; the headquarters were at Akassa, at the mouth of the River Nun, about 50 miles further along the Coast from Forcados.

Several renderings of a snake story have appeared in English papers. An old number of *The Engineer's Gazette*, dated May 1893, has furnished me with what is evidently the correct account. The appended quotation is taken from a contribution by John Parkin, who in the text describes himself as " Superintendent of an engineering repairing shop." I gather that the period of which he has written was 1880 or thereabouts.

" My next adventure in the snake line was at Akassa, while in charge of the engineering workshop there. The shop was built between the river and the jungle and the boiler fixed outside the building and close to rank vegetation. One day, after making my usual inspection of the boiler, I was startled to see a large snake making tracks for me. For the moment I was half-paralysed with fear, but instantly recovering myself and deeming prudence the better part of valour, I took to my heels. I was soon arrested in my inglorious flight by the derisive laughter of a fellow engineer, who, with characteristic pluck and presence of mind, picked up a shovel and chased the serpent that was chasing me, and with one well-aimed blow cut it in two. That daring engineer was John Burns, now of the L.C.C. and M.P. for Battersea.

" That was not the only occasion on which Burns showed his intrepidity. One day he and I were returning from the Brass River, through the creeks, in a steam launch. The propeller had only two blades. . . . They worked loose and fell off. The situation was alarming, as we were near a small village inhabited by cannibals, whilst the creek was teeming with sharks and reptiles. Fortunately the creek was not deep, it being low tide. The bottom was composed of soft, stinking mud and decayed vegetable matter; so we had but faint hopes of finding either of the blades. I proposed testing my skill as a diver, but Burns wouldn't hear of it. 'No,' said he, 'you are married and I am single. If either of us risks his life I'm the man'; and, immediately stripping, he plunged in. To my delighted surprise he found one blade, and we managed to fix it in the boss and proceeded on our course, arriving at Akassa in safety, though several hours late. We had been a long time without food and were ravenously hungry. Both of us did our duty at the table, but I was not in it with Burns, who ate nearly the entire leg of a goat."

The launch of my very good friend, Mr Price, of Burutu, took me from there the five miles to the sea, and once more I steamed away from the land of Nigeria, which, notwithstanding the privations and hardships undergone, and the bad name the climate is given, retains for me a continual attraction and fascination to revisit.

INDEX

A

ABIGAH junior, 120-2
Abigah, King of Lokoja, 327-8
Aboh, 337, 343
Aborigines, Preface viii
Accra, 11
African World, 149, 211, 218
Agent (in West Africa), 6
Aiki Square, 20
Akabo, 2
Akassa, 351-3
Algeria, 102
Alkali, 68, 70, 71, 107, 114-15, 123, 239, 325-6
Amadu, 153, 158-9, 161, 166, 172
Anjim men, 100
Ashanti, military contingent for, 88
Ashanti War, 88
Awai, 134
Axim, 8

B

BADEGI, railway from Baro to, 300
Badiko, 161, 163, 165, 195
Baikie, R.N., Dr, 317
Baker, Major E. M., Preface x
Bakin Kasua, 50
Bank of British West Africa, 118, 319
Bannerman, Mr D., 135
Barijuko, 133
Baro, 103, 145; railway from, to Badegi, 300; 306-11
Barth, Dr, 316, 327
Bassa, 68
Bauchi, 40; as the Capital, 42; Province of, 155, 205; expedition against Emir of, 195; Plateau, 223, 245;

BAUCHI—*continued*
266, 269, 334; escarpment, 224-5
Beit-el-Mal, *See* Native Treasuries
Bell, Sir Hesketh, Preface ix, 67, 73, 294, 325
Bensusan, Mr F. L., 171-2
Benue River, 187, 224, 316, 319, 321, 335
Berbushay, 86
Beri-Beri country, 8
Beri-Beris, 63, 112, 121
Berrida, 134
Bibin, 136
Bida, 15, 40; Emir of, 88; railway through Province of, 300; battle of, 318
Biffen, Mr E. H., 46
Biscay, Bay of, 3
Bland, Mr E. M., Preface ix, 52
Borgu, 63
Bornu, Resident at, 26, 63, 69
Bourke, Mr F. D., Preface x, 174
Boussa, 314
Boyce, Sir Rupert, 5
Boyle, Mr A. G., C.M.G., Preface ix
Brass River, 352
Brayscher, Mr A. W., 58, 59
Brocklebank, D.S.O., Capt. J. J., Preface x, 81-85, 128, 192
Brown, Mr Richard, 137-8
Brown, Mr Robert, 137-8
Bugi, 175
Bukuru, 196, 247-268
Burns, M.P., the Right Honourable John, 351-3
Burutu, 348-353
Bush fires, 222-3
Byfield, Mr Bertram D., Preface x, 325-7
Byrd, Mr W. P., Preface x, 60, 128

INDEX

C

CACTUS, 248-9, 251
Camel transport, 191-2
Camera, 60, 160
Canary Islands, 5
Cannibalism, 246
Cantonment Magistrates, 28-9, 30-2, 325-6
Cape Coast, 11
Cape Palmas, 9
Cape Verde, 6
Carriers, 139-40, 146-180, 185, 219; pace of 226; 237-242; *See* also Dan Sokoto and Gotum Karo
Caruso, 300
Catholics, 39
Central Province, 205
Ch'Kardi, Adamu, Preface x, 94, 129
Chief Justice, the acting, 24; the, 114
Christian, Messrs G. W., 319
Clerks, Gold Coast and Sierra Leone, 38, 350-1
Climate, 5, 236
"Coast, call to the."
Coast towns, Preface viii, 118, 324, 349
Coasters, 5, 6
Coleman, Mr E. N., 305, 308-9, 312
Coombe, Mr A., 313
Costello, Dr, 201, 219
Cotton growing, 305; British Cotton Growing Association, 319
Cowries, 104, 322
Crowther, Bishop, 330
Cyclops cement-block machine, 310

D

DAGO RIVER, 35
Daka-Keri, 36
Dalla, 86
Dan Sokoto, 239-41
David, 86
Deleme River, 173, 195
Donisthorpe, Mr Loder, 80
Donkey transport, 142-3, 192-3
Driver, Mr T. H., Preface x, 232-4
Dyer, Lieutenant, 91
Duchi-n-Wai, 134, 135

E

EAGLESOME, Mr John, 25, 49, 133
East Africa, 2
Egerton, Sir Walter, Preface ix
Egypt, 2
Emirs, 26, 64, 65, 66, 67, 68, 70, 296, 299-301
Emlyn, Dr A., 199-200
Emperor William I. of Germany, 327
Engineer's Gazette, The, 352
English Channel, 2, 3
Euston, 131
Evans, Mr E., 258
Exclusive Prospecting Licence, the first, 195

F

FAIRLEY, Messrs J. D., 319
Farms, Hausa, 55; Pagan, 253-4
Fedderi, 178-80
Forcados, 103, 118, 348
Fox, the late Rev. C., 56
Francis, Mr A. C., Preface x, 298
Fremantle, Captain, 298
French Company, the, 73, 74, 75, 76, 292
Frontier, of Southern and Northern Nigeria, 15
Fulani, Preface viii, 67, 100, 112, 116, 121, 154, 207, 263-6, 318

G

GALL, Mr F. Beckles, Preface x, 205-8, 213
Gambia River, 7
Gana-Gana, 344
Garrard, Mr Percy, 143-4, 147-9, 242
Gascoyne, Lieutenant, 91
Geiser and Company, 292

INDEX 857

Gidan Gombo, 148, 149, 150-2, 257
Girouard, D.S.O., Sir Percy, 49, 300, 303, 306
Glasgow, 348
Godwin, Captain, F. A. E., 36
Gold Coast Colony, kola nuts from, 302
Gold discoveries, the, 293-4
Goldie, Sir George Taubman, Preface viii, 63, 66, 281, 318
Goldsmith, C.M.G., Mr H. S., 25
Goron Dutsi, 86
Gotum Karo, 179-80
Government House, 27
Governor, authority of, 19; 245
Graham, Mr F. G., 166
Grand Bassa, 9
Grant-in-aid, 23, 205
Gurum River, 175-7, 231, 233
Gussum, 153, 154

H

Hanington, Dr, 3, 4
Hanza, 153-4, 156-168, 172, 174, 178
Harmattan, 14, 223
Harrison, Mr W., 3, 4
Hausa, Preface viii, 36; traders on the railway, 49; 63, 64, 67, 100, 112, 116, 121, 137, 154, 162, 207, 226-8, 237, 243-4, 247-8; house, 251; 254, 262-6, 280-1, 290, 318
Herodotus, 314
Hibbert, Mr W. H., Preface x, 312, 321
Hill Division, 207
Holt, Messrs John, 73, 292, 319, 337
Horses, 108, 109, 141-2, 164, 216-18, 249, 253, 255-7
Hos, 225, 228
Hospital Sisters, 5
Hospitals, Jos, 200; Baro, 311; Lokoja, 328-9
House of Commons Resolution, 317
House of Lords, the, 308
Huddart, Mr L. H. L., 293-4

I

Ibadan, 15, 309
Iddo Wharf, 11-13
Ijaw, 350
Imperial Yeomanry, 8th, 81
Inspector of Mines, Government, 21

J

James, Mr F. Seton, C.M.G., Preface ix
Jebba, 16, 40; as the Capital, 41; 88, 319
Jemma, 223-4
Johnson, Captain, A. E., D.S.O., 35, 36
Johnson, Dr, 201, 298
Jos, 174, 181-93, 196, 221, 230
Judd, Colonel, 22
Juga, 154, 167, 169

K

Kabba, expedition against, 281, 318; Province of, 319; City of, 325
Kadaura, 169
Kaduna Bridge, 52
Kanduna River, 41; tributaries of, 50
Kano, 57-129
Kantagora, 40; Emir of, 88
Karre, 134
Karshi, 225, 228
Katsina, 70; Emir of, 89; 103, 107
Keffi, Magasi of, 89
Kelly, Captain G. C., Preface ix, 24, 26
Kendall, Mr, 191
King, the Great White, 65
King's Dragoon Guards, 81
Kogin Serekin Pawa, 50
Kogini Rahama, 149
Kolo, 215-16, 238-9
Kooty-Wenji, 17
Krumen, 7-8, 11
Kudara, 134, 136, 137
Kugo River, 50
Kukuruku, 36

L

LAFEE SALA, 163
Lagos, 11, 12; as the capital, 42; Colony of, 63; 73, 75, 103, 118
Lagos Stores, Ltd., 73, 75, 76, 292
Laird, McGregor, 315-17
Lake Chad, 54, 316
Lander, the brothers, 314-16
Langslow-Cock, Mr A. E., 204-5
Laundryman, 9
Laws, Mr H. W., 195-6
"Lazy negroes," 55
Lefanu, Sergeant, 91
Leighton, Mr, 175
Lenthall, Mr Robert, Preface x
Liberia, 9
Liverpool, 2, 11, 315
Liverpool, 103
Lokoja, as the capital, 41; 311, 313-33; distance from Forcados, 335
Loko-Keffi route, 187-8, 224
London and Kano Trading Company, 80-85, 292
Lugard, Lady, Preface viii
Lugard, Sir F., Preface viii, 25, 36, 39, 40, 49, 64, 65, 66, 88, 89, 90, 92, 127, 133, 142, 194-5

M

MACDONALD, Mr George, 195-6
Macintyre, Archdeacon, J. L., 330-2
Maclaverty, Captain C. F. S., Preface ix, 24, 151, 282
Maclean, Mr C., Preface ix
Magama, 165
Mail services, 37
Malarial fever, 5, 329
Mal-de-mer, 3
Mallam, 280-1; on railway, 301-2; 318
Mama, 238-9
Manchester, 103
Manson, Sir Patrick, 5
Marsh, Mr W. J., 59, 60
McDowell, Mr J. B., Preface x

McQueen, James, 315
Medical staff, 5
Melba, Madame, 300
Migeod, Mr C. L., 207
Military, 1st Northern Nigeria Regiment, 24; West African Frontier Force, 36; artillery, 36; operations, 65; Northern Nigeria Regiment, 81; contingent for Ashanti, 88, 278-90; marriage in the service, 281; the guns, 282-4; sports, 284-5; signalling, 285-7; the bands, 287-8; classification of white civilians, 289-9; expedition against Kabba, 318; Battle of Bida, 318
Minerals royalty, 198
Minna, 16; station, 44-5-6, 302; distance from Zaria, 302
Missionaries, 45, 125-9, 258-9, 316, 324, 329-332
Mockler-Ferryman, Colonel, Preface viii
Mohamedan and Moslem, 38, 39, 44; clothing, 64; 66, 68, 102, 114, 127, 243, 249, 280-1, 318, 324, 338, 350
Molyneux, Mr S. A., 179-80
Money, 117-8, 185, 322
Monrovia, 9
Morel, Mr E. D., Preface viii
Morland, Colonel, 90-1
Morocco, 101, 102, 103
Mosques, 120
Motor lorry transport, 191-2
Mungo Park, the, 336-7, 339-40
Musical instruments, Pagan, 249, 250

N

NARAGUTA, 169, 173, 195-6; extended, 196; 197, 205, 214
Nasaru, 338-9, 346
Nassarawa, 40; Province of, 223, 225
Navy, the Royal, 315
Newport, Mr A., 45
N'Gell, 196
Nicolaus, Mr G., 195

INDEX 859

Niger Company, 33; constabulary, 36; 61, 63, 66, 73, 74, 75, 76, 77, 139-145; finance department, 184-6; transport department, 186-193; mining department, 194-8; 293, 307, 310, 318-19, 321, 336-7, 348-51
Niger River, 16; ferry, 16; bridge, 17; 103, 145; at Baro, 315; exploration of and early trading on, 314-17; 319, 321; navigating the, 334-47
"Niggers," 13
Nun River, 351
Nupés, 63, 100, 112, 312, 338
Nursing, feminine, 200-1, 328

O

OFFA, 15
Officials, English, number of, 67
Oil Rivers, 11
Oje, divines water, 46; 59, 170, 182, 211-15, 238, 309-10
Oldfield, Mr J., 46
Ollivant and Company, 292
Olokemeji, 15
Onitsha, 337, 340
Orr, Captain, Preface viii
Oshogbo, 15
Overweg, Dr, 316
Oxen transport, 142, 191-2

P

PADDINGTON, 131
Pagans, Preface vii, 36, 38, 63, 64, 69, 154, 177-8, 207, 224, 226-8, 243-77; musical instruments, 250; houses, 251-3; fuel, 252; farms, 253-4; cattle and herds, 255; public celebrations, 255; races, 256; as horse-masters, 256-7; hunting, 257; sign language, 257-8; administering justice, 260-6; authority of Kings and Chiefs, 260, 270-1; trial by ordeal, 262; taxation, 266-8; marriage customs, 271-3; death customs, 273-5; can-

PAGANS—*continued*
nibalism, 275-7; military, 280; 350
Pagenstecher and Company, 292, 319
Park, Mungo, 314
Parkin, Mr John, 352
Paterson and Zochonis, 292
Pleiad, the, 316
Police, Northern Nigeria, 35-6; Emir's, 36, 245
Polygamy, 120
Pooley, Captain, 10, 11
Population, number of, 67; decrease of, 88
Porch, Mr M. P., 298
Porter, Major, 91
Postmaster-General, the, 24, 37
Price, Mr A. E., Preface x, 347, 353
Probis, Mr, 195
Public Works Department, 20

R

RADCLIFF, Captain J., 29
Rahama, 134, 138-145, 147, 231
Railway, Anchou, 54; Baro-Kano, Preface vii, 48, 58-9, 145, 299-305; Bauchi Light, Preface vii, 17, 131-8, 145, 154; Boat train, 12, 14, 131; Deputy Director of, 24-5; Dumbi, 54; extension from Jebba to Kano, 20-1; fares, 18; ferry, 16; gauges, 132; Hausa traders on the, 49; Kaduna station, 50-1; Kaduna bridge, 52; Kano, approach to, 56; Kano station, 58; Kano and the desert route for Arab merchants, 102; Lagos Government, the, Preface vii, 15; locomotive and elephants, 302; locomotive and horse, 302; meals on the, 18; Nigerian, Preface vii; proportion of travellers per class, 49; Rahama, trains from, 231; receipts, 48-9; Rigachikun, 54; road transport contrasted with the, 235; rolling-stock, demand for, 48; Shallawa River, 55; terminus, 11, 12, 13; 3rd

RAILWAY—*continued*
  class coaches, 49; track repair, 51; water for engines, 51; Zaria junction, 291; Zaria Plateau, 50; Zungeru, 17; Zungeru station, 43; Zungeru to Kano train, 44
Rats, as food, 309-10
Rattler, the, 312-13
Reichard, Herr, 314-15
Residents, discretion to, 26; 67, 205-8, 245-6, 247-8, 260-1, 263, 266-8, 297
Rest-houses, 22, 57, 109, 150-1, 164, 297-8
Rhodesia, 236
Richards, Mr Cyril, 14
Richardson, Mr, 316
Rigachikun, 187
Ross, Major Sir Ronald, 5
Raffan Governor, 234
" Rule of the road " at sea, 10

S

SAHARA DESERT, 7, 102
Salah, the, 216, 219-220
Scarbrough, Lord, 197
Schools, Government and Missionary, 39
Secondee, 11
Selander, Mr J. E., 107
Shallawa River, 90
Sierra Leone, 7, 8, 9, 118
Sign language, 257-8
Signalled message, 290
Simmonds, Mr E. B., 186
Slave-raiding, 50, 243, 262-4
Slaves, domestic, 122
Soba, 134, 135
Sokoto, 15; resident at, 26; mails to, 37; 40, 67, 68, 91, 103
Soper, Captain, F. P., 224
South African War, 81
Speed, Mr, 235-7
Stephenson, Captain, W. H., 336, 339, 343, 347
Stobart, Mr S. E. M., Preface, x, 261-7
Sudan United Mission, 258-9
Suly, Preface x, 129
Sussex scenery, 223
Swainson, Mr J., 137-8
Syrian trader, a, 73, 75, 76, 78

T

TAXATION, native, 67, 207, 245, 266-8, 295-7
Temperature, 7, 14, 159-60, 225-6, 252-3
Temple, Mr Charles L., C.M.G., Preface ix, 25, 27, 300
Territory, extent of, 63, 67, 278
Tetrazzini, Madame, 300
Tilde Fulani, 171, 180, 195
Tin areas of Nigeria, 73, 75, 76, 292, 319
Tin fields, travellers for, 17; inception of, 194-8; mining regulations, 202-5; Government Inspector of Mines, 204-5; travellers to, 307
Toner, Mr James, 4
Toro, 169, 170
Trading firms, European, 6, 73
Transvaal scenery, 221
Treasuries, native, 34, 68, 69, 70, 115, 295-6
Tremearne, Major, Preface viii
Trial by ordeal, 262
Trigge, Mr Joseph E., Preface x
Tripoli, 101, 102, 103, 316
Tunis, 101
Turegs, 100

V

VULTURES, 117

W

WALKDEN AND COMPANY, John, 292
Wallace, Sir William, 195-6
Waller, Mr F. W., Preface, ix
Wassaku Concessions, 134
Waterloo, 131
Watson, Dr, 199-200
Watts, Mr Walter, Preface x, 194-5
Weinthal, Mr Leo, Preface ix

West African Frontier Force, 36
White, Mr, 80
Wilks, Mr, 61
Women traders, 119
Woolloy, Mr H. M., 37
Worroko, 134

Y

YOLA, 316
Yorubas, 30, 63, 309, 350

Z

ZARIA, 15, 17, 40, 89, 90; station, 130-1; 182, 291-8; native taxation, 295-7; Emir of, 296; railway through

ZARIA—*continued*
Province of, 300; kola nuts for, 303
Zungeru, 19-20; character of, 21; living accommodation in, 21-2; houses and food, 22-3; rest-houses at, 22; future of, as Capital, 23, 39; hours of work at, 26; Secretariat, 26; Government House, 27; Governor's motor-car, 27-8; Cantonment Magistrate, 29-32; Chief of, 31-2; Niger Company's store, 33; native town, 34; prison, 35-6; mail services, 37; sports, 38; native and other coloured inhabitants, 38; strategic position of, 40-1; 73